1987

The Essential Articles Series

Essential Articles for the study of
Jonathan Swift's Poetry

Edited by
DAVID M. VIETH
Southern Illinois University
at Carbondale

Archon Books
1984

© 1984 by The Shoe String Press, Inc.
All rights reserved
First published 1984 as an Archon Book,
an imprint of The Shoe String Press, Inc.
Hamden, Connecticut 06514

Printed in the United States of America

The paper in this book meets the guidelines for
performance and durability of the Committee on
Production Guidelines for Book Longevity of the
Council on Library Resources.

Library of Congress Cataloging in Publication Data

Essential articles for the study of Jonathan Swift's
   poetry.

   Includes bibliographical references.
   1. Swift, Jonathan, 1667–1745—Poetic works—
Addresses, essays, lectures. I. Vieth,
David M. II. Title. III. Title: Jonathan Swift's
poetry.
PR3728.P58E84 1984   821′.5.   84-18511
ISBN 0-208-01979-0

Contents

IV. The *Description* Poems

V. *Cadenus and Vanessa*

VI. The Stella Poems

VII. *A Satirical Elegy*

VIII. The "Scatological" Poems

CONTENTS

IX. *On Poetry: A Rapsody*

X. *Verses on the Death of Dr. Swift*

Foreword

The resources available for the study of literature are so vast as to be almost overwhelming, particularly in the case of major authors. Few libraries have copies of all the important articles a serious student might wish to read, and fewer still can keep them easily accessible. The aim of the Essential Articles series is to bring together from learned journals and scholarly studies those essays on a standard writer or area of English literature which are genuinely essential—which will continue to appear on syllabus and reading list.

Introduction

The plan for this collection grew out of my activity as associate editor of *Contemporary Studies of Swift's Poetry,* edited by John Irwin Fischer and Donald C. Mell, Jr., published by the University of Delaware Press in 1981, and out of my compilation *Swift's Poetry 1900–1980: An Annotated Bibliography of Studies,* issued by Garland Publishing, Inc., in 1982. Worthwhile though the Delaware essays are, they are mostly brief pieces commissioned for a series of Special Sessions at meetings of the Modern Language Association of America, whereas there are almost two dozen earlier essays, of pivotal significance for the study of Swift's poetry, that are cited constantly by specialists in the field. Of the nineteen such essays included in this collection, only one has ever been reprinted.

The primary criterion used in selecting most of these essays is an impressionistic judgment of the frequency with which they are cited, which I take to be an index not only of their continuing usefulness but of their high quality and the contribution they have made to the astonishing surge of interest in Swift's poetry during the two decades 1960–1980. Excluded from consideration, occasionally with regret, are all sixteen essays in the Delaware volume and those in single-author book-length critical studies of the poetry: Maurice Johnson's *The Sin of Wit* (1950), Nora Crow Jaffe's *The Poet Swift* (1977), John Irwin Fischer's *On Swift's Poetry* (1978), Peter J. Schakel's *The Poetry of Jonathan Swift* (1978), A. B. England's *Energy and Order in the Poetry of Swift* (1980), Louise K. Barnett's *Swift's Poetic Worlds* (1981), Arno Löffler's *"The Rebel Muse"—Studien zu Swifts kritischer Dichtung* (1981), and Carole Fabricant's *Swift's Landscape* (1982). Also excluded are all other essays that have been frequently or at least conveniently reprinted, such as Norman O. Brown's "The Excremental Vision" and Herbert Davis's essays in his *Jonathan Swift: Essays on His Satire and Other Studies* (1964). The sole exception is Claude

Rawson's discussion, here reprinted (slightly condensed) in recognition of his unique impact on other critics of the poetry.

Although the only real criterion for choosing these essays has been frequency of citation, they happen to be distributed in representative fashion. Each essay is by a different critic, and collectively these twenty critics (there is one joint article) represent a majority of those who have contributed significantly to the growing interest in Swift's poetry. Coverage of the poems is also representative, ranging from three sections of general essays—on Swift's "anti-poetry," his "biographical presence," and his verse style—to seven sections focused more narrowly upon individual poems or groups of poems. The arrangement of these seven sections is chronological, from Swift's two early *Description* poems to *Verses on the Death of Dr. Swift*. Within sections containing more than one essay, the arrangement is according to date of publication.

Thanks are due to the authors and publishers who generously allowed us to reprint this material. Thanks are also due to the following Swiftians who offered suggestions concerning the makeup of the volume: John Aden, Louise Barnett, Bliss Carnochan, John R. Clark, A. B. England, John Irwin Fischer, Donna Fricke, Thomas Gilmore, Donald Greene, Robert Hume, W. R. Irwin, Nora Crow Jaffe, Mackie Jarrell, Maynard Mack, Donald Mell, Felicity Nussbaum, Clive T. Probyn, Christine Rees, Richard Rodino, Pat Rogers, E. San Juan, Jr., Peter Schakel, Arthur Scouten, David Sheehan, James Tyne, Marshall Waingrow, and James Woolley. In spite of the skepticism about the open-mindedness of the editor expressed by several of them, their advice resulted in more than a half-dozen changes in the original table of contents.

D. M. V.
April 1984

I. Poetry and Anti-Poetry

OSWALD JOHNSTON

Swift and the
Common Reader

One of the more gratifying things about neoclassical poetry is that reading it is normally a process of having one's reasonable expectations fulfilled. Granted, there is a preliminary difficulty, which all modern readers have to get over, in the formality of neoclassical poetic language. But once one realizes that its conventions—such as epithets and periphrases, the decorums of "elevated" and "low" words, the modes of heroic and pastoral, the forms of epic, epistle, and ode—are theoretically inviolable, their very predictability becomes a positive advantage. Behind all these conventions is an assumption that both poet and reader share a confidence in the values and beliefs of a regulated civilization. Style, in other words, is a medium of moral judgment. Of course, in the case of a poet like Addison, who is so completely submerged in conventionalities as to be anonymous, the values of civilization could adequately be expressed by solemn platitudes about being correct. But a poet like Pope, who does not reduce style to a conveyance for moralistic generalities and polite learning, requires that a fuller, more discriminating attention be paid to uses of formal language. The conventions are all present, and Pope's reader is certainly expected to have the same confidence in them that Addison's reader does: but he must also re-

This essay is reprinted from *In Defense of Reading: A Reader's Approach to Literary Criticism*, edited and copyright © 1962 by Reuben A. Brower and Richard Poirier, by permission of E. P. Dutton, Inc.

spond to modulations of style—often with the same quickness of understanding that enables him to respond to inflections and changes of tone in a clever conversation. Being sensitive to Pope's poetic language means imaginatively sharing the social brilliance of his wit at the same time that one accepts his profound belief in the moral values of civilization. Lacking the former qualification puts one in danger of calling *The Rape of the Lock* a dull satire on High Life; lacking the second tempts one to call it a trivial parody of heroic poetry. But such dangers are real only if the reader fails of the confidence that neoclassical poetic language extends, and on which neoclassical poetry relies for its effects.

Therefore, a reader equipped with the reassuring knowledge that Swift, in his long life, was a contemporary of both Dryden and Pope might well feel that his normal expectations will be fulfilled by Swift's poetry. His prose is notorious for its tricks and pitfalls: but neoclassical poetry is in the long run predictable—particularly when, as in "A Description of a City Shower," it is written in the early eighteenth century, and in heroic couplets. The "Description" bears a subtitle, "*In Imitation of* VIRGIL's Georg.," which, by confirming the prejudice that eighteenth century verse has something to do with the classics, seems to invite any reader to rely on his expectations. Just as Dryden, in *MacFlecknoe*, and Pope, in the *Dunciad*, use Virgil as a means of making a judgment about bad poets, so here Swift, one might suppose, is using Virgil's pastoral-descriptive style to make some point about rainstorms in the city of London. All that is needed, it appears, to place this poem in the literary-historical categories that seem natural to it is to decide what point about rainstorms Swift is making, and the job is done:

> Careful Observers may fortel the Hour
> (By sure Prognosticks) when to dread a Show'r:
> While Rain depends, the pensive Cat gives o'er
> Her Frolicks, and pursues her Tail no more.
> (1–4)

By attending to the elevated solemnity of these lines, with their suggestion that the coming shower will be as dreadful an event as a hurricane or a flood or even Judgment Day, and by noticing

4

the way in which the elevated word "pensive," reinforced in its line by the Latinate "depends," collapses into the description of the tailchasing alley cat, one might reasonably conclude that Swift, through the disparity between style and subject, is evoking a standard against which homely details of city life can be placed. There is more evidence for such a conclusion further on:

> Mean while the South rising with dabbled Wings,
> A Sable Cloud a-thwart the Welkin flings,
> That swill'd more Liquor than it could contain,
> And like a Drunkard gives it up again.
>
> (13–16)

The collapse here, from the elevated poetic language describing the sky to the ill-behaved drunkard, is even more drastic; and if it is reasonable to consider that ill-behaved drunkards are characteristic of city landscapes in the same way that alley cats are, it is likely that these lines are repeating the procedure of the earlier passage.

> Now in contiguous Drops the Flood comes down,
> Threat'ning with Deluge this *Devoted* Town.
>
> (31–32)

Here the Latinate "contiguous" gives the rain enough poetic dignity to justify the hyperbolical "Deluge"; and since "Devoted," in an older use, can mean literally "doomed" even while it is making an ironic reference to the Londoners' churchgoing habits, Swift seems to be implying that the city of London in some way deserves both the judgment and the catastrophe of Noah's Flood.

Up to now, so many preliminary expectations about the poem have been fulfilled that it would be reasonable to expect even more: for instance, a grand climax that asserts absolutely the moral standard that the style of the poem has evidently been evoking. Pope himself does no more than this in the conclusions to, say, the fourth *Moral Essay* and the *Dunciad*. Here is Swift's conclusion:

> Now from all Parts the swelling Kennels flow,
> And bear their Trophies with them as they go:

5

Filth of all Hues and Odours seem to tell
What Street they sail'd from, by their Sight and Smell.
They, as each Torrent drives, with rapid Force
From *Smithfield,* or *St. Pulchre*'s shape their Course,
And in huge Confluent join at *Snow-Hill* Ridge,
Fall from the *Conduit* prone to *Holborn-Bridge.*
Sweepings from Butchers Stalls, Dung, Guts, and Blood,
Drown'd Puppies, stinking Sprats, all drench'd in Mud,
Dead Cats and Turnip-Tops come tumbling down the Flood.

(53–63)

The reader's normal expectations, whose fulfillment I have apparently been demonstrating, seem undermined by this passage. Of course, it remains possible to point out that the language is still alluding to a more elevated style: the reference to the garbage as "Trophies" and the metaphorical suggestion that the colors and smells of the flooded gutters serve the same function as heraldic ensigns indicate that Swift is thinking of Virgilian, or even Homeric, fleets. But such an explanation tells us nothing of the moral judgment that the "normal" reader, with his solemn assumption that an elevated style must evoke a moral standard, has been expecting. The most direct answer, that Swift is using the style of Virgilian pastoral and heroic description in order to judge London's sewage system, is absurd; and, considering the virtuosity that even my purposely fallacious argument has managed to uncover in the poem, it would be unsatisfactory, not to say simple-minded, to conclude that Swift likes the country better than the city. Obviously, something that the normal reader does not expect has been going on in the poem. It is time to discard the pretense and find out what Swift is up to.

If, at the beginning of the poem, one does not stop short at line 4, one finds this:

Returning Home at Night, you'll find the Sink
Strike your offended Sense with double Stink.

(5–6)

It should be evident, from the bluntly unembarrassed recognition that cesspools "Stink" more than usual when there is moisture in the air, that Swift is perfectly willing to give us any homely

6

detail he wants, without having recourse to more elevated—more poetic—uses of language. There is a suggestion that he is not even interested in maintaining a style of poetic decorum—either for the sake of Virgil, whom he is supposed to be imitating, or for the moral standard such a style might be expected to embody. Much the same point can be demonstrated from Swift's use of the word "swilled" in the lines on the drunkard and the "Sable Cloud":

> Mean while the South rising with dabbled Wings,
> A Sable Cloud a-thwart the Welkin flings,
> That swill'd more Liquor than it could contain,
> And like a Drunkard gives it up again.

In its context the single coarse word deflates the elevated language of the previous lines perfectly well by itself: the drunkard is, so to speak, an embellishment. Evidently a good bit of the pleasure of reading the poem comes from the outrageous ways in which Swift makes fun of the poetic language he pretends to be using. Because we are told that it is "swill'd," we have no choice but to take "Liquor" in its colloquially limited sense of strong drink rather than in the elevated, general sense that the poetic "Sable Cloud" would seem to demand. Once this is admitted— once the elevated style has collapsed so irrevocably—the logic of the statement demands that it be completed by the undignified simile—the drunkard—with which it ends. One thing at least is clear: the drunkard is in no way being judged by the elevation of the style. If anything, the reverse has taken place; and if it is too much to say that the drunkard provides a standard by which the style can be judged, it seems inescapable that Swift's point here is to play some kind of practical joke on poetic language.

The conclusion one must draw from all this is that Swift is intent upon pushing his readers into a decidedly peculiar relationship with his poem. Contrary to our normal expectations, he does not allow us to settle upon a recognizable poetic style as a means of judgment—as a fixed standard whose values we share and against which we can measure divergences. The judgments that are made are delivered in a direct, conversational style that is pointedly antipoetical; and if we make the mistake of looking for a poetic "norm" to gratify our moral requirements, the judgment is likely to turn against us—or at least the joke will be at our expense. At any rate, the normal procedures of a reader of neoclassical verse have to be followed with extreme tact and discrimination, if not discarded. The more one relies on the conventional attitude of reverence for the classics and for the moral values of poetry, the more one is likely to be made fun of.

If the procedure of "A Description of a City Shower" is characteristic, rather than merely perverse, it will appear that Swift had an equivalent attitude to all the grander, more solemn pretensions of poetry. One would not expect, for instance, anything remotely resembling the invocation to the muse in Book I of *Paradise Lost*. Such a supposition would almost be right. The exception is to be found among the elaborate and unreadable Pindaric Odes and contemplative epistles that Swift wrote as a young man in the early 1690s, before *A Tale of a Tub* or anything else that one would normally recognize as his. It is the rare kind of exception that really does "prove" the rule, because this address to the muse, which serves as the conclusion of the last of these serious poems, is actually a dismissal, not an invocation:

> There thy enchantment broke, and from this hour
> I here renounce thy visionary pow'r;
> And since thy essence on my breath depends,
> Thus with a puff the whole delusion ends.

The passage is prophetic in more ways than one. All the poems written after this are in some manner reflections of the attitudes and procedures indicated by "A Description of a City Shower": in fact, the majority of them, measured in bulk, consist of private jokes, political libels, epigrams, and puns in a kind of pig Latin. Prophetic in a more interesting way is the disparaging implication that poetic inspiration is, literally, breath—that is, wind. From this point on, Swift was consistently rude to muses—his own or anybody else's. In a poem called "On Poetry: a Rapsody" he offers this recipe for an invocation:

> Be mindful, when Invention fails,
> To scratch your Head, and bite your Nails.
> (89–90)

And one could place beside Milton's elevation of poets to a

8

prophetic priesthood this celebration, from the same poem, of bardic dignity:

> Not Beggar's Brat, on Bulk begot;
> Nor Bastard of a Pedlar *Scot;*
> Nor Boy brought up to cleaning Shoes,
> The Spawn of *Bridewell,* or the Stews;
> Nor Infants dropt, the spurious Pledges
> Of *Gipsies* littering under Hedges,
> Are so disqualified by Fate
> To rise in *Church,* or *Law,* or *State,*
> As he, whom *Phebus* in his Ire
> Hath *blasted* with poetick Fire.
>
> (33–42)

There is more involved here than the fact that Swift made irreverent fun of poets for striking self-important attitudes. Irreverence is not in itself unusual. In fact, were one to take Milton's high solemnity as a model for poetic deportment, it would be hard to avoid accusing, say, Pope of being churlish in the same way as Swift—only to a lesser degree. But it is the degree that is all-important. There is never any question but that Pope, for all his comparatively un-Miltonic irreverence, has a full confidence in the capacity of serious poetic forms—of poetic language—to express all that he needs to express. This is tautologically obvious: poets believe in poetry; otherwise they would do something else. And such confidence, it should be evident, is only another way of defining the expectations with which we, as readers of neoclassical verse, first approached "A Description of a City Shower." As we now know, those expectations were bound to be upset. Swift has none of Pope's confidence in the language of poetry: in "A Description of a City Shower" he uses expertly many of the available resources of poetic language only in order to engineer its own collapse. Formal language, by the peculiar logic of its construction, which insists upon elevated, figurative abstractions to the exclusion of the undignified and the literal, contains the seeds of its own destruction. All Swift need do is emphasize the meanings that are normally excluded, and "Liquor" automatically refers to drunkards, and "inspiration" to windbags.

Considering his attitude toward the serious pretensions of poetry and his capacity for using, as his main weapon, the resources of poetic language against itself, it would seem quite reasonable to suppose that much of Swift's verse is simply parody. In a way, it would be accurate to call the imitations of Virgilian styles in "A Description of a City Shower" parody. But doing so would only fix a useful label to certain details of procedure. It would not supply a category for the whole poem, which we now realize cannot be dismissed by so simple a formula. It was evidently written with other objectives in mind—objectives that go beyond the capacities of parody alone. By itself, parody is too much confined within the style it is making fun of—so much so that, as the old saying goes, it pays the style a compliment. Swift always remains enough outside the style he parodies to place it in a comic perspective, to impose on it a logic of his own, and to turn it against itself.

The first stanza of "A Love Song in the Modern Taste," one of the few pure parodies that Swift wrote, runs:

> Flutt'ring spread thy purple Pinions,
> Gentle *Cupid* o'er my Heart;
> I a Slave in thy Dominions;
> Nature must give Way to Art.

The conventions of pastoral love poetry that Swift is making fun of are illustrated conveniently enough by these lines describing the bower of Adam and Eve in *Paradise Lost*:

> Here Love his gold'n shafts emploies, here lights
> His constant Lamp, and waves his purple wings,
> Reigns here and revels . . .
>
> (IV, 763–765)

In the contrast, the scorn expressed by Swift's mock simplicity of tone is inescapable. But the last line of Swift's stanza makes a criticism of pastoral conventions that is at once more explicit and more provocative than anything parody alone can convey: "Nature must give Way to Art." Some of the importance of this criticism is suggested by another passage from the same book of *Paradise Lost*:

But rather to tell how, if Art could tell,
How from that Saphire Fount the crisped Brooks,
Rowling on Orient Pearl and sands of Gold,
With mazie error under pendant shades
Ran Nectar, visiting each plant, and fed
Flours worthy of Paradise, which not nice Art
In Beds and curious Knots, but Nature boon
Powrd forth profuse on Hill and Dale and Plaine . . .
(236–243)

Milton is doubting the capacity of Art—a function of knowledge and civilization—to describe Nature in a state of innocence, in the Garden of Eden. Yet after the disclaimer in the first line he goes ahead with his description of Eden, uses all the pastoral imagery at his disposal, pauses again to insist that the flowers of Paradise are arranged naturally, and continues after that for fifty lines more. In spite of his moral doubts about art, Milton cannot avoid using the pastoral conventions because, as a poet, he must depend upon the resources of his art and count on the language of poetry as the one indispensable area of agreement with his readers. Swift, as we know, is determined to break down this kind of relationship between poet and reader. Besides, the "Nature" he is referring to in his stanza is not innocent nature. It is not even pastoral nature, since pastoral is art, and the point of his statement is to suggest that art and nature are not only distinguishable but also in fundamental opposition. Because art seeks to embellish nature with formalities of pastoral language, it is not telling the truth; and because poetry, with its artfulness, is supposed to be pretty, truth, or nature, is likely to be ugly. It is as though Swift were serving notice on all readers of poetry, warning them that he will systematically demolish the standards of poetic language that they normally rely on. All he will offer as a substitute for those comfortable standards will be a far less pleasant set of assertions, which he here calls nature, or truth.

The sum of all these suggestions is tantamount to a declaration of war on readers; for that reason alone one might find them somewhat disquieting. In particular, the implication that art is only a disguise for a natural but unpleasant truth seems to threaten a direct assault on our politer sensibilities—and any one

11

who has read the fourth book of *Gulliver's Travels* will realize the lengths to which Swift can go to fulfill a threat of that kind. Gulliver's avowal of his debt to the Houyhnhnm master could stand as a kind of boundary line, marking the extreme limits Swift's attitude to poetry is liable to attain:

> I had likewise learned from his Example an utter Detestation of all Falsehood or Disguise; and *Truth* appeared so amiable to me, that I determined upon sacrificing every thing to it.

"Sacrificing everything" includes the reader; and the fact that Swift never goes quite so far as Gulliver will not prevent us from being, on occasion, placed in a very precarious position.

An especially precarious approach to these limits is made by a poem called "The Progress of Beauty," which even in its opening stanzas seems to give a clear sign of the direction it will take:

> When first Diana leaves her Bed
> Vapors and Steams her Looks disgrace,
> A frouzy dirty colour'd red
> Sits on her cloudy wrinckled Face.
>
> But by degrees when mounted high
> Her artificiall Face appears
> Down from her Window in the Sky,
> Her Spots are gone, her Visage clears.

One of the more remarkable things about the beginning of this poem is that it is not absolutely necessary to notice that Swift is talking about the moon until one reads the third stanza:

> 'Twixt earthly Females and the Moon
> All Parallells exactly run;
> If Celia should appear too soon
> Alas, the Nymph would be undone.

Only now is it quite certain that the cloudy and discolored complexion of the first stanza is an atmospheric phenomenon, and that the degrees and spots of the second are astronomical details. When Swift tells us that parallels between "earthly Females and the Moon" are exact, he is giving fair warning that the poetic logic of the usual hyperbolic comparison between the pastoral mistress and the moon will be drastically redefined. Conventionally, the moon is beautiful but remote, chaste but inconstant, aloof and serene, but productive of amorous frenzy and high tides. But Swift picks on details that have a distinctly unliterary kind of appropriateness. The possibility that the first two stanzas are describing an earthly female instead of the moon is emphasized by the fourth, and becomes a definite indication of the direction in which these exact parallels will run:

> To see her from her Pillow rise
> All reeking in a cloudy Steam,
> Crackt Lips, foul Teeth, and gummy Eyes,
> Poor Strephon, how would he blaspheme!

Evidently the antipoetic logic of Swift's simile here will leave few details unexplored. For instance, one might observe in passing that, if Celia and the moon rise at the same time, and if they both, consequently, appear only at night, the traditional association of the virtue of chastity with the moon goddess has a special ironic inappropriateness. Swift remarks later on:

> Take pattern by your Sister Star,
> Delude at once and Bless our Sight,
> When you are seen, be seen from far,
> And chiefly chuse to shine by Night.
> (Stanza 18)

No threat of this kind is left unfulfilled, and Celia becomes a streetwalker before the poem is over. But for the time being Swift is interested in describing the artificial face that Celia, as well as the moon, must provide for herself before she can show herself in public:

> Three Colours, Black, and Red, and White,
> So gracefull in their proper Place,
> Remove them to a diff'rent Light
> They form a frightfull hideous Face,

For instance; when the Lilly slipps
Into the Precincts of the Rose,
And takes Possession of the Lips,
Leaving the Purple to the Nose.

(6–7)

It is entirely appropriate to the logic of the antipastoral Swift is developing that Celia's face should imitate a catalogue of flowers; just as, further on, it is equally logical that Venus should be the heavenly power to whom Celia owes the materials used in her cosmetic transformation:

Thus after four important Hours
Celia's the Wonder of her Sex;
Say, which among the Heav'nly Pow'rs
Could cause such wonderfull Effects.

Venus, indulgent to her Kind
Gave Women all their Hearts could wish
When first she taught them where to find
White Lead, and Lusitanian Dish.

(14–15)

It might be worthwhile pausing at this point to take stock of what is going on and, in so doing, contrast another, more familiar, cosmetic triumph: Belinda in *The Rape of the Lock*. I say "contrast" because Celia and Belinda are not strictly comparable, any more than it is appropriate to conclude from the dressing-table scene in the first canto that Belinda is, so to speak, a "painted hussy." Of course Pope criticized her for being silly, and wantonly prideful, and trivial; but we are certainly expected to find her charming all the same. Disapproval of face powder, in this context, is altogether too unimportant as an attitude to come anywhere near being serious disapproval of Belinda. Similarly, the marvelously supple and varied fun that Pope has with elevated poetic styles in *The Rape of the Lock* is in no way an indication that he has lost confidence in their ability to express feelings and embody values. But Swift considers that the poetic language he is reversing in "The Progress of Beauty" is in its normal state nothing less than a deception. By the logic of his reversal, the qualities opposite to those that pastoral poetry would maintain are the ones he asserts. Calling Belinda a nymph is a charming extravagance; calling Celia a nymph is a sardonic indication that she is a whore. Similarly, since cosmetics are literally a means of applying physical beauty artificially, Celia's use of them inevitably means that she is not only not beautiful, but positively disgusting. Art, which includes cosmetics as well as the language of pastoral convention, is discarded as a false embellishment of nature; and nature is presented as corrupt, ugly, and decadent.

By now, any reader who looks to the language of the poem for some kind of moral refuge from Swift's unpleasant details should be almost forcibly disabused. On the other hand, if the reader is knowing, if he is aware of Swift's tricks, and realizes that neither the nymph nor the moon is likely to be rescued from the antipoetic simile in which Swift has placed it—that is, if he is suspicious of art and seeks a refuge in nature—there is still nothing to feel comfortable about. Nature is too distasteful. The moon wanes as well as waxes—and, in the context of Swift's simile, that means that Celia's real face is even more vulnerable to disease and corruption than her painted one:

> But, Art no longer can prevayl
> When the Materialls all are gone,
> The best Mechanick Hand must fayl
> Where Nothing's left to work upon.

> Matter, as wise Logicians say,
> Cannot without a Form subsist,
> And Form, say I, as well as They,
> Must fayl if Matter brings no Grist.

> And this is fair Diana's Case
> For, all Astrologers maintain
> Each Night a Bit drops off her Face
> When Mortals say she's in her Wain.

> While Partridge wisely shews the Cause
> Efficient of the Moon's Decay,
> That Cancer with his pois'nous Claws
> Attacks her in the milky Way:
> But Gadbury in Art profound
> From her pale Cheeks pretends to show

That Swain Endymion is not sound,
Or else, that Mercury's her Foe.

. . . .

Yet as she wasts, she grows discreet,
Till Midnight never shows her Head;
So rotting Celia stroles the Street
When sober Folks are all a-bed.

(20–24; 26)

Swift has made our relationship with the poem a dilemma: Celia
is either "poetical" or revolting. The only "honorable" way out,
apparently, is to stay at a distance and try to enjoy the ruthless
ingenuity with which Swift develops the perverse logic of his
antipoetic simile. But it is difficult to do this. As long as one is
following the development of the poem, it is hard to contain one's
feelings of revulsion within Swift's tone of rational unconcern—
unless one is prepared to surrender altogether, and abandon
onself to the consequences of such an argument:

Two Balls of Glass may serve for Eyes,
White Lead can plaister up a Cleft,
But these alas, are poor Supplyes
If neither Cheeks, nor Lips be left.

(29)

Such a conclusion is inescapable: but any amusement it gives
takes the form, I suspect, of nervous laughter. We are not too
far from "A Modest Proposal" here—or, for that matter, from
the Yahoos.

It would, of course, be perversely naïve to base any final
claim for Swift as a poet simply on the fact that he makes his
readers nervous—just as it would be improper to declare that
Gulliver's Travels owes all its effectiveness to the revulsion aroused
by the Yahoos. And, although I have so far been heading in the
direction of such a claim, it requires no desperate ingenuity to
correct the balance of my argument. There are several poems,
among them the poems addressed to Stella, in which Swift makes
use of the same procedures that extend to such drastic lengths
in "The Progress of Beauty," but in which he achieves a totally
different effect. Simply mentioning Stella's name is enough to

suggest "the other side" of Swift's personality. The "private life" of the Dean of St. Patrick's is, of course, a celebrated literary mystery, responsible for much speculation as to whether Stella was really his half-sister, or his mistress in everything but in fact, or secretly his wife. But more important than such unanswerable questions is the actual quality—the style—of Swift's personality; of this, thanks to poems in which he expresses thoughts and feelings that are direct and private, it is possible to know a great deal.

Such a poem is the first of the yearly tributes "On Stella's Birthday," dated 1718/19; although it will tell us nothing about the legal definition of Stella's relation to Swift, it will tell us what no biographical theory ever can: something about the quality of that relationship.

> Stella this Day is thirty four,
> (We won't dispute a Year or more)
> However Stella, be not troubled,
> Although thy Size and Years are doubled,
> Since first I saw Thee at Sixteen
> The brightest Virgin of the Green,
> So little is thy Form declin'd
> Made up so largely in thy Mind.
> Oh, would it please the Gods to split
> Thy Beauty, Size, and Years, and Wit,
> No Age could furnish out a Pair
> Of Nymphs so gracefull, Wise and fair
> With half the Lustre of Your Eyes,
> With half thy Wit, thy Years and Size:
> And then before it grew too late,
> How should I beg of gentle Fate,
> (That either Nymph might have her Swain,)
> To split my Worship too in twain.

The main procedures of this poem are characteristic. Swift is evidently making fun of elegant poetic compliments. Along with the easily recognizable mock-pastoral talk about nymphs—and one is suspicious of all Swift's nymphs—one can observe inelegantly precise references to the lady's age and shape; a characteristically impolite word, "split," which is used twice; and an extended joke at the expense of poetic conceits that quite literally equates increased virtue with enlarged size and additional years. But there is something else to notice as well: something that is involved in the absolute distinction between Stella and the unspeakable Celia that the tone of easy intimacy requires the reader to make. Celia was a nymph also; but the collapse of poetic language in "The Progress of Beauty" is inseparable from all the dreadful revelations about Celia's true nature. In this poem the clumsy variations from the manner of poetic compliment that Swift pretends to assume—the size, the years, the "Form declin'd"—only serve to make the compliment more genuine. There is none of the ruthless urgency that, in "The Progress of Beauty," forces the reader into an impossible choice between false art and monstrous nature. Here art is, perhaps, no less false; and Stella, for all that one loves her, is by no means an embodiment of chivalric ideals. Nevertheless, in this poem a good bit of the irony that accompanies the collapse of the poetic language is directed back at Swift himself, speaking the poem. It is as though he were pretending to show off by turning an elegant compliment, but instead kept making awkward mistakes, dropping inadvertent insults about age and size, and using impolite words. The reader, who with his habits and prejudices is usually a primary target of Swift's irony, is almost completely ignored. The poem seems to be an actual conversation that we overhear only by chance. There is no hindrance to an address that is intimate and direct, spoken with full confidence that every inflection will be appreciated and every private joke understood. That is what I mean by saying that the poem can tell us something about the quality of their relationship: Swift is revealed as an actual participant in a moment of communication rather than as a literary lover assuming for his mistress a posture of poetic address. It is, I think, a rare thing to find a love poem that expresses so unpretentiously, so effortlessly, and so honestly an intimacy of this order.

One might add that it is an even rarer thing to find such a poem by Swift. But the discovery is less surprising if one considers what is known about his capacity for friendship, and his delight in private jokes and games with words—and if one considers also the *Journal to Stella*. That running account of Swift's political career during Queen Anne's last years, written in a special language that consists of a punning baby talk, is actually the kind of private correspondence that the poems to Stella imitate. The last entry in the *Journal* is relevant here. It was written on the inside of the cover of Swift's last letter to Stella, shortly before he sailed from Chester on his return to Ireland: ". . . when I read the Passage upon Chester walls, as I was coming into Town, & just receivd the Lettr: I sd aloud—Agreable B—tch." Fifteen years after this, and nearly ten years after the birthday poem, in a private reminiscence begun on the day of Stella's death, Swift had another occasion to remember her as "the brightest Virgin of the Green":

> I knew her from six years old, and had some share in her education, by directing what books she should read, and perpetually instructing her in the principles of honour and virtue; from which she never swerved in any one action or moment of her life. She was sickly from her childhood until about the age of fifteen: But then grew into perfect health, and was looked upon as one of the most beautiful, graceful, and agreeable young women in London, only a little too fat.

"On the Death of Mrs. Johnson" was not published until many years after Swift's own death: it may be presumed to have been written for no readers at all. Even here the voice is recognizable as characteristic.

There is, besides, a characteristic perverseness in the fact that Swift appears to us as most congenial when he is paying least attention to us. In the Stella poems—and the *Journal* and the other private writings—the anonymous common reader is ignored, and the irony that often turns all its force against the language readers normally trust is instead contained by a familiar situation. But Swift is usually addressing readers, not friends; and he addresses them in a voice that one cannot identify as "his own," and certainly not as congenial. The congenial moments constitute a sort of parenthesis in his career. It is, of course, a most distinguished parenthesis since, besides the Stella poems, it includes "Cadenus and Vanessa" and "Verses on the Death of Dr. Swift." If the old-fashioned question, "whether Pope was a poet," were ever seriously asked about Swift, it would be to such poems that one would point to support the Johnsonian rejoinder, "If this be not poetry, where is poetry to be found?" Yet Celia is more likely to be the heroine of his poems than is Stella. And one would not dream of adapting Johnson's reply to a defense of "The Progress of Beauty": if the interlocutor were sufficiently shocked by the poem, the answer might well come back, "Anywhere else."

But such colloquies should remain purely hypothetical. Swift simply is not interested in "being a poet." If there is any truth at all in the legend of Dryden's observation ("Cousin Swift, you will never be a poet"), it is that Swift was still writing Pindaric Odes when Dryden is supposed to have discouraged him. After that, the whole question becomes irrelevant. All the procedures that Swift follows in his poems demonstrate how little the stricter canons of neoclassical poetry apply to him. We have seen what happens to readers who are so stubborn as to try holding him to account, asking that their normal expectations be gratified. If anything, his poems demonstrate all the limits, and none of the uses, of the conventional literary categories. If at this point a category is still wanted, it had better be looked for in the prose satires. Whereas the canons of neoclassical poetry can provide only extreme contrasts, "A Modest Proposal," *A Tale of a Tub,* or *Gulliver's Travels* will suggest repeatedly that the procedures of the poems are as essential to Swift as irony itself. The same brutal rationality that dismembers Celia is employed by the projector of "A Modest Proposal"; the same confusion of logic and language that turns pastoral metaphors upside down and converts compliments into insults characterizes the courtiers of Lilliput and the academicians of Lagado; and, finally, the same alarming tendency to turn poetic language against itself is apparent in *A Tale of a Tub,* where all formal uses of language become self-destructive. In effect, the prose satires are expansions of procedures that are often only suggested in the poems. Thus, if one continues to be frustrated by Swift's refusal to fulfill any conventional expectations—not to mention the contempt that accompanies the refusal—one can always take a kind of Gulliverian comfort in the reflection, "If you can get used to the Yahoos, you can get used to Celia." And if one prefers to remember Stella, all the better.

E. SAN JUAN, JR.

The Anti-Poetry of
Jonathan Swift

The sense of the immediate, the acute responsiveness to concrete actuality, the energetic control exercised over elements of immediate sensory experience so as to organize them into a harmonious structure of meanings—these qualities characterize, in general, Swift's poetic achievement. To an extent we may consider poems like "Description of the Morning," "Description of a City Shower," the early Pindaric odes and the later self-portraits in verse (to name only a handful) modern in their inclusiveness, ambiguous complexity, and profound intellectual involvement with life. What hinders an intelligent estimate of Swift's poems is, among other prejudices, the naive belief that neoclassical poetry consists of no more than literal statements. That of course is far from the truth.

We know that "poetic diction" cannot be confined to any rigid category. For Pope, "poetic diction would cover all the words used in the dictionary, except those which nobody knew the meaning of without intense specialization in technical fields."[1] A random page of *The Dunciad* shows such "low" words as : *mustard, bowl, catcall, brangling, snip-snap,* juxtaposed with such deliberately mock-poetic words as *clarion* and *welkin.* Pope's criterion of correct usage implies appropriateness. This attribute,

This essay first appeared in *Philological Quarterly* 44 (1965): 387–96. Reprinted by permission.

however, falls short of precisely designating the subtlety of tone and ironic obliqueness in "Death and Daphne," "Day of Judgment," or "On Poetry: a Rhapsody," to cite a few cases. F. R. Leavis' estimate of Swift's stylistic technique contents itself with Dr. Johnson's praise of the artistry of Swift's poems, whose value lies in the "justness of their similes and the minuteness as well as exactness of their description."[2] That is all to the point. But could we not take this exactitude as a point of departure for a more intensive analysis of Swift's poems?

What strikes the reader of a piece like "The Progress of Beauty," for instance, may be found in its metaphysical manner of expression. This involves the power to see and hear what is felt, to convey such feelings or attitudes in multivalent correlatives that are accessible to everyone. The framework of analogy between the moon's appearance and the nymph's beauty functions as the principal vehicle for the ideational conflict between nature's dictates and human perversity. But the parallel also operates in such a way as to make perversity conform to natural phenomena:

> Take Pattern by your Sister Star,
> Delude at once and Bless our Sight,
> When you are seen, be seen from far,
> And chiefly chuse to shine by Night.
> (69–72)

This certainly proves how Swift's attitude to human vanity and self-deception cannot be definitely fixed or paraphrased.

To be sure, Swift's position is all-inclusive. Nature is supposed to serve as a guide for rational conduct, but the natural constitution of the nymph suffers "Crakt lips, Foul teeth, and gummy Eyes." There is the form imaged by the moon, but the corruptible substance of Celia appeals strongly to our humanity. And Luna's fate impresses us only with its remoteness from the pain of mortal shame, wretchedness, and death. The speaker, in spite of the implicit mockery at man's pretentiousness, confronts his cowardice in refusing to accept the human condition. He affirms the pattern he would reject:

Ye Pow'rs who over Love preside
Since mortal Beautyes drop so soon,
If you would have us well-supply'd,
Send us new Nymphs with each new Moon.

(117–20)

With an undertone of humorous flippancy in his invocation, he counterpoints the serious elevated tone of the address with the prosaic "drop" and "well-supply'd." Both terms allude to the mechanical artifice which represents pride and the degradation of the human body. And we assume in this context that the body has been originally cast in a divine mold.

No doubt Swift achieves an equilibrium of opposing emotional impulses through the ambiguity of the extended analogy. He knows that the ironical development of material brings in the opposite, but complimentary, impulses to the surface intent, which is confirmed mainly by the prevailing tone. Out of this process he produces an "intricately wrought composure" of surface and pattern. The poem thus effects a synthesis of disparities derived from experience. But as a rule the resolution of attitudes remains manifold, inexhaustible, and susceptible of limitless interpretations. Beneath the negative impact of *saeva indignatio*, the positive wit of his comic vision, Swift's "comedy of discontinuity," exerts its evocative richness, its density of suggestion.

Few have called attention to the extraordinary mass of details in Swift's poetry. Yet we must not ignore his intense scrutiny, his apathetically hostile but vigilant and minute attention focused on everyday actuality. This fidelity to perception serves as an appeal to the reader's disposition for fantastic details, his curiosity for microscopic particulars, yet it must be stressed that the sensory immediacy manifested by the texture of most of Swift's poems is by no means a photographic "slice of life." The aesthetic pattern imposed on the discordant qualities of the material, reconciling antithetical values, arises from his singular unity of tone; and the total meaning of a poem results from his establishment of meaningful relationships among the discordant elements. Consequently, poetic meaning refers more precisely to the total interaction of all the qualities of language. With these points in mind, we may further qualify the "realistic" or "anti-poetic" strategy of Swift's poems.

23

Ricardo Quintana, commenting on the anti-poetic movement in "A Description of the Morning," points to the curious
perspective established to bring all details into accord, and says
"Any work of art which discloses a point of view markedly individualistic or eccentric partakes of a certain dramatic quality:
it is not the artist's presence that we are aware of so much as
that of some person who is forcing us to experience the world
on his own terms."[3] Such a statement provokes two questions:
how do we verify the individualistic quality of Swift's point of
view, and by what means shall we ascertain the dramatic force
of his poems? I submit two ways of approach: first, through tone,
which forms the person's point of view; second, through language, which indicates the tonal modulations.

The concept of the anti-poetic signifies, according to Wallace
Stevens, who first defined it, "that truth, that reality to which all
of us are forever fleeing."[4] This flight *to* reality, to the world given
us by our senses and by our sensitive grasp of life, reveals itself
in the language of many poets. Shakespeare, for example, was
beset by the need to penetrate through the facade of abstractions
and conventions. He expressed his anti-poetic drive through his
protagonist: "Henceforth my wooing mind shall be express'd/In
russet yeas and honest kersey noes." And in Wallace Stevens:
". . . heads/Of the floweriest flowers dewed with the dewiest dew./
One grows to hate these things except on the dump." "Is it
peace," he asks, "is it the philosopher's honeymoon one finds/On
the dump?"[5]

Juxtapose with Stevens Swift's coda to "The Lady's Dressing
Room":[6]

> Such Order from Confusion sprung
> Such gaudy Tulips rais'd from Dung.
> (143–44)

Confronted with the filth of the biological, repulsed by the "excremental smell" of "sweet Celia," Swift, via his mask Strephon,
tones down his ruthless "stripping" of hypocritical veils. He executes this by indirectly acquiescing in the natural place and basis
of human affections. He alludes to Aphrodite's mythical birth—
with a side-glance at Botticelli's painting for greater irony:
"Should I the Queen of Love refuse,/Because she rose from

stinking Ooze?" Between an idyllic purism (which is all brain and no breath, e.g., the Houyhnhnms) and a sensual, primitive animalism, Swift mediates by presenting a purification trope in terms of cooking. From lines 99 to 114, he builds up an analogy: whereas "Mutton Cutlets, Prime of Meat," put on "clearest Fire," would turn the flame to "stinking Smoak," "Pois'ning the Flesh from whence it came," if its fat drops on the cinders,

> So things, which must not be exprest,
> When plumpt into the reeking Chest,
> Send up an excremental Smell
> To taint the parts from whence they fell.
> (109–12)

In comparing Celia's chest to Pandora's box, Swift affects our associations with each, and thus while Celia's chest denigrates Pandora's myth, the myth deodorizes Celia's room. Such a process occurs also in Pope's *The Dunciad,* where the salient mock-heroic metaphor "springs from holding the tone and often the circumstances of heroic poetry against the triviality of the dunces and their activities."[7]

Among modern poets, T. S. Eliot frequently exhibits this convergence of myth and experience through mock-heroic protagonists like Prufrock, Sweeney, and the young man carbuncular. Swift's poems commonly foreshadow this counter-pointing so fruitfully exploited by modern poetry. His technique deploys thematic material according to patterns suggested by the Biblical deluge ("Ode to the Athenian Society," "Description of a City Shower"), Aesop's fables ("The Beasts' Confession to the Priest"), Horace's satires ("Imitation of Horace I, vii"), the story of Cynthia and Endymion obliquely referred to ("Strephon and Chloe"), and Virgil's *Georgics* ("Description of a City Shower"). Particularly with "A Beautiful Young Nymph Going to Bed," a whole line of pastoral idylls, plus Ovid's *Art of Love,* asserts itself to provide the background of classical culture. Allusive intensification lent by Milton's Eve, her frailty and errors, and her Biblical counterpart; and Virgil's sibyl with her prophetic ecstasy, may be detected in lines 8–9: "Four stories Climbing to her Bow'r; Then, seated on a three-legg'd Chair. . . ."

On the whole, the vision of descrepitude is staggering. The

epic catalogue of artificial bodily parts, a faithful record of grotesque appendages that reduce the status of the human body, forms the substance of Swift's analysis. He dissects to reveal the hidden anatomy of human character. Yet in spite of the accumulation of harsh objects there are also lyrical modulations, as in these lines: "And then between two Blankets creeps/With pains of Love tormented lies"; or, "Shew the Anguish, Toil, and Pain/Of gath'ring up herself again?" To obviate the peril of overstatement or gross sentimentalism, Swift conceals the pathos of the situation and his sympathy toward it in the sustained impetus of his matter-of-fact rhythm.

In mode of presentation and technique, "On Dreams"[8] has the tact of "A Beautiful Young Nymph Going to Bed." Here dreams do not rise from "infernal Mansions" but from a "busy Head" that "with mimick Art runs o'er/The Scenes and Actions of the Day before." As Swift ranges over a panorama of degradation, the "false flitting Shades" he alleges capable of deluding our minds appear as agents who perform a factual inventory of deeds. These deeds defy the horrors of nightmare in their sordidness. When "with equal terrors; not with equal guilt,/The Murd'rer dreams of all the Blood he spilt," the murderer is surely not dreaming, he is remembering. In short, dreams are or metamorphose into facts. And the frightful thing is not the dream but the fact. Swift epitomizes the evil that shows through the prosaic routine of everyday life, by juxtaposing crimes with non-moral acts, as in

> The Soldier smiling hears the Widow's cries,
> And stabs the Son before the Mother's Eyes.
> With like Remorse his Brother of the Trade,
> The Butcher, feels the Lamb beneath his Blade.
>
> (15–18)

In this imaginative world, everything is moral since every fact connotes a human attitude or decision. In "The Author upon Himself,"[9] Swift describes himself dealing in "Vices of the graver sort;/Tobacco, censure, coffee, pride, and port." Like the "infernal Mansion," the oxymoronic "nauseous Praise" telescopes the social disorder in which tyrant and murderer, soldier and butcher, lawyer and pick-purse, physician and hangman, Divine and mountebank, hireling senator and Dick the scavenger, are all brothers in one riotous family. Swift's anti-poetic vision perceives that fact, the objective stuff of the newspaper, is more nightmarish. Objects are never opaque, they are always transparent: "The sleeping Hangman ties the fatal Noose,/Nor unsuccessful waits for dead Men's Shoes." An apocalyptic truth is delivered by "false-flitting Shades" in a typical Swiftian irony whose ambivalent antithesis traps the reader ("The kind Physician grants the Husband's Prayers") and cuts him when caught ("Or gives relief to long-expecting heirs").

We can see that Swift's method is unfailingly anti-poetic in the handling of material. Its implications tend to counteract the eighteenth-century tendency to narrow the language of poetry and its range of subject matter. Far from excluding matters of daily life, Swift includes the normal environment however brutish or filthy. His light verse seriously concerns itself with problems in a social context. While his imagination orders details into an ideal harmony, the substance is always solid: his poetry presents "imaginary gardens with real toads in them."

Swift's anti-poetic temper tends to exhibit a definitely ironic disposition and a satiric tone. For example, in "Verses Wrote in a Lady's Table-Book,"[10] the ivory table-book is made to speak out with a sincerity that insults the sham and social pretense of its owner. Placing awkward clichés and mis-spelled stock phrases that convey affections—"Here in Beau spelling (tru tel deth),/ There in her own (far an el breth)"—side by side with objective notations of practical life, Swift presents his moral attitude toward the trivial, petty, and vulgar mind of a society goddess. Though the incongruity of arrangement—

> Here you may read (*Dear Charming Saint*)
> Beneath (A new Receit for Paint)
>
> (*Madam, I dye without your Grace*)
> (*Item, for half a Yard of Lace*)
>
> (7–8, 15–16)

—effectively lampoons the disclosed stupidity and insensibility of the lady, Swift also attacks the prospective reader, "the peeping Fop," who would fling his "excrement" or "clap his own Nonsence" on the pages. He who will accept the depravity of the

27

human situation rendered here is "a Gold Pencil Tipt with Lead." Ultimately the attitude expressed through the table-book and its voice involves an ambiguity that escapes simple paraphrase.

Similarly, in "Mrs. Harris' Petition,"[11] the colloquial, ballad-like raciness of the uneducated servant's speech measures the personality of those whom she consults as they express their attitudes toward her lost purse. Through her coarse naivete, she caricatures the ways of her class and burlesques the manners of those above her. The statistical accuracy of her absurd chatter—"'Tis true, seven Pound, four Shillings, and six Pence, makes a great Hole in my Wages"—travesties her anxiety as well as the feelings of anger and of sympathy shown by others. On the other hand, "The Day of Judgment"[12] denies mankind's claim to the dignity and importance implicit in heroic rhetoric. The Miltonic ring of "Jove, arm'd with Terrors, burst the Skies,/And Thunder roars, and Light'ning flies!" yields to "I to such Blockheads set my Wit!/I damn such Fools!—Go, go, you're bit!" The surprising end abruptly shatters the grand vision. It provokes at once the comic disgust which Death also feels upon touching Daphne's hand in "Death and Daphne." Consequently, we get a parody of the traditional formula of tragic reversal:

> The matrimonial Spirit fled;
>
> Away the frighted Spectre scuds,
> And leaves my Lady in the suds.
>   (99, 103–04)

Swift's attraction to the anti-poetic led him from early imitations of Cowley to scathing lampoons and occasional verses dealing with public issues. Sometimes his "sin of wit" leads to doggerel, but in "Helter Skelter," for instance, tension exists between the ease of the metrics and the stark dissonance of the material: rapacity, lechery, murder. The galloping trochaic beat and the harmonizing rhyme scheme (e.g., houses, spouses; wenches, benches) compose what William Carlos Williams describes as "the complement tranquil and chaste," that is, the idealizing aesthetic pattern. Here the movement is quick in order to fit the "hue and cry," the chaos. Swift's technique of juxtaposing low descriptions ("Thorow stinking Lanes and allies") with morally reprehensible acts ("Some to Cuckold Farmers Spouses") resembles that of

"The Description of an Irish Feast."[13] Amid the innocent revelry, thievery and violence—even Death's laughter—masquerade as episodes of the merriment:

> They rise from their Feast,
>   And hot are their Brains.
>
> Come down with that Beam,
>   If Cudgels are scarce,
> A Blow on the Wean
>   Or a kick on the A—se.
>   (61–62, 85–88)

In other places, Swift's burlesque style may seem too occasional and detached. As a more familiar and intimate way of communication, his verse displays a severe plainness of speech. One detects a flat tonelessness in "Cadenus and Vanessa," for example.[14] The frame of fantasy makes the matter seem a "cavalier business,"or "a private humorsome thing." When we come to "Epistle to a Lady"[15]—"Still to lash, and lashing smile,/Ill befits a lofty style"—the violence of Swift's recurrent image of lashing "borders upon grandeur." While his ardor elevates the tone, his sensitivity never loses sight of the physical: e.g., Stella's face appears "an angel's face a little crak'd." Swift indeed "aimed at the head, but reached the heart":[16]

> My hate, whose lash just heaven has long decreed
> Shall on a day make sin and folly bleed.
>   (133–34)

Despite Swift's keen consciousness of the physical, Huxley's and D. H. Lawrence's accusations that his mind was diseased by "terror of the body" seem unfounded. On the other hand, though he used no tabooed words in "The Problem"[17] or in "The Virtues of Sid Hamet the Magician's Rod," Swift must have shocked the readers of his time through his emphasis upon man's sexual and gustatory urges. He rejected romantic mawkishness and exposed the loathsome and the unsavory. Thus while John and Phillis (in "The Progress of Love") end up keeping "at Stains the old Blue Boar/Are cat and Dog, and Rogue and Whore,"[18] the widow (in "The Progress of Marriage") marries a scoundrel[19]:

> To turn her Naked out of Doors,
> And spend her Joynture on his Whores:
> But for a parting Present leave her
> A rooted Pox to last for ever.
>
> (163–66)

Clearly Swift is anti-romantic in thinking that spurious fancies distort reality and introduce anarchy rather than any order to which they aspire. One such fancy is exemplified in "The Bubble"[20] with its images of confusion, Icarus, deluded mariners, and cheating jugglers. As humorist and wit, Swift continues the tradition of "Hudibras." His aim of reforming errors is always directed by experience: "Thus I find it by experiment/Scolding moves you less than merriment." Indeed, his method, Shavian in satiric bite, is "raillery to nettle/Sets your thoughts upon their mettle." Reacting against the heroic view of poetry and of the poet's function (e.g., Dryden's "furor poeticus"), Swift uses a casual, direct, and simple manner "spit wholly out of himself," enhanced "by feeding upon the insects and vermin of the age."

One critic calls attention to Swift's compromise with reality in acknowledging the physical nature of man.[21] But I think this acknowledgment is merely a function of Swift's attempt to represent the human condition, which is that human bodies—often loathsome—are engaged in dramatic action. Where is the compromise? Swift's moral theme employs the human body as a means to suggest the "necessity and hazard of the search of truth." Man being a mingled mass of good and bad, moral confusion can be resolved not abstractly but concretely, through the image of natural man: the human body thus becomes a plastic metaphor through which ideas achieve concrete correlatives. In "To Mr. Congreve,"[22] consider the lines:

> Those beds of dung, where schoolboys sprout up beaus
>
> (99)

or:

> . . . diseas'd conceptions, weak and wild,
> Sick lust of souls, and an abortive child,
> Born between whores and fops, by lewd compacts . . .
>
> (123–25)

Consistently Swift believed that reason and the passions form a precarious unity whose tension is a perpetual moral, aesthetic, and social problem.

To conclude: the anti-poetic element in Swift's poetry manifests itself in the intense awareness of a unifying sensibility. Swift accepted facts and delivered in highly charged language the de-idealizing meaning of facts. He exploited the spiritual implications, values, and attitudes that facts provoked, until finally consciousness became conscience. Swift's anti-poetic vision, in embodying his sense of proportion between justice and reality, still has relevance.

Notes

1. Geoffrey Tillotson, "Eighteenth-Century Poetic Diction," *Eighteenth-Century English Literature,* ed. James Clifford (New York, 1959), p. 214. Compare Irvin Ehrenpreis, *Swift: The Man, His Works, and The Age* (London, 1962), pp. 109–41. Francis Elrington Ball, *Swift's Verse* (London, 1929) may still be found useful.

2. *The Common Pursuit* (London, 1952), p. 84.

3. *Swift: An Introduction* (New York, 1955), pp. 92–93; see also Quintana's *The Mind and Art of Jonathan Swift* (London, 1936), pp. 49–74. I intentionally omit here any discussion of the two well-known pieces, "A Description of the Morning" and "Description of a City Shower"; see the discussion in F. W. Bateson, *English Poetry: A Critical Introduction* (London, 1951), pp. 177 ff., and in Maurice O. Johnson, *The Sin of Wit* (Syracuse University Press, 1950).

4. *The Necessary Angel* (New York, 1951), p. 25.

5. "The Man on the Dump," *Parts of A World* (New York, 1945), p. 23. Stevens adds in a postscript: "The poetry of a work of the imagination constantly illustrates the fundamental and endless struggle with fact" (p. 183).

6. *The Poems of Jonathan Swift,* ed. Harold Williams (Oxford: Clarendon Press, 1958), p. 530. All quotations of Swift's poetry are from this edition.

7. Maynard Mack, "Wit and Poetry and Pope: Some Observations on His Imagery," *Eighteenth-Century English Literature,* p. 37.

8. *Poems,* pp. 363–64.

9. Ibid., p. 164.

10. Ibid., p. 60.

11. Ibid., pp. 69–73.

12. Ibid., p. 543.

13. Ibid., pp. 245–47.

14. Ibid., pp. 686–714.

15. Ibid., pp. 629–38.

16. Ibid., p. 47.

17. Ibid., pp. 65–67.

18. Ibid., pp. 131–35, 222–25.

19. Ibid., pp. 289–95.

20. Ibid., pp. 248–59.

21. Kathleen Williams, *Jonathan Swift and the Age of Compromise* (University of Kansas Press, 1958), pp. 153 ff. On Swift's obscenity and bawdiness, see the discussions of: Irvin Ehrenpreis, *The Personality Of Jonathan Swift* (London, 1958), pp. 29–49; Edward W. Rosenheim, Jr., *Swift and the Satirist's Art* (University of Chicago Press, 1963), pp. 230–38; and John Middleton Murry, *Jonathan Swift, A Critical Biography* (New York, 1955), especially chapter 28, "The Excremental Vision," pp. 432–48.

22. *Poems,* pp. 46–47.

A. B. ENGLAND

World without Order: Some Thoughts on the Poetry of Swift

The complexity of Swift's satire is now recognised; the savage misanthrope has given way to the detached manipulator of ironic ambiguities. If perhaps inevitable in the change of critical climate a more devious response is clearly demanded anyhow by the work itself; the unresolved oppositions of *Gulliver's Travels* simply *have* to be held in a state of tension. It is this shifting inconclusiveness, a refusal (or incapacity) to define with the normal Augustan authority that is responsible for the peculiarly disconcerting effect of his writings. That Swift doesn't organise his material with any decisive clarity may suggest that his hold on the Popian ideal of a simplifying 'Order' was less than confident. Just how far this satiric apprehension of disunity extends can perhaps be seen by re-examining some of his most familiar poems.

'The Lady's Dressing Room' is a poem which seems for most of its length to be handled with the thematic discipline of a moral tract, until its solid coherence finally dissolves in irony. Strephon's idealising vision of Celia's divinity is ruthlessly broken down through contact with the inside of his 'Goddess''s chamber:

This essay first appeared in *Essays in Criticism* 16 (1966): 32–43. Reprinted with permission.

> Strephon, who found the Room was void,
> And Betty otherwise employ'd;
> Stole in, and took a strict Survey,
> Of all the Litter as it lay;
> Whereof, to make the Matter clear,
> An Inventory follows here.
>
> (5–10)

We are to have a 'strict Survey', an 'Inventory', just as in another poem we have an informative but unorganised 'Journal'; the use of the versified catalogue is important for Swift's special purpose. He is merely to report observed fact, coldly and impartially. In consequence Strephon's process of discovery is conveyed through a random succession of unassimilated details. Swift amasses the hideousnesses with bare physical precision. No sense of urgency or stress is felt in the words. He evokes a carefully particularised confusion by being all the time insistently specific. Strephon's experience is characterised by an obsessive determination to be thorough:

> No Object Strephon's Eye escapes,
> Here Pettycoats and frowzy Heaps;
> Nor be the Handkerchiefs forgot
> All varnished o'er with Snuff and Snot.
> The Stockings, why should I expose,
> Stain'd with the Marks of stinking Toes;—
>
> (47–52)

The sensory concreteness of Swift's description is unremitting, as detail is added to detail under a kind of mechanical pressure. This confused filth is what lies behind the carefully arranged surface implied in the ironic 'varnished o'er'. Swift draws attention to his concern for complete and accurate reportage, dwelling on physical minutiae, trying to get them right. When he lingers on Celia's use of her magnifying glass the apparently gratuitous elaboration of her delicate technique of extracting 'Worms' from her skin is intended to suggest an exhaustive care for detail.

It is finally in the image of Celia's lavatory that Swift condenses the simple scatological meaning. Disguised as a cabinet, covered with decorative trappings ('Rings' and 'Hinges'), it has a superficial elegance. The smell soon announces the unpleasant truth to Strephon, but he is masochistically 'Resolv'd to go thro' thick and thin'. The vague abstraction, 'Hope', which leads him on, is abruptly displaced by a recognition of concrete fact:

> The Vapours flew out from the Vent,
> But Strephon cautious never meant
> The Bottom of the Pan to grope,
> And fowl his Hands in Search of Hope.
> (91–94)

The symbolism is obvious to the point of being over-explicit. It is characteristic of Swift's elusive technique that his most distasteful poems should also be his most didactic. Here reality is opposed to unreality with crude emphasis. Strephon's mistake is like that of the 'Fool' in 'The Bubble', Swift's verse-attack on the South-Sea Project, who through relying on an optical illusion is bespattered with the mud of actuality. The image concentrates Swift's anti-romantic theme, summing up all its contrasts of inside and outside, dirt and decoration. Strephon is quite incapable of assimilating the juxtaposition:

> Thus finishing his grand Survey
> Disgusted Strephon stole away
> Repeating in his amorous Fits,
> Oh! Celia, Celia, Celia shits!
> (115–18)

In the last line Swift's satiric point is made with bald directness, as Strephon clings longingly to the incantation of Celia's lovely name, but can only finish his sentence with an absurd stress on the fact of excrement. He has been subjected to a process of total disillusionment and his reaction is grotesquely unbalanced:

> His foul Imagination links
> Each Dame he sees with all her stinks:
> And, if unsav'ry Odours fly,
> Conceives a Lady standing by—
> (121–24)

When his initially distorted vision is shattered the failure to discriminate is only intensified and extended. Imbalance leads to

35

imbalance; Strephon's reaction is objectively placed and laughed at. D. H. Lawrence's irritated assumption that Strephon is Swift speaking to his own mistress typifies a common reaction (*Selected Literary Criticism,* ed. A. Beal, London, 1955, p. 29). Lawrence's attitude is in fact the same as Swift's, only a little more violent. The identity of the reaction is not surprising: Swift and Lawrence both tried to accept the human body without making it other than what it is—as well as to destroy the linguistic inhibitions of taboo-words.

II

Though the thematic structure of 'The Lady's Dressing Room' is ordered with some formality and its central antithesis stated clearly, Swift's personal attitude is not made explicit. Strephon's shock at being made to realise the fact of excrement effects a violent reversal in his approach to woman, and Swift concludes the poem by expressing pity for this new and indiscriminate loathing and by recommending a compromise solution that he has adopted himself:

> Should I the Queen of Love refuse,
> Because she rose from stinking Ooze?
> To him that looks behind the Scene,
> Satira's but some pocky Quean.
> When Celia in her Glory shows,
> If Strephon would but stop his Nose;
> (Who now so impiously blasphemes
> Her Ointments, Daubs, and Paints and Creams,
> Her Washes, Slops, and every Clout,
> With which she makes so foul a Rout;)
> He soon would learn to think like me,
> And bless his ravisht Sight to see
> Such Order from Confusion sprung,
> Such gaudy Tulips rais'd from Dung.
>
> (131–144)

The irony here is as difficult to follow as that with which Swift works out the same theme in the 'Digression on Madness' of *A*

Tale of a Tub. There it is 'Reason' which comes to cut away the beautiful surface and reveal the hideousness within; and the writer urges the necessity of either disregarding its findings or not using it for this incisive purpose at all. Here Swift is suggesting that the fact of 'Stinking Ooze' should be assimilated into a generally admiring attitude towards women. He deliberately mixes up his language. The 'Queen of Love' is still a relevant phrase, and the poet looks on woman with 'ravisht Sight'. Yet her origin is at the same time recognised as 'Dung'; and 'Gaudy Tulips' suggests a heavily coloured artificiality. Swift is in fact being tortuously ambiguous. Strephon has been subjected to an overwhelming impression of physical repulsiveness, but the author can still assert that in cursing Celia's 'Washes' and 'Slops' he 'impiously blasphemes'. The religious ceremonies of cosmetic self-adornment, Pope's 'Sacred Rites of Pride', are deplored only by the profane. The voice that Swift momentarily assumes accepts at its face value the pretended reverence with which Pope approaches Belinda's dressing-table. Yet the compromise that is suggested to Strephon is obviously healthier than his present state. So the ground persistently shifts beneath our feet; after each ostensible attitude has been progressively modified we have in the end nothing whatever to hold on to. The kind of language that is used makes it clear that the advice is being given with conscious irony. But just where Swift stands in relation to the author's voice cannot be ascertained. Though he asserts his delight in the created 'Order', it would appear that he has a much stronger sense of the 'Confusion' which is being falsified, and which most of the poem has been devoted to presenting. To suggest that Strephon should 'stop his Nose' is merely to incite him to non-recognition. Evidently, then, this final passage manifests a tension and uncertainty that are not visible in the firm thematic shape of the narrative (there is much the same submerged unease in 'Cadenus and Vanessa'). Swift makes his exposure with vigorous clarity, but he is not sure what attitude to take towards it.

What he does, in this poem and in others that bear the same theme, is to juxtapose two laughably over-simplified concepts of woman and to suggest that a right attitude lies somewhere in between, this somewhere not being precisely located. Exactly the same technique is employed in the fourth book of *Gulliver's Travels*. The Houyhnhnms and the Yahoos are the structural equivalents of woman unreally idealised and woman unreally debased. Strephon makes the same kind of mistake as Gulliver and appears equally absurd. Swift builds up a pattern of oppositions without establishing his own preferences.

III

These persistently antithetical structures are related to the form of the verse-couplet, and we can see the same satiric patterning on a smaller scale from line to line in most of his poetry. In 'Verses Wrote in a Lady's Ivory Table Book' Swift works out his meaning through a series of repeated juxtapositions. The table-book becomes a sharp, clear image of the Lady's moral idiocy that is developed with dry precision:

> Here you may read (Dear Charming Saint)
> Beneath (A new Receit for Paint)
> Here in Beau-spelling (tru tel deth)
> There in her own (far an el breth)
> Here (lovely Nymph pronounce my doom)
> There (A safe way to use Perfume)
> Here, a Page fill'd with Billet Doux;
> On t'other side (Laid out for Shoes)
> (Madam, I dye without your Grace)
> (Item, for half a Yard of Lace.)
>
> (7–16)

The table-book reveals a senseless chaos. Exaggerated expressions of romantic love jostle with notes on cosmetics, bad breath, perfume and the price of shoes. The two voices, sounding alternately, create an impression of dissonance through grating rhymes like 'Billet Doux/Shoes' and 'Saint'/'Paint'. This apparent disharmony in the mélange of seeming passion and trivial expense-accounts conveys the immediate sense of an irrational confusion of values in much the same way as a similarly constructed passage in 'The Rape of the Lock'.

Not youthful kings in battle seized alive,
Not scornful virgins who their charm survive,
Not ardent lovers robb'd of all their bliss,
Not ancient ladies when refus'd a kiss,
Not tyrants fierce that unrepenting die,
Not Cynthia when her manteau's pinn'd awry,
E'er felt such rage, resentment, and despair,
As thou, sad Virgin! for thy ravish'd Hair,
                                        (Canto IV. 3–10)

By moving rapidly between areas where extreme emotions are
valid and areas where they are ridiculous Pope satirises Belinda
for the kind of misplaced emphasis that derives from a distorted
sense of values. The two sets of incidents are utterly separate,
and the point made by the passage is that Belinda's world fails
to recognise the incongruity of placing them together. Swift also
moves between two apparently different levels, but he conveys
meaning less through laughing at the unrecognised separateness
than through revealing the actual congruity. For there is a chime
of harmony in the second couplet that indicates the way in which
the two voices blur into one another. The passion that the beau
expresses is really no more than a fashionable display of feeling
in conventionally decorative phrases and is just as shallow as the
lady's concern for her recipes. The values of the lady and the
beau are distorted in that they have reduced emotion to mechanical phrase-making, and the final impression is not of contrast between feeling and non-feeling but of uniform sterility.
Instead of sharply isolating one level from another, in Pope's
manner, Swift merges two apparently different modes. Pope and
Swift both use the same formalised rhetoric of opposition that is
invited by the shape of the couplet; but whereas the one makes
through it a precise series of separations, the other reflects an
indistinctly jumbled confusion.

A much later poem, 'On Dreams', embodies in its careful
structure a similar process of implicit evaluation by means of
pointed juxtaposition. In each stanza two activities are set neatly
against one another; always however the second image, persistently taken from an area of 'low' life, has a powerfully concrete
quality that purports to stress what is basic in the first:

The kind Physician grants the Husband's Prayers,
Or gives Relief to long-expecting Heirs.
The sleeping Hangman ties the fatal Noose,
Nor unsuccessful waits for dead Mens Shoes.
(27–30)

The pattern is again formalised and repetitive, placing one couplet with another in a regular progression of pairs. While the two sets of activities would seem on the surface to belong to quite separate levels, their difference in social stature only masks a moral homogeneity. Swift implies his satiric statement through a series of carefully weighted oppositions; it is one of a pervasive baseness in human life. One thing shades imperceptibly into another, and distinctions become hard to make. Accepted lines of demarcation are in reality obscured.

This recurring structural technique is operated with greater compression and economy in 'On Poetry: A Rapsody'. Advising the poet against the vague substitution of initials for the full name of the person satirised, Swift says that readers will not understand whom he is talking about:

A publick, or a private Robber;
A Statesman, or a South-Sea Jobber,
A Prelate who no God believes;
A (Parliament), or Den of Thieves.
A Pick-purse at the Bar, or Bench;
A Duchess, or a Suburb-Wench.
(161–66)

Here the juxtapositions are made within the line, and their import is precisely the same as in the last poem. If the poet does not specifically state the identity of the people he writes about we shall be unable to ascertain whether they are statesmen or thieves, lawyers or pick-pockets, duchesses or prostitutes. Only a name distinguishes the morally coalescing levels. Butler had dealt with the same theme in like manner:

There's but the twinkling of a star
Between a man of peace and war:
A thief and justice, fool and knave,
A huffing off'cer and a slave;

A crafty lawyer and pick-pocket,
A great philosopher and a blockhead;
A formal preacher and a player,
A learn'd physician and man-slayer.
                ('Hudibras', II, iii, 957–64.)

Swift clearly echoes this passage both here and in the previous poem. Butler was beset by the same sense of uniformity in apparent diversity, and expressed it in a similar rhetoric of merging oppositions. Swift exploits the antithetical structures suggested by the couplet form, not to bring sharp separates ironically together and to mock those who don't see the falsity, but to throw apparent unlikes into conjunctions that are valid and real. In doing so he conveys a sense of actuality as something amorphous and indistinct, not to be resolved into simple partitions.

IV

In these passages a kind of ordered shape is created in the repetitive pattern of seeming contrasts, only to be made irrelevant by the shapelessness which results from the contrasts being broken down. In 'A Description of the Morning' there is not even this superficial order. The poem is on one level a specific parody of pretty descriptions of pastoral dawns, such as Cotton's 'Morning Quatrains' which is echoed in the last line. Only hackney-coaches make people conscious of the coming dawn. No one is susceptible to it as a natural phenomenon causing an aesthetic response. Day is not felt in streaks of gold in the eastern sky, but in the first rattling noises of the street. Nor do we have Aurora creeping from the lap of Tithonus, only Swift's characteristic equivalent:

Now hardly here and there an Hackney-Coach
Appearing, show'd the Ruddy Morns Approach.
Now Betty from her Masters Bed had flown,
And softly stole to discompose her own.
The slipshod Prentice from his Masters Door
Had par'd the Dirt, and Sprinkled round the Floor.
Now Moll had whirl'd her Mop with dext'rous Airs,

Prepar'd to Scrub the Entry and the Stairs.
The Youth with Broomy Stumps began to trace
The Kennel-Edge, where Wheels had worn the Place.
The Smallcoal-Man was heard with Cadence deep,
'Till drown'd in Shriller Notes of Chimney-Sweep.
Duns at his Lordships Gate began to meet,
And Brickdust Moll had Scream'd through half the Street.
The Turnkey now his Flock returning sees,
Duly let out a Nights to Steal for Fees.
The watchful Bailiffs take their silent Stands,
And School-Boys lag with Satchels in their Hands.

The first intention of this drably realistic picture is to ridicule the kind of natural description that seeks no more than a surface attractiveness. There is no point in complaining with W. D. Taylor that even in a city there is more to the dawn than this (*Jonathan Swift: a critical essay*, London, 1933, pp. 243–4). A limiting point of view is adopted for a special purpose. The element of parody is stressed by the use of a vocabulary alien to Swift but common in pastoral poetry. The coalman shouts 'with Cadence deep', the chimney-sweep 'in Shriller Notes', and the gaoler sees his 'Flock' of prisoners return after a night's thieving.

Though the various activities are not so formally interrelated as in the previous passages they do imply a kind of comment on one another in much the same way. Instead of building up a series of apparently radical oppositions, Swift works through a number of unemphatic variations from couplet to couplet. For though the activities that Swift brings together do not come from dramatically different levels, they do diverge in a more subtle way, varying between menial servant work, gutter-combing, prostitution, delivering coal, bankruptcy, theft and loitering. None of these are particularly attractive, but obviously some are more distasteful than others, and some are simply criminal. F. W. Bateson rationalises the catalogue into the juxtaposition of the 'morally neutral' and 'real social evils' (*English Poetry*, London, 1950, pp. 176–77). This is, I think, to make an ordered separation which the poem itself does not quite effect. Swift does not so much distinguish between two kinds of activity, pointing out how they have ceased to be differentiated, as present a variousness that cannot properly be resolved at all. Bateson is right, however, to suggest that the point Swift is making is that society tends to take these various things equally for granted. The flat, steady movement of the verse, the similarly unemphatic statement of each activity, suggest the uniform indifference with which they are all regarded. The poem does not really conclude; it just peters out, lazily. A world which sees these incidents with equal unconcern has lost its sense of values. Swift's achievement in this poem is, without losing the fragmentary, confused effect of realism, also to attain a kind of thematic pattern. For the picture is so near to being an undifferentiated reflection of disorder that it makes a satiric point without seeming tailored to a didactic end.

This kind of realism, through which Swift presents details without seeming to order them, amounts in 'Mrs. Harris's Petition' to an apparently complete abdication from the artist's selective responsibility. Here Swift brings the kind of faithfulness to the recording of a mind's moment by moment activity that has become familiar in the twentieth century 'stream of consciousness' technique. The poem announces itself as a formal petition in which it is to be expected that a series of argumentative points will be logically ordered towards a certain conclusion. But Mrs. Harris is incapable of discriminating between her experiences, and everything that comes into her head has to be put down. For her to state her case the only possibility is a painstakingly detailed narrative that accumulates relevancies and irrelevancies in a random associative flow:

> Lord! Madam, says Mary, how d'ye do? Indeed, says I,
>   never worse;
> But pray, Mary, can you tell me what I have done with my
>   Purse!
> Lord help me, said Mary, I never stirr'd out of this Place!
> Nay, said I, I had it in Lady Betty's chamber, that's a plain
>   Case.
> So Mary got me to Bed, and cover'd me up warm,
> However, she stole away my Garters, that I might do my-
>   self no Harm:

So I tumbl'd and toss'd all Night, and you may very well
    think,
But hardly ever set my Eyes together, or slept a Wink.

                                (14–21)

Emile Pons compares the humour of this poem with that of
Chaucer and distinguishes it for its exhaustively detailed realism,
for 'une notation plus sèche, plus incisive des motifs et des ar-
rières-pensées,—une insistence plus grande sur ce qui n'est que
mesquin' (*Les Années de jeunesse et le 'Conte du Tonneau'*, Stras-
bourg, 1925, p. 231). The voice meanders on and on without
purpose or direction. Abandoning order in the progression of
thought, Swift also abandons order in the structure of his verse.
Regular metre is replaced by limping doggerel. Occasionally a
line moves with an apparent rhythm (line 38 or 51, for example)
only to emphasise the disharmony of those around it by momentarily setting up expectations that are not realised. Imitating
Mrs. Harris's aimless gabble, Swift records an inane confusion.

    The pictures that Swift draws have particularity without
shape. The contents of Celia's dressing-chamber accumulate
without being made to add up to a unified description. We are
not given an impression of what the chamber is like as a room,
only a catalogue of the bits and pieces that litter it. 'A Description
of the Morning' presents the same multifariousness, as Swift
enumerates a series of common sights with almost random un-
selectiveness, noting details without bringing them together.
Again in 'The Description of a City Shower' Swift's naturalism
demands a profusion of detail and a vivid sense of disorder. The
shower is not the vast generalised downpour described in the
First Book of Virgil's 'Georgics' which Swift intermittently parodies, but a certain quantity of water which is felt as coming
down through individual 'Spouts' rather than from the limitless
heavens, and as falling upon specific umbrellas and sheds rather
than over a wide landscape. It does not bring universal terror
and humility, but an endless series of minor discomforts and
irritations. Swift lists a number of individual people and situations without in any way resolving their fragmentary separateness into a total picture. The shower falls onto the infinitely
detailed city, and it is these details which are important rather
than the shower as a single phenomenon. We are simply pre-

sented with its localised effects upon a number of concrete particulars. The borders of the composition are blurred, and the specific elements seem likely to spill over the edges of any frame that might irrelevantly be imposed on them. Such poems, pictorially and sometimes structurally indecisive, are in a sense images that illustrate one of Swift's reactions to his world.

ROBERT W. UPHAUS

Swift's Poetry:
The Making of Meaning

A number of Swift's poems have often been used as evidence of
his opposition to poetry—his "anti-poetic" it is most often called.
Such assertions, regrettably, have tended to assume that Swift's
poems "demonstrate all the limits, and none of the uses, of conventional literary categories."[1] By measuring a selection of Swift's
poems against this assumption, I intend to show how Swift makes
poetry by projecting his own vision of reality—a simultaneous
opposition to the visionary imagination and a firm commitment
to the material world as the primary source of human knowledge—within certain traditional literary conventions. That Swift
alters or reshapes poetic conventions should not be surprising,
for this is the traditional prerogative and responsibility of poets.
Indeed, this is how good poets make meaning.

  The following well-known passage from *A Tale of A Tub* gives
a premonition of the theme of "Verses wrote on a Lady's Ivory
Table-Book":

> Last week I saw a Woman *flay'd,* and you will hardly
> believe, how much it altered her Person for the worse.
> Yesterday I ordered the Carcass of a *Beau* to be stript
> in my Presence; when we were all amazed to find so

This essay first appeared in *Eighteenth-Century Studies* 5 (1972): 569–86. Permission to reprint it has been granted by the American Society for Eighteenth-
Century Studies.

many unsuspected Faults under one Suit of Cloaths:
Then I laid open his *Brain,* his *Heart,* and his *Spleen*;
But, I plainly perceived at every Operation, that the
farther we proceeded, we found the Defects encrease
upon us in Number and Bulk . . .[2]

In a miniature way, "Verses wrote on a Lady's Ivory Table-Book"
similarly flays a woman, only the approach is witty rather than
severe. For Swift is here less interested in shocking his ostensibly
naive reader than in envisioning the triviality of a "modern"
lady's heart. (This is a topic, by the way, which attracted Swift's
interest in a number of poems.) The theme of this poem is the
dislocation between a lady's charming image and the dullness
and triviality of her feelings. This dislocation is reinforced by
Swift's contrast of his own precise language with the vapid entries
in the lady's ivory table-book which are italicized in the poem.

> Peruse my Leaves thro' ev'ry Part,
> And think thou seest my owners Heart,
> Scrawl'd o'er with Trifles thus; and quite
> As hard, as senseless, and as light;
> Expos'd to every Coxcomb's Eyes,
> But hid with Caution from the Wise.
> Here you may read (*Dear Charming Saint*)
> Beneath (*A new Receipt for Paint*)
> Here in Beau-spelling (*tru tel deth*)
> There in her own (*far an el breth*)
> Here (*lovely Nymph pronounce my doom*)
> There (*A safe way to use Perfume*)
> Here, a Page fill'd with Billet Doux;
> On t'other side (*laid out for Shoes*)
> (*Madam, I dye without your Grace*)
> (*Item, for half a Yard of Lace.*)[3]

What Swift has done here is simply to identify the woman's
heart with the book in which trifles are recorded. The book
conceit is a well-established literary convention, one which Ernst
Curtius devotes an entire chapter to in *European Literature and
the Latin Middle Ages.* Let me quote some examples from Shakespeare's plays which Curtius cites[4]—first from *A Midsummer*

Night's Dream:

> Reason becomes the marshal to my will
> And leads me to your eyes, where I o'erlook
> Love's stories written in Love's richest book.
>   (II.ii.120–22)

Or this from *Romeo and Juliet*:

> Read o'er the volume of young Paris' face
> And find delight writ there with beauty's pen;
> Examine every married lineament
> And see how one another lends content,
> And what obscur'd in this fair volume lies
> Find written in the margent of his eyes.
> This precious book of love, this unbound lover,
> To beautify him, only lacks a cover.
>   (I.iii.81–88)

And as a final example, although more occur in Shakespeare's plays, there is Othello's well-remembered outburst: "Was this fair paper, this most goodly book,/Made to write 'whore' upon?" (IV.ii.71–72). Swift would also know this convention from many poets of the seventeenth century, among them Jonson, Herrick, Waller, Donne, and Marvell. The question, then, is not whether Swift uses literary conventions to advance meaning (he obviously does), but rather how he transforms a popular convention and extends its potential. Just as the above conceits extend to a seemingly "logical" conclusion, so Swift advances the conceit, in his own way, to its inevitable, trivializing conclusion, which is fully in accord with the poem's contrast between a woman's beguiling appearance and her mind crowded with minutiae:

> Whoe're expects to hold his part
> In such a Book and such a Heart,
> If he be Wealthy and a Fool
> Is in all Points the fittest Tool,
> Of whom it may be justly said,
> He's a Gold Pencil tipt with Lead.

What image could be more consistent and more apt to summarize the poem's juxtaposition of glitter and triviality? The woman's heart is a book, in which the man, who is a pencil, scrawls trifles.

It is possible to make a fairly plausible case for the veiled obscenity in this poem. After all, Swift is fond of visualizing his male victims in terms of images of impotence or sterility; seen in this light the image of a "Gold Pencil tipt with Lead" is wonderfully suggestive. But when Swift finds this procedure necessary, as in "The Description of a Salamander" or "The Virtues of Sid Hamet the Magician's Rod," he is usually explicit. Now it is not my intention to philosophize about the profundity or the inherent poetic magic of obscenity, but since Swift's obscenity is often used as evidence of his "anti-poetic" attitude, I would like to suggest that the obscenity in "The Description of a Salamander" is both conventional (that is, it has poetic precedents) and thematically necessary. As much as I may agree with Sir Harold Williams that this poem about Lord John Cutts is a "scurrilous invective against a brave man,"[5] I do not find the poem "inexcusable," because, given the conventions of invective, the one thing I do *not* expect is fairness and impartiality.

The creation of this poem appears to have occurred this way. Swift, capitalizing on the nickname "Salamander" which Cutts had won at the siege of Namur and remembering Pliny's description of a salamander in his *Natural History*, seized the opportunity to exploit the parallels between a mythical salamander, alleged to have the power to endure fire, and Lord Cutts, who is also said to have endured fire—gunfire. From this parallel, as the following lines show, Swift quickly points to the dislocation between the titles of classical heroes and the ironic appropriateness, in his view, of calling a "modern" hero a salamander:

> So men have got from Bird and Brute
> Names that would best their Natures suit:
> The *Lyon, Eagle, Fox* and *Boar*
> Were Hero's Titles heretofore,
> Bestow'd as Hi'roglyphicks fit
> To shew their Valor, Strength or Wit.
> For, what is understood by *Fame*
> Besides the getting of a Name?
> But e're since Men invented Guns,

> A different way their Fancy runs;
> To paint a Hero, we enquire
> For something that will conquer fire.
>
> (ll. 7–18)

Two lines later he writes a couplet whose rhyme words "grander" and "Salamander" effectively disclose the poem's ironic version of Cutts's heroism. By invoking what Irvin Ehrenpreis has called "parallel history," Swift uses Cutts as an example of his culture's trivialization of genuine heroism; among other things, the poem suggests that any warfare which uses guns is distinctly unheroic. But there are two other characteristics of a salamander which Swift applies to Cutts—its gaudy skin and serpentine shape, and its resistance to heat.

In the first instance, the parallel is both general and obvious:

> So when the War has rais'd a Storm
> I've seen a *Snake* in human Form,
> All stain'd with Infamy and Vice,
> Leap from the Dunghill in a trice,
> Burnish and make a gaudy show,
> Become a General, Peer and Beau,
> Till Peace hath made the Sky serene,
> Then shrink into it's Hole again.
>
> (ll. 37–44)

But for the second characteristic, the salamander's coolness, Swift may well have had in mind the opening lines of John Cleveland's "The Antiplatonic," which employs a popular seventeenth-century literary figure for a lover's coolness to passion. I quote some lines from Cleveland's poem:

> For shame, thou everlasting Woer,
> Still saying Grace and ne're fall to her!
> Love that's in Contemplation plac't,
> Is *Venus* drawn but to the Wast.
> Unless your Flame confesse its Gender,
> And your Parley cause surrender,
> Y'are Salamanders of a cold desire,
> That live untouch't amid the hottest fire.[6]

Cleveland's military metaphor (parley, surrender, fire) is, of course, appropriate to Swift's subject. But Swift goes several steps beyond the genial wit of Cleveland's poem. Here is *his* obscene version of Cutts's alleged coolness amid love's "hottest fire":

> SO have I seen a batter'd Beau
> By Age and Claps grown cold as Snow,
> Whose Breath or Touch, where e'er he came,
> Blew out Love's Torch or chill'd the Flame:
>
> (ll. 57–60)

And Swift continues in a more explicitly syphilitic vein for a few more lines. What seems to me decidedly worth noticing, in light of the assumptions about Swift's alleged "anti-poetry," is that this poem is firmly rooted in the conventions of invective; as nasty as the poem may be, its meaning emerges and is shaped by recognizable literary precedents. Swift certainly has worked at collapsing Cutts's grandeur, but he has not "engineered" the collapse of poetic language.

It would appear, at first reading, that "A Satirical Elegy on the Death of a late Famous General" (namely, Marlborough) is nothing more than a repetition of "The Description of a Salamander." Such, however, is not the case. This poem is much more than an invective; it is an inverted elegy in which Swift contrasts Marlborough's military greatness (a fact Swift seems willing to concede) with the mundane circumstances of Marlborough's unheroic death. If Swift had stopped at this point, the poem would certainly have resembled an invective. But the fact is, he uses Marlborough's pride to reinforce the lesson of Ecclesiastes: "Vanity of vanities; all is vanity. What profit hath a man of all his labour which he taketh under the sun?"

To begin my discussion of this poem, I would like to contrast the opening of Swift's "Satirical Elegy" with Henry King's elegy, "The Anniversarie." Both poems are based on similar literary conventions (down to almost the last image), although their thematic intent clearly differs. I may be laboring the obvious, but it seems to me that the difference between the two poems does not necessitate our calling one poem poetry and the other "anti-poetry." Rather, the two poems are an effective object lesson of the expansiveness of the language and conventions of poetry. Here are the opening lines of King's elegy:

So soone grow'n old? Hast thou bin six yeares dead?
Poore Earth, once by my Love inhabited!
And must I live to calculate the time
To which thy blooming Youth could never climbe,
But fell in the ascent? Yet have not I
Study'd enough Thy Losse's History?
   How happy were mankind, if Death's strict Lawes
Consum'd our Lamentations like the Cause!
Or that our grief, turning to dust, might end
With the dissolved body of a friend![7]

And here are the first sixteen lines of Swift's elegy:

His grace! impossible! what dead!
Of old age too, and in his bed!
And could that Mighty Warrior fall?
And so inglorious, after all!
Well, since he's gone, no matter how,
The last loud trump must wake him now:
And, trust me, as the noise grows stronger,
He'd wish to sleep a little longer.
And could he be indeed so old
As by the news-papers we're told?
Threescore, I think, is pretty high;
'Twas time in conscience he should die.
This world he cumber'd long enough;
He burnt his candle to the snuff;
And that's the reason, some folks think,
He left behind *so great a stink.*

   The conventional three-part structure of the elegy[8]—praise, lament, consolation—has dropped out of sight, but not out of mind. Swift knows what the usual procedures of elegy require, but he plays the reader's expectations against the obvious informality of the poem. The commonness of Marlborough's death suggests, once again, that Swift is suspicious of public greatness because it leads men to overestimate their inherent worth. In this regard, Swift is actually writing in the main line of Augustan poetry; one recalls, for example, Dr. Johnson's harsh lines in *The Vanity of Human Wishes* about the distinctly unheroic last days of

Swift and Marlborough: "From Marlb'rough's eyes the streams of dotage flow/And Swift expires a driv'ler and a show" (ll. 317–18). Moreover, the final lines of "A Satirical Elegy" use Marlborough in much the same way that Dr. Johnson uses Charles XII of Sweden: "He left the name, at which the world grew pale,/To point a moral, or adorn a tale" (ll. 221–22). One need only compare these lines with the conclusion of Swift's elegy:

> Come hither, all ye empty things,
> Ye bubbles rais'd by breath of Kings;
> Who float upon the tide of state,
> Come hither, and behold your fate.
> Let pride be taught by this rebuke,
> How very mean a thing's a Duke;
> From all his ill-got honours flung,
> Turn'd to that dirt from whence he sprung.

The images of dirt and water, coupled with the verb "sprung," precisely locate the incongruity between man's common origin and his grand aspirations. This is a poem written with Old Testament fervor and poetic tact: that Swift turns the dust of King's elegy into dirt, that he reduces the conventional restorative waters of weeping to the airy bubbles of the vanity of human wishes, in no way compels us to conclude that he was writing anything other than effective poetry.

At this point, we might wonder whether Swift is capable of, or even interested in, writing poetry of approval, a poetry in which he can align a wholly affirmative vision within certain literary conventions. The answer is, yes, he can, and he does so in a variety of ways. "Stella's Birth-day 1727," for example, is the last poem in a series of birthday poems which Swift began writing Esther Johnson ("Stella") in 1719. Unlike the conventional amatory poetry of the late sixteenth and seventeenth centuries, which often depicts the passion and instability of love, Swift's "love" poems concentrate on friendship as a way of stabilizing the fluctuations of passion. To do this, however, Swift neither parodies nor satirizes conventional amatory verse. He simply projects his views of love as friendship against the traditions of amatory verse, and then allows the reader to note the differences. Let me quote some lines from Swift's poem which both allude to and quietly reject the notion of *carpe diem* often embedded in amatory verse. I should also mention that when Swift wrote this poem Esther Johnson was mortally ill.

> This Day, whate'er the Fates decree,
> Shall still be kept with Joy by me:
> This Day then, let us not be told,
> That you are sick, and I grown old,
> Nor think on our approaching Ills,
> And talk of Spectacles and Pills;
> To morrow will be Time enough
> To hear such mortifying Stuff.
> (ll. 1–8)

> Although we now can form no more
> Long Schemes of Life, as heretofore;
> Yet you, while Time is running fast,
> Can look with Joy on what is past.
> (ll. 15–18)

In these lines Swift may well be alluding to, say, the following passage from Marvell's "To His Coy Mistress":

> Now let us sport us while we may;
> And now, like am'rous birds of prey,
> Rather at once our time devour,
> Than languish in his slow-chapped power.[9]

Yet the language of poetry can easily accommodate both views, without our having to reject one poem as "anti-poetry." Where Marvell, given the intent of his poem, emphasizes time as a threat to love, Swift transforms the threat into a reaffirmation of the stability of friendship and proof of the invulnerable wholeness of a virtuous life. Swift is not interested in the transient pleasures of passion; he is concerned with the strength of friendship, where time is devoted to "Reflecting on a Life well spent" (l. 36). Unlike the life of passion, the life of virtue can look back and also move with "Courage on" because such a life is a continuous flow of self-fulfillment. Happiness is not sensual pleasure; it is the knowledge that attends consciousness of virtue:

> Does not the Body thrive and grow
> By Food of twenty Years ago?
> And, had it not been still supply'd,
> It must a thousand Times have dy'd.
> Then, who with Reason can maintain,
> That no Effects of Food remain?
> And, is not Virtue in Mankind
> The Nutriment that feeds the Mind?
> Upheld by each good Action past,
> And still continued by the last:
> Then, who with Reason can pretend,
> That all Effects of Virtue end?
>
> (ll. 55–66)

This is not the sort of passage which Marvell was about to include in "To His Coy Mistress." After all, much of the wit of Marvell's poem relies on his presenting a seemingly well-reasoned argument to engage in immediate passion. In Marvell's poem the woman's mind, or reason, is represented as "coyness," an obstacle to pleasure, but Swift, in the concluding lines of his poem, urges Stella to use her mind so as to take comfort in the knowledge that her friends are loyal and her life remains stable:

> O then, whatever Heav'n intends,
> Take Pity on your pitying Friends;
> Nor let your Ills affect your Mind,
> To fancy they can be unkind.
> Me, surely me, you ought to spare,
> Who gladly would your Suff'ring share;
> Or give my Scrap of Life to you,
> And think it far beneath your Due;
> You, to whose Care so oft I owe,
> That I'm alive to tell you so.

To sum up: both Swift and Marvell root their thematically divergent poems in the same poetic conventions. Yet the one poem holds the body supreme, the other the mind.

Now Swift has other, less gentle ways, of writing about women who seize the day, as in "A Beautiful Young Nymph Going to Bed," which could be subtitled a day in the life of a whore. When, however, Swift uses scatological imagery, the "anti-poetry" critics are quick to seize a cliché. And if he isn't dogged by the "anti-poetry" enthusiasts, he receives even less help from John Middleton Murry, who finds such imagery evidence of a "sick" mind, and Norman O. Brown, who loudly applauds Swift's keen, anal insights.[10] Without going into the genealogy of scatological imagery, we can see that Swift has a number of poetic models in mind when he uses such imagery. For example, here are some lines from Juvenal's *Sixth Satire* (Dryden's translation, ll. 173–89):

> To the known Brothel-house she takes her way;
> And for a nasty Room gives double pay;
> That Room in which the rankest Harlot lay.
> Prepar'd for fight, expectingly she lies,
> With heaving Breasts, and with desiring Eyes:
> Still as one drops, another takes his place,
> And baffled still succeeds to like disgrace.
> At length, when friendly darkness is expir'd,
> And every Strumpet from her Cell retir'd,
> She lags behind, and lingring at the Gate,
> With a repining Sigh, submits to Fate:
> All Filth without and all a Fire within,
> Tir'd with Toyl, unsated with the Sin.
> Old *Caesar*'s Bed the modest Matron seeks;
> The steam of Lamps still hanging on her Cheeks
> In ropy Smut; thus foul, and thus bedight,
> She brings him back the Product of the Night.[11]

So, too, does Swift's poem benefit from Spenser's description of Arthur's stripping of Duessa:

> Her craftie head was altogether bald,
> > And as in hate of honorable eld,
> > Was overgrowne with scurfe and filthy scald;
> > Her teethe out of her rotten gummes were feld,
> > And her sowre breath abhominably smeld;
> > Her dried dugs, like bladders lacking wind,
> > Hong downe, and filthy matter from them weld;

> Her wrizled skin as rough, as maple rind,
> So scabby was, that would have loathed all womankind.[12]

And from this description, which is a mock-blazon[13] in part—
Una draws the following moral lesson which *exactly* parallels
Swift's theme:

> Such then (said *Una*) as she seemeth here,
> Such is the face of falshood, such the sight
> Of fowle Duessa, when her borrowed light
> Is laid away, and counterfesaunce knowne.
> (Book I, viii, 49)

Here are the opening lines of Swift's poem, a poem which
not only capitalizes on the models of Juvenal and Spenser, but
which also draws much of its strength from reversing the descriptions of those well-known nymphs in, say, Herrick's "No
loathsomnesse in love," "Corinna's Going a Maying," and especially his poem "Delight in Disorder."

> CORINNA, Pride of *Drury-Lane,*
> For whom no Shepherd sighs in vain;
> Never did *Covent Garden* boast
> So bright a batter'd, strolling Toast;
> No drunken Rake to pick her up,
> No cellar where on Tick to sup;
> Returning at the Midnight Hour;
> Four Stories climbing to her Bow'r;
> Then, seated on a three-legg'd Chair,
> Takes off her artificial Hair:
> Now, picking out a Crystal Eye,
> She wipes it clean, and lays it by.
> Her Eye-Brows from a Mouse's Hyde,
> Stuck on with Art on either Side,
> Pulls off with Care, and first displays 'em,
> Then in a Play-Book smoothly lays 'em.
> Now dextrously her Plumpers draws,
> That serve to fill her hollow Jaws.
> Untwists a Wire; and from her Gums
> A Set of Teeth completely comes.

Swift is picking apart her image because Corinna's *is* the face of falsehood. There is no delight in this disorder, for this is Swift's portrait of a modern Duessa. Never in Swift's poetry has detail been so well aligned with poetic function. The "Pride of *Drury-Lane*" (which means that Corinna is the most "beautiful" whore of either Drury-Lane or Covent Garden)[14] extends beyond Corinna to the self-deception and falsehood of the modish belles and beaux who frequent Drury-Lane and Covent Garden; the word "Bow'r" (with its courtly overtones) and the Miltonic "dextrously" are effectively contrasted with the underlying degradation of Corinna's life; and finally Swift poses the disturbing incongruity between Corinna's loving care for her own frail imposition of order and the mechanics by which she maintains her image.

Obviously, the kind of tyrannous detail elicited in this poem is much more than an irreverent shower of epithets designed, as some critics presumably believe, to collapse the language of poetry. Corinna's life is symbolic of the life of those who *do* seize the day, who choose the body to the complete exclusion of the mind, who choose pleasure alone and hence *must* live from day to day, for unlike Stella they have no solid foundation on which to build their life. In one of his essays Swift, in speaking of those people who base their life entirely on the body's appearance and pleasures, remarks on the "vain Endeavours to repair by Art and Dress the Ruins of Time."[15] This is the theme Swift is getting at—the vicious cycle of a life contemptuous of virtue, the horrible disorder and falsehood that hounds the life of a person committed exclusively to the body. This theme is made especially clear in the poem's conclusion:

> The Nymph, tho' in this mangled Plight,
> Must ev'ry Morn her Limbs unite.
> But how shall I describe her Arts
> To recollect the scatter'd Parts?
> Or shew the Anguish, Toil and Pain,
> Of gath'ring up herself again?
> The bashful Muse will never bear
> In such a Scene to interfere.
> *Corinna,* in the Morning dizen'd,
> Who sees, will spew; who smells, be poisn'd.

This is, evidently, a less joyful version of "gathering rosebuds"; it is, rather, a grim depiction of starting from scratch. If Swift's poem seems too strong, a case of overkill, let me remind the reader, as the conclusion to my discussion of this poem, of some lines from Robert Frost's version of a beautiful young nymph, "Provide, Provide":

> The witch that came (the withered hag)
> To wash the steps with pail and rag,
> Was once the beauty Abishag,
>
> The picture pride of Hollywood.
> Too many fall from great and good
> For you to doubt the likelihood.
>
> Die early and avoid the fate.
> Or if predestined to die late,
> Make up your mind to die in state.[16]

Since, up to this point, I have not examined a poem which explicitly deals with Swift's own sense of what poetry is and what, in his own time, it needed to do, let us look at "On Poetry: A Rapsody," a poem which I think is both a defense of Swift's use of poetry and a critical estimate of the verse of many of his contemporaries. Interestingly, the very accusation that Oswald Johnston has brought against Swift's verse—namely, that "his poems demonstrate all the limits, and none of the uses, of the conventional literary categories"[17]—parallels Swift's indictment of those "moderns" who are "Jobbers in the Poets Art" (l. 312) and "Creatures of the rhiming Race" (l. 386). To borrow from Pope's much-admired "Epistle To Augustus," a poem directly influenced by "On Poetry," Swift is attempting to preserve the distinction between "The Poet" and the "Man of Rhymes." [18]

Before I move directly to the content of Swift's poem, I would like to discuss the literary conventions which shape the meaning of "On Poetry." However, I entertain no hope of having detected all the literary precedents which Swift uses to make meaning. The opening proposition of this poem is that a combination of pride and folly best accounts for the abundance of trivial verse written during Swift's time.

> What Reason can there be assign'd
> For this Perverseness in the Mind?
> *Brutes* find out where their Talents lie:
> A *Bear* will not attempt to fly:
> A founder'd *Horse* will oft debate,
> Before he tries a five-barr'd Gate:
> A *Dog* by Instinct turns aside,
> Who sees the Ditch too deep and wide.
> But *Man* we find the only Creature,
> Who, led by *Folly*, combats *Nature*;
> Who, when *she* loudly cries, *Forbear*,
> With Obstinacy fixes there;
> And, where his *Genius* least inclines,
> Absurdly bends his whole Designs.
>
> (ll. 11–24)

Besides drawing on Edward Young's *Universal Passion* and Pope's *Essay on Criticism* and *Dunciad*, Swift has used at least three seventeenth-century poets to help shape the theme of his poem. From the Earl of Roscommon's "Essay on Translated Verse" he has benefited from such lines as "How justly then will impious Mortals fall,/Whose *Pride* would soar to *Heav'n* without a Call."[19] He has clearly been influenced by the following lines from Dryden's translation of Boileau's *The Art of Poetry*:

> Rash Author, 'tis a vain presumptuous Crime
> To undertake the Sacred Art of Rhyme;
> If at thy Birth the Stars that rul'd thy Sence
> Shone not with a Poetic Influence:
> In thy strait Genius thou wilt still be bound,
> Find *Phoebus* deaf, and *Pegasus* unsound.
>
> You then, that burn with the desire to try
> The dangerous Course of charming Poetry;
> Forbear in fruitless Verse to lose your time,
> Or take for Genius the desire to Rhyme:[20]

And I am confident that Swift was familiar with both the Latin original and John Oldham's imitation of Horace's *Art of Poetry*, whose concluding lines read:

> 'Tis hard to guess, and harder to allege,

Whether for parricide, or sacrilege,
Or some strange, unknown, and horrid crime,
Done in their own, or their forefathers' time,
These scribbling wretches have been damned to rhyme:
But certain 'tis, for such a cracked-brained race
Bedlam, or Hogsdon, is the fittest place.

. . . .

Remorseless they to no entreaties yield,
Till you are with inhuman nonsense killed.[21]

It is precisely this distinction between "Genius" and "the desire to Rhyme," between genuine poetry and what Oldham calls "scribbling" and "inhuman nonsense," that Swift wishes to uphold. For Swift realizes that, without this distinction, poetry will slip into the hands of men whose verse *will* demonstrate all of the limits and none of the uses of literary categories. Let me quote from Swift's address to a young beginner in "On Poetry":

How shall a new Attempter learn
Of diff'rent Spirits to discern,
And how distinguish, which is which,
The Poet's Vein, or scribling Itch?
(ll. 71–74)

Again, I think it's instructive to realize the literary precedents from which Swift inherits this distinction between the "Poet's Vein" and "scribling Itch," for his attack on bad poetry could mistakenly be called "anti-poetry." (Herbert Davis, for example, has said that "Swift is of course not concerned in this poem with any poetic ideal.")[22] The Latin origin of "scribling Itch" ("scribendi cacoethes") occurs in Juvenal's *Seventh Satire* (l. 52).[23] The exact phrase also occurs in Oldham's imitation of Boileau's *Eighth Satire,* and other variations of this phrase are in Rochester's "An Allusion to Horace," Dryden's translation of Boileau's *Art of Poetry,* and Roscommon's "Essay on Translated Verse." Looking beyond Swift's poem, the phrase "Poetick Itch" appears in Pope's "Epistle to Augustus." I mention these occurrences only as evidence of Swift's intent, which is not to collapse poetry, but to align himself with poets and poems written in defense of poetry.

The terrible distortion of the "anti-poetry" thesis, then, is this: the charge has been brought against a poet who is himself attempting to preserve the distinction between genuine poetry and derivative scribbling. Swift attacks those men whose lack of talent subverts the dignity of poetry, and yet in doing so he has been mistakenly called an "anti-poet." But even a cursory look at "On Poetry: A Rapsody," I hope, has demonstrated that Swift's attack on *bad* poetry ought not to be taken as an attempt to collapse the resources of poetic language. It would require a "Perverseness in the Mind" to misconstrue the intent of the following passages from "On Poetry":

> *Hobbes* clearly proves that ev'ry Creature
> Lives in a State of War by Nature.
> The Greater for the Smaller watch,
> But meddle seldom with their Match.
> (ll. 319–22)

> . . . .

> But search among the rhiming Race,
> The Brave are worried by the Base.
> If, on *Parnassus'* Top you sit,
> You rarely bite, are always bit:
> (ll. 327–30)

> . . . .

> Thus ev'ry Poet in his Kind,
> Is bit by him that comes behind;
> Who, tho' too little to be seen,
> Can teaze, and gall, and give the Spleen;
> Call Dunces, Fools, and Sons of Whores,
> Lay *Grubstreet* at each others Doors;
> Extol the *Greek* and *Roman* Masters,
> And curse our modern Poetasters.
> Complain, as many an ancient Bard did,
> How Genius is no more rewarded;
> How wrong a Taste prevails among us;
> How much our Ancestors out-sung us;
> Can personate an awkward Scorn
> For those who are not Poets born:

And all their Brother Dunces lash,
Who crowd the Press with hourly Trash.
(ll. 341–56)

There is another way that we can look at "On Poetry: A Rapsody," one that best summarizes all that I have been trying to say in this paper. This poem does not simply depict the presence of good and bad poetry; it suggests, as well, that only through the careful preservation of the distinction between the "Poet's Vein" and "scribling Itch" will truthful language remain invulnerable to barbarism and decadence. This poem, together with the others I have examined, deals ultimately with one basic conflict—that between mankind's susceptibility to the language of pride and flattery and the poet's obligation to uphold the language of virtue and truth. In an age darkened by uncreating words (to use Pope's phrase), the best a sensitive poet could do was either to retreat into a highly private kind of poetry and defend his own integrity (which Pope was tempted to do) or else aggressively seek out the causes of such decadence and publicly expose them as Pope did in *The Dunciad*. I think in his late career the choice for Swift was even narrower than this: it was either silence or satire, complete abdication or militant attack. That Swift chose to attack the scribblers who were progressively corrupting the resources of poetry is wholly consistent with the responsibilities of the poet. That he aligned his verse with, rather than against, the traditional uses of poetry is ample evidence of his faith in poetry as a vehicle for truth.

Notes

This paper was read to the Eighteenth-Century Conference held at Michigan State University on 9 May 1970. I would like to thank Professors Howard Anderson, Phillip Harth, and Arthur Sherbo for their helpful and encouraging remarks.

1. Oswald Johnston, "Swift and the Common Reader," in *In Defense of Reading*, ed. Reuben A. Brower and Richard Poirier (New York, 1963), p. 189. [Reprinted in this volume.] For other variations of the "anti-poetry" approach, see Herbert Davis' essay, "Swift's View of Poetry," in *Jonathan Swift: Essays on his Satire and other Studies* (New York,

1964), and E. San Juan, Jr.'s article [reprinted in this volume], "The Anti-Poetry of Jonathan Swift," *PQ*, 44 (July 1965), 387–96.

2. *The Prose Works of Jonathan Swift*, ed. Herbert Davis, 14 vols. (Oxford, 1939–62), I, 109–10. Hereafter cited as *Prose*.

3. Jonathan Swift, *Poetical Works*, ed. Herbert Davis (London, New York, and Toronto, 1967), p. 45. I use this edition throughout my essay, although I often depend on the helpful notes in Sir Harold Williams' edition of Swift's poems.

4. See Ch. xvi of *European Literature and the Latin Middle Ages* (New York and Evanston, 1963). Curtius only cites the act and scene of the quoted passages. However, I have collated the passages with the line numbers in *The Complete Plays and Poems of William Shakespeare*, ed. William Allan Nelson and Charles Jarvis Hill (Cambridge, Mass., 1942).

5. Sir Harold Williams, *The Poems of Jonathan Swift*, 2nd ed., 3 vols. (Oxford, 1958), I, 82.

6. *The Poems of John Cleveland*, ed. Brian Morris and Eleanor Withington (Oxford, 1967), p. 54. For a brief discussion of the conventions behind this poem, see the editors' commentary on p. 146. That Swift associates Cutts with "Salamanders of a cold desire" is especially ironic because Cutts himself had written love poetry.

7. *The Poems of Henry King*, ed. Margaret Crum (Oxford, 1965), pp. 72–73.

8. See O. B. Hardison, Jr., *The Enduring Monument* (Chapel Hill, 1962), pp. 113–16, 122.

9. *The Poems and Letters of Andrew Marvell*, ed. H. M. Margoliouth, 2 vols. (Oxford, 1963), I, 27. It is possible that lines 17–18 of Swift's poem were also influenced by Denham's "Look forward what's to come and back what's past" ("Of Prudence," l. 217). See *Poetical Works of Sir John Denham*, ed. Theodore Banks, Jr. (New Haven, 1928), p. 196. I have examined the Stella poems in more detail in my article, "Swift's Stella Poems and Fidelity to Experience," *The Dublin Magazine*, 8 (Spring 1970), 31–42.

10. See John Middleton Murry, *Jonathan Swift* (New York, 1955), and Norman O. Brown, *Life Against Death* (Middletown, 1959).

11. *The Poems of John Dryden*, ed. James Kinsley, 4 vols. (Oxford, 1958), II, 700–701. Hereafter cited as *Dryden*.

12. *The Poetical Works of Edmund Spenser*, ed. J. C. Smith and E. De Selincourt (London, New York, and Toronto, 1965), p. 44 (Book I, viii, 47).

13. See Hallett Smith, *Elizabethan Poetry* (Ann Arbor, 1968), pp. 26–27, 53. Of course, Spenser's description is much more than a mock-blazon, and the same should be said for Swift's "A Beautiful Young Nymph Going to Bed."

14. Professor Arthur Sherbo brought this meaning to my attention.

15. *Prose*, IX, 92.

16. Robert Frost, *The Complete Poems* (New York, 1964), p. 404.

17. Johnston, "Swift and the Common Reader," pp. 178, 180, 189.

18. *The Poems of Alexander Pope*, ed. John Butt (New Haven, 1963), p. 647.

19. The edition I have used of Roscommon's "Essay on Translated Verse," which is in the Special Collections of the Michigan State University Library, was printed together with some of Dryden's poems for Jacob Tonson in 1685. There are no line numbers in the text.

20. *Dryden*, I, 332.

21. *The Poems of John Oldham*, ed. Bonamy Dobrée (Carbondale, Ill., 1960), p. 167. There are no line numbers printed in the text.

22. *Jonathan Swift: Essays on his Satire and other Studies*, p. 170.

23. I am indebted to the editors of *Eighteenth-Century English Literature* (New York, 1969) for this gloss on Swift's phrase.

II. The "Biographical Presence"

MAURICE JOHNSON

Swift's Poetry Reconsidered

I

Existing autographs of Jonathan Swift's poems show three different styles of handwriting. There is a formal, impersonal script like that engraved in metal for frontispieces to eighteenth-century books, with precise, elegant capitals and uniform *d*'s, each with an overhead flourish. There is Swift's easier script, more relaxed and less rigorously employed. And there is his cruder and somewhat hesitating script, the so-called disguised hand, though it might perhaps be called a "private" hand. For it is in the painfully formed letters of this third style that one finds, on the final page of the Morgan Library autograph of "The Discovery" (1699), the poet's vexed rejection of his pen: *"this i i is impossible to mend this is/so sog goo/for nothing/ . . . . this must not/not not one once upon a/time isi iis impossible."*[1] The manuscripts, whether they appear as works of calligraphic art or as impatient outcries, are valuable because they contain the texts of Swift's poems in his own hand. But they are significant as well because of what they reveal to us about Swift's methods and attitudes—for what they suggest about Swift biographically.

Like the manuscripts, the poems themselves have a bio-

This essay first appeared in *English Writers of the Eighteenth Century,* ed. John H. Middendorf (New York and London: Columbia University Press, 1971), pp. 233–48. Reprinted with permission.

graphical interest. Some, indeed, meant as off-the-cuff jokes, doodles, jingles, and private mutterings, have little interest of any other kind. Many of the deservedly famous poems are self-dramatizations of personality, depicting Jonathan Swift not only in the ways he looked to himself but as he imagined he appeared to other eyes. Some of the more formal, impersonal poems, though they seem detached from Swift's career and the historical background of his time, can perhaps achieve deeper interest and meaning when read in a biographical context.

For almost fifty years critics have warned against the tendency to infer events of a poet's life from his poem. They have also warned against the temptation to project into a poem the "true" events and experiences of the poet's life as we know or imagine them to be. A proper reader, many of us have been convinced, does not imagine his relationship with the poet to be that between one man and another. A poem is to be read not as self-expression but as a rendering of certain principles of rhetoric: not as illumination on aspects of the author's identity but as a "verbal contraption" (the term is W. H. Auden's).

There was certainly a real need to rescue Swift's works, both in prose and verse, from the prejudicially biographical "Swift"—neurotic and malevolent—invented by nineteenth-century commentators who were exquisitely fascinated by his negative qualities. Even T. S. Eliot, who, perhaps more than any other single critic in the twentieth century pressed the discrediting of the biographical approach to literature, saw behind Swift's writings an "amazing madman," a master of disgust whose *Gulliver* manifests "the progressive cynicism of the mature and disappointed man of the world."[2] Eliot read Swift under the influence of nineteenth-century commentators. Those commentators or their ghosts are still with us, though they nowadays especially praise a "Swift" who was fashionably mad with sex and excrement obsessions.

Considering Swift's poetry more or less from the "verbal contraption" point of view, and rejecting the nineteenth-century idea of a "mad" Swift, recent studies have some new things to say about conscious craftsmanship in the poems. Not that such studies are frequent. In the past twenty years there have been only my own general book on the subject; an appreciation in the

Oxford History of English Literature; and four or five independently published critical explications of any length that deal with individual poems.[3] Quite properly a recent assessment of unexplored areas for future study in Restoration and eighteenth-century literature opens by noting that interpretation of "many of Swift's poems has scarcely begun."[4]

II

In modern studies it has been demonstrated that Swift's versification is expert and his phonetic effects and meter are skilfully adjusted to enforce his meaning. To suit his theme and mood he effectively employs devices like alliteration: sometimes he diffuses alliteration throughout a passage, sometimes he concentrates it in a single line. Experimenting with a variety of styles, he works most characteristically in the octosyllabic couplet, which he can attune to Hudibrastic high (or low) jinks, or to the tender delicacy of seventeenth-century lyrics, or—unusual in the work of any poet—to an intersecting and blending of these two disparate modes. Such a blending is most readily recognized in the poems addressed to Stella, which join loving-kindness and laughter. After relinquishing his early experiments with the Pindaric form, Swift surprises the ear with audacious rhymes and parodies, deliberately avoiding the pretentious and would-be sublime. He employs almost no ornamental imagery seriously intended. Instead, he confers unexpected interpretations upon conventional metaphors, which suddenly are shown to be canting or empty. He borrows elevated images only to twist, shrink, shred, or dissolve them, altering clichés into puns by treating them as though they were not verbal abstractions but palpable things to be sat on, cooked and eaten, made love to, mailed in a letter, slammed down like a window, or watched flying away through the sky. His diction and syntax are colloquial and often elliptical, especially when they imitate the rhythms and language of garrulous monologuists, town gossips, and persons trapped in the false etiquette of social intercourse.

There is no question, either, about the formal complexity of structure in Swift's best poems, often at tension with the racy colloquial diction and familiar style. An able strategist in his verse as well as in his more famous prose, Swift proceeds in a manner shaped by an energetic and conscious art. Three general patterns or schemes control the structure in those poems that seem of permanent interest.

One pattern is that of mutually exclusive opposites, often in a satiric confrontation of opposed exaggerations. In certain poems a middle ground of common sense is made explicit, as in Swift's delineation of contrasting events on a wedding night. The bridegroom's exaggerated embarrassment at being bedded with a "cold and snowy" goddess "unsusceptible of Stain" is contrasted with his sudden change to an exaggerated state of reciprocated bedroom animality in which "They soon from all Constraint are freed." But more than a third of the poem goes on to outline a lesson of mutual respect and common sense: "Let Prudence with Good Nature strive,/To keep Esteem and Love alive."[5] Other poems, more characteristic of Swift, leave the middle ground of intention to be inferred. In "Verses on the Death of Dr. Swift," for instance, the pretended weaknesses of character Swift imputes to himself, as well as the pretended account of general indifference to the news of his death, are balanced by the shamelessly exaggerated praise for the "dead" Dean with which the poem concludes. Elsewhere in his prose and verse Swift similarly dramatizes a need for moderation when he poses an impossible choice between Fool and Knave or between Yahoo and Houyhnhnm. Such a confrontation must be resolved in the mind of the reader. In poems of this first pattern, that of locking irreconcilable extremes in opposition, the thematic or structural device is ultimately moral in its implications.[6]

Another structural pattern is exemplified by his verses on the death of the Duke of Marlborough, which in only thirty-two lines stun the reader by offering an elegiac ode of conventional patriotic piety and then debasing it, item by item. As we read, we descend from the exclamatory announcement "His Grace! impossible! what dead!" to his Grace's unmourned funeral and thence to his Grace's ignominious interment: "From all his *ill-got* honours flung,/Turn'd to that *dirt* from whence he sprung" [italics mine].[7] The device is that of deflation, unmasking, and stripping bare. One of the high points of wisdom for Swift, it is well known, lies in the art of exposing weak sides and publishing infirmities. As in the metaphorical prose of *A Tale of a Tub* the carcass of a beau is stripped of its clothes, its brain laid open, and its heart and spleen dissected to discover more defects, in a number of poems the stripping bare is literally achieved. The prosthetic whore in "A Beautiful Young Nymph Going to Bed" is dreadfully allowed to take herself apart. She is not, after all, a beautiful young nymph. Sometimes, especially in the shorter poems like "The Day of Judgement," exposure is accomplished by a sudden twist in the concluding couplet, altering all that has preceded. A curtain is flicked up to reveal things as they are. Exposure by reversal, undercutting, or moral unmasking is intensified in its effect by an abruptly altered tone, plummeting from the elevated to diction that is rudely colloquial, earthy, and real.

A third pattern in Swift's poetry has been termed that of "a comedy of continuity."[8] For example, in "Verses wrote in a Lady's Ivory Table-Book" and "The Furniture of a Woman's Mind," with their amusingly incongruous parallels to insinuate a confusion of values, the method is often that of a seemingly undiscriminating continuum of items. Incongruous catalogues, inventories, connections, and correspondences accumulate with a total effect of strong force. "I am not in the least provoked [Lemuel Gulliver writes when his travels are ended] at the sight of a Lawyer, a Pick-pocket, a Colonel, a Fool, a Lord, a Gamester, a Politician, a Whoremunger, a Physician, an Evidence, a Suborner, an Attorney, a Traytor, or the like."[9] The reader is confounded to imagine what "the like" would be in order to fit into such an outrageous list. The point of course is that Pick-pocket, Colonel, Fool, and the rest are truly indistinguishable as fallen creatures "smitten with *Pride*." Such an incongruous catalogue can provide the entire structural outline for a poem like "The Beasts Confession to the Priest," where distinctions between one man and another, as well as between man and animal, are blurred. Or, concentrated in an eighteen-line paragraph, there is the better-known tour de force in which the Dean's "female Friends" interruptedly discuss his demise while they pursue a game of cards. Through a series of five parallel stages, death and the business of playing cards are exactly equated, beginning with "'The Dean is dead, (*and what is Trumps?*)'" and concluding with "'He lov'd the Dean. (*I lead a Heart.*),'" each uttered in a single undiscriminating breath.[10] With alternatives each of which is equatable and interchangeable with the others, the seriate construction acts as a testing of the reader's powers of discrimination.

There is, then, a good deal to be said about craftsmanship in the poems. Criticism in its chilliest aspect, as methodological doctrine or systematic process, will find matters for analysis in many of the poems that have never yet been studied.

III

Commentators sympathetic to Swift's verse are likely to conclude their discussions with the observation that it is puzzlingly unique, or with an admission of critical inadequacy or bafflement. In the language and structure alone they do not find sufficient warrant for the peculiar emotional effect of some of the poems. Certain poems by Swift are characterized as "unlike anything else in our language" or "without quite their like in our literature"; and "we have not yet attained to an adequate appraisal" of Swift's poetic art; "for exact discussion of those very aspects of poetry in which Swift excels we still lack adequate tools." He is "a poet of a special kind."[11]

On reconsideration, I wonder whether the special quality in Swift's poems may not work through his own biographical presence.

All of Swift's poems—those with critical interest and those with none—may be said to evoke response beyond that implicit in the imaginative constructs they represent, simply because we know them to come from the author of *Gulliver's Travels* and *The Conduct of the Allies*. To gain control over the "difficult" poems of any author, we read them in relationship to his other works, which are likely to interact among themselves and are all, taken together, one manifestation of their author's life. We do this in spite of any wish for critical "purity." For Swift as poet such a reading seems especially desirable, as it does also for Herman

Melville as poet: Melville's "Billy in the Darbies" may have been originally intended to stand alone; but part of its impact for us comes from its relationship now to *Billy Budd, Moby Dick,* and Melville's own career.

The moving events of Swift's life cannot be dissociated from his writings; as much as for any poet of his day, his own identity and his poetry seem inseparable. In the drama of many of his poems Swift deliberately creates a character for himself and plays the leading role. He explores, defines, and identifies himself in his poems, using that identity as a sort of intermediary to dramatize the human predicaments his poems deal with.

One of Swift's most striking poems bears the open-faced title "The Author upon Himself," but many of his other poems could share that title, including "The Author's Manner of Living," "In Sickness," "The Dean's Reasons," "The Dean to Himself on St. Cecilia's Day," "Written by Dr. Swift on his Own Deafness," and of course "The Life and Genuine Character of Doctor Swift" and "Verses on the Death of Dr. Swift." He poses himself alongside friends in "The Dean of St. Patrick's to Thomas Sheridan" and "Dr. Swift to Mr. Pope While he was Writing the *Dunciad.*" In three of his liveliest poems he describes himself by means of an altered perspective as though seen by Lady Acheson: "My Lady's Lamentation and Complaint against the Dean," "Lady Acheson Weary of the Dean," and "A Panegyrick on the Dean in the Person of a Lady in the North"; in another poem, "To Dean Swift," he assumes the guise of her husband Sir Arthur to address himself. Usually referring to himself in the third person in these and other poems, as though recording what he sees in a mirror, he appears—often humorously—as "The Chaplain," "Parson Swift," "Poor S—t," "Good Dr. S—t," "Cadenus," "Good Mr. Dean," "the DRAPIER," "thy Deanship," "the Dean," or "St. P—'s D—n." The important exception is in the eleven poems to Stella, all but one of which use the first person singular. Thus in his most affecting and personally tender group of poems the focus is properly on the woman to whom they are addressed. Use of third-person seems more self-conscious in its effect than the use of "I"; and Lord Hervey, who egotistically refers to himself as "Hervey" in his *Memoirs,* is unconvincing when he explains his use of the third-person as a wish to avoid "the disagreeable egotisms with which almost all memoir writers so tiresomely abound."[12]

Openly egotistic like Montaigne in prose, Swift in poetry models his central figure upon himself, painting himself for others. Like Montaigne, Swift might have said he had written a body of work "consubstantial with its author, concerned with my own self, an integral part of my life"; and he might have noted with Montaigne that by training himself "to see my own life mirrored in that of others, I have acquired a studious bent in that subject, and when I am thinking about it, I let few things around me which are useful for that purpose escape my notice."[13] Montaigne was well known to Swift.[14] To symbolize Vanessa's superiority over most other females, Swift writes that in the shrill company of fashionable 'glitt'ring Dames" of her acquaintance she quietly "held *Montaigne,* and read."[15] Montaigne could teach the art of self-scrutiny and self-depiction.

IV

Throughout his poetical career Swift showed himself in a series of remarkably varied lights and postures. His changing states of mind form a constant subject, but his visualized depictions of himself as he ages are numerous. A few examples will suggest his method. As a gowned young chaplain in Lord Berkeley's household in Ireland, he has Frances Harris, the lady-in-waiting who is attracted to him, describe how "he twisted his Girdle at me like a Rope." In London he makes Robert Harley, Lord Oxford, first see him as a priest who "shew'd some Humour in his Face" and "Look'd with an easie, careless Mien." Once installed by Oxford as an influential figure in the Tory government, Swift now "mov'd and bow'd, and talk't with too much Grace;/Nor shew'd the Parson in his Gait or Face"; when he enters the room at Windsor, "Waiters stand in Ranks; the Yeomen cry,/*Make Room*; as if a Duke were passing by." He is out of favor and is returned to favor, so that "*Delaware* again familiar grows;/And, in *Sw—t*'s Ear thrusts half his powder'd Nose." Elevated in the church, he becomes "a *Dean* compleat,/Devoutly lolling in his

Seat." After he assumes his duties as Dean in Ireland, however, he pretends to "College Aukwardness" with Lady Carteret and arrives sheepishly at her residence "by slow Approaches,/Thro' Crowds of Coxcombs & of Coaches." He is renowned as patriot and author, both loved and feared, but when he is a guest of Lord and Lady Acheson in the north of Ireland, his pleasures are simple, rural ones: he helps to churn the butter and "He's all the day saunt'ring,/With labourers bant'ring."[16] Finally, in his sixties, he versifies Lady Acheson's complaints about his incessant punning and railing at her, and provides an arresting face-to-face confrontation with him in his old age with

> Tallow Face and Wainscot Paws,
> . . . Beetle-brows and Eyes of Wall.[17]

The heavy, oppressive terms he chooses here, displaying himself with eyes staring out from under frowning brows in a pale face, his clumsy hands embrowned with age, are all humorously contemptuous and self-depreciating. "Wainscot" is the only unfamiliar term in the passage. In "Dick, A Maggot," written at about the same time, Swift uses "wainscot" again as a contemptuous adjective synonymous with "hazel," "tawney," and "Gypsey"; and his use is cited in the OED to illustrate an obsolete meaning for "wainscot." Although he causes Lady Acheson to describe him contemptuously in his poem, the description (except for the hands) is true to the portrait painted by Francis Bindon in Swift's old age and now in the Irish National Gallery. The Earl of Orrery wrote that "Dr. Swift had a natural severity of face, which even his smiles could scarce soften."[18]

Tested by his portraits, letters, and other people's accounts of him, the autobiographical glimpses of Swift in the preceding paragraph seem true to life. Yet some of them are taken from one of his imitations of Horace, so that the "Swift" who appears there—though perhaps absolutely true to life—is acting a role in a Latin poem brought up to date. Possibly, as other authors have been, Swift was assisted in formulating an idea of himself by taking clues from Horace and slightly altering the models Horace provides. Although he had reason to pride himself on his originality, Swift's "autobiographical" presentation of himself in his poems must have been associated in his consciousness with

77

similar presentations elsewhere in literature. Perhaps he sometimes thought of himself in terms of Montaigne. Occasionally he seems to have imagined himself in verse as a Restoration wit manqué. His name is linked with that of Juvenal. He certainly associated the character "Swift" with characterizations in Horace's poetry, and Swift's contemporaries appreciated many of his poems by locating them in reference to the Latin Satires, Epistles, and Odes, as they were understood in eighteenth-century England.

> Had he lived in the same age with HORACE, he would have approached nearer to him, than any other poet. . . . Each poet was the delight of the principal persons of the age. *Cum magnis vixisse* was not more applicable to HORACE, than to SWIFT. They both were temperate: both were frugal; and both were of the same Epicurean taste. HORACE had his LYDIA, SWIFT had his VANESSA. HORACE had his MÆCENAS and his AGRIPPA. SWIFT had his OXFORD and his BOLINGBROKE. HORACE had his VIRGIL, SWIFT had his POPE.[19]

Two out of Swift's eight adaptations from Horace place him in his relationship with Robert Harley, Eart of Oxford, who qualifies as nearly as any other contemporary to be called patron and hero to Swift. In "Part of the Seventh Epistle of the First Book of Horace Imitated and Addressed to the Earl of Oxford," the role of the famous Roman lawyer, orator, and consul, L. Marcus Philippus, is taken over by Oxford; that of the freedman auctioneer Vulteius Mena—respectable, discreet, and lacking a fortune—is taken by Swift. The ruinous gift to Vulteius of a farm he does not want makes a nice parallel for Swift's preferment to his unwanted deanery in Ireland. Vulteius, first seen by Philippus in a barber's booth, is altered to Swift pricing books at a stall near the palace in Westminster.

> Harley, the Nation's great Support,
> Returning home one Day from Court,
> (His Mind with Publick Cares possest,
> All *Europe*'s Bus'ness in his Breast)

> Observ'd a *Parson* near *Whitehall*,
> Cheapning old Authors on a Stall.
>   (1–6)

Although Swift has himself, like Vulteius, not responding to the initial invitation from his future patron, the historical fact is that it was Oxford who postponed their meeting.[20] Otherwise, the account seems close to the truth, and its effect is enhanced by what we bring to it from Swift's accounts of himself and Oxford in other poems, the *Journal to Stella*, pamphlets, and tracts. His *History of the Four Last Years of the Queen* incorporates a formal "character" of Oxford as a person who "hath been so highly Instrumental in changing the Face of Affairs in *Europe*; And hath Deserved so well of his own Prince and Country."[21] The poem cleverly versifies this prose matter, using Horace for a continuing line of reference.

In his *History* Swift goes out of his way to praise Oxford's "agreeable Conversation in a private Capacity."[22] Samples of that conversation, or "Tattle," shared with Parson Swift,

> As once a week we travel down
> To *Windsor*, and again to Town,

provide realistic entertainment in "Horace, *Lib*. 2 *Sat*. 6. Part of It Imitated."[23] Elsewhere Swift depicts himself as a suffering wit, a demanding friend, or a scourge of corruption; but in these two adaptations from Horace he is the naive parson, humorously put upon in the great world of Lords, Whitehall, Windsor, petitions, and Court secrets. Swift's Horatian poems, because they are based on models less familiar now than in the eighteenth century, and because they introduce public persons whose fame has faded, are in need of footnotes to explain their references.

The poems to Stella, however, need no explanation. They are as honestly affecting nowadays as when they were written. Perhaps it is not very surprising after all that Swift's most private and personal poems are his most universal. Biographically, their subject is the enduring power of affectionate friendship between a man and a women as they grow old. Stella is pictured as she patiently attends him in his recurrent illnesses, while he lies "Lamenting in unmanly Strains," with "sinking Spirits," "Tormented with incessant Pains."[24] Concern with personal ills in some modern "confessional" poetry is likely to encourage a mood apocalyptic and nearly hysterical. Swift's personal ills are introduced to explain a world in which mutual loyalty and assistance can make decay and dissolution endurable.

The last birthday poem to Stella before her death was written when she was ill and Swift was fifty-nine. The birthday itself is conventionally a day of "Joy," but it is also the annual reminder that "Time is running fast"; and Swift attempts in his poem to reconcile those two concepts. Acts of benevolent virtue, like those of Stella, he says, are neither chimeras nor merely their own reward. Such acts leave "lasting Pleasure in the Mind" to sustain us in "Grief, Sickness, Poverty, and Age."

> This Day then, let us not be told,
> That you are sick, and I grown old,
> Nor think on our approaching Ills,
> And talk of Spectacles and Pills;
> To morrow will be Time enough
> To hear such mortifying Stuff.[25]

When, at the age of seventy-five, Samuel Johnson had recovered from an illness, he recited the central couplet from this passage, "assuming a gay air," according to Boswell.[26] Johnson, grown old and sick, could enter into Swift's words precisely because they are so truly private, biographically personal, and universal in their application.

V

Swift's voice in his poems is like that which Montaigne praised, "succulent and sinewy, brief and compressed, not so much dainty and well-combed as vehement and brusque."[27] It is speech that suggests an identifying presence and gesture. The brusque accents of Swift's voice can be heard even in the slightest of the trivia that one is often tempted to prune, lop off, and clear away from the overgrown canon of his verse. But it was Coleridge, the formulator of a new, "serious" concept of poetry after Swift's day, who suspected that he was "not perhaps the only one who has derived an innocent amusement from the riddles, conundrums, trisyllable lines, etc. etc., of Swift and his correspondents."[28]

Such an item is Swift's couplet of invitation to Lord Oxford to join members of the Scriblerus Club in Dr. Arbuthnot's rooms in St. James's Palace, where, Oxford is promised, he will encounter mirth and can assist in the ridicule of false learning. Arbuthnot addresses Oxford in a couplet, as does Thomas Parnell. John Gay's couplet, which he seems to have had trouble in versifying, alludes self-consciously to his own *Shepherd's Week*. Alexander Pope's couplet is even more complicated and allusive than Gay's. In Alexandrines and trisyllabic rhymes, Pope imposes a veneer of elegance by reminding Oxford of lines from the *Iliad* describing how Jove himself would willingly descend to consort with mortals and appear at "Feasts of *Æthiopia's* blameless Race" (as Pope's own translation has it). Pope writes: "My Lord, forsake your Politick Utopians,/To sup, like Jove, with blameless Ethiopians."

Perhaps the friendly insolence of Swift's voice is as much an affectation as Pope's well-combed elegance, but one is not aware of it. The voice comes through with an authentic sound:

> In other words, You with the Staff,
> Leave John of Bucks, come here and laugh.[29]

Intentionally, Swift restates in bare language, vehement and brusque, exactly what Pope has insinuated under a tissue of "poetic" allusion. Exchange of Pope's formal "My Lord" for the blunt "You" characterizes the difference between Pope's poetic voice here and that in which Swift speaks. It is like the exchange of the humorously vague "Politick Utopians" for the vulgarized and specific "John of Bucks." Pope's couplet is good-naturedly mocking, for Oxford is neither a Lord engaged among ambiguous "Utopians" nor a God receiving an invitation from "blameless" outsiders. In Swift's doggerel couplet a real Lord Treasurer, holding a real staff of office, is brusquely commanded to excuse himself from the real company of John Sheffield, Duke of Buckingham, and other political planners, to join the merriment of real Scriblerians. Oxford is addressed as himself; Swift speaks as himself.

In hundreds of other lines that Swift revised with care—not lines dashed off in a hurry among friends—there is still the immediate effect of a voice that singularly speaks concisely and outright, so that "In other Words" could serve as a kind of general epithet for Swift's verse.

"In other Words" suggests a man impatient with conceits, one who clarifies, exposes, and cuts through pretense. It represents the biographical presence that one strongly feels but cannot quite account for in much of Swift's poetry.

Notes

1. The Fountaine MS. of "The Discovery," 3 pp., now in the Pierpont Morgan Library, New York. Courtesy of the Pierpont Morgan Library.

2. T. S. Eliot, "Charles Whibley" and "Cyril Tourneur," in *Selected Essays 1917–1932* (New York, 1932), pp. 404, 166–67.

3. Maurice Johnson, *The Sin of Wit: Jonathan Swift as a Poet* (Syracuse, 1950; reprinted with corrections, New York, 1966); Bonamy Dobrée, *English Literature in the Early Eighteenth Century: 1700–1740* (Oxford, 1959); notably Brendan O Hehir, "Meaning in Swift's 'Description of a City Shower'," *ELH*, XXVII (1960), 194–207 [reprinted in this volume]; Charles Peake, "Swift's 'Satirical Elegy on a Late Famous General'," *Review of English Literature*, III (1962), 80–89 [reprinted in this volume]; Barry Slepian, "The Ironic Intention of Swift's Verses on His Own Death," *Review of English Studies*, XIV (1963), 249–56 [reprinted in this volume]; John M. Aden, "Corinna and the Sterner Muse of Swift," *English Language Notes*, IV (1966), 23–31 [reprinted in this volume]. All take their text from *The Poems of Jonathan Swift*, ed. Harold Williams (Oxford, 1937, 2nd ed. 1958), 3 vols.

4. David M. Vieth, "Introductory Note," *Papers on Language and Literature*, special issue, II (1966), 291.

5. "Strephon and Chloe," ll. 205, 309–10.

6. I have noticed this pattern elsewhere (*Notes and Queries*, CXCIX [1954], 473–74, rephrased here).

7. "A Satirical Elegy on the Death of a Late Famous General," ll. 1, 31–32.

8. Ricardo Quintana, "*The Rape of the Lock* as a Comedy of Continuity," *REL*, VII (1966), 9–19. Quintana earlier characterized Swift's "The Lady's Dressing-Room" and similar works as "completely ruthless studies in *discontinuity*" [italics mine] (*Swift: An Introduction* [Oxford, 1955], p. 185).

9. *Gulliver's Travels,* ed. Herbert Davis (Oxford, 1941, rev. ed. 1959), p. 296.

10. "Verses on the Death of Dr. Swift," ll. 228–39.

11. Dobrée, pp. 472, 473; Aden, p. 23; Peake, p. 88; Edmund Wilson, *The Shores of Light* (New York, 1952), p. 697.

12. *Lord Hervey's Memoirs,* ed. Romney Sedgwick (New York, 1963), p. 5n.

13. Montaigne, "Of Giving the Lie," II:18, and "Of Experience," III:13, *Complete Works,* transl. Donald M. Frame (Stanford, 1957), pp. 504, 825.

14. See Harold Williams, *Dean Swift's Library, with a Facsimile of the Original Sale Catalogue* (Cambridge, 1932), p. 66.

15. "Cadenus and Vanessa," l. 372.

16. "The Humble Petition of Frances Harris" (1701), l. 62; "Part of the Seventh Epistle of the First Book of Horace Imitated" (1713), ll. 8–9; "The Author upon Himself" (1714), ll. 13–14, 35–36, 67–68; "Part of the Seventh Epistle of the First Book of Horace Imitated," ll. 97–98; "An Apology to the Lady Carteret" (1725), ll. 148, 151–52; "My Lady's Lamentation and Complaint against the Dean" (1728), ll. 159–60.

17. "Lady Acheson Weary of the Dean" (1728?), ll. 38–39.

18. John Boyle, fifth Earl of Orrery, *Remarks on the Life and Writings of Dr. Jonathan Swift* (London, 5th ed. 1752), p. 78.

19. Ibid., pp. 44–45.

20. Letter IV, September 29 and 30, 1710, *Journal to Stella,* ed. Harold Williams (Oxford, 1948), I, 33–35.

21. *The History of the Four Last Years of the Queen,* ed. Herbert Davis (Oxford, 1951), p. 75.

22. Ibid.

23. ll. 77–78.

24. "To Stella, Visiting Me in My Sickness," ll. 99, 109; "To Stella, March 13, 1724," l. 1.

25. "Stella's Birth-Day, March 13, 1727," ll. 17, 30, 32, 3–8.

26. *Boswell's Life of Johnson,* ed. George Birkbeck Hill, rev. L. F. Powell (Oxford, 1934–50), IV, 285.

27. Montaigne, "Of the Education of Children," I:26, p. 127.

28. *Biographia Literaria,* ed. George Watson (Everyman's Library, 1956, corrected 1965), p. 37.

29. See *Poems,* ed. Williams, I, 187; *Memoirs of Martinus Scriblerus,* ed. Charles Kerby-Miller (New Haven, 1950), p. 353. The exact date of the invitation, in April, 1714, is uncertain.

III. Swift's Verse Style

WILLIAM K. WIMSATT

Rhetoric and Poems
The Example of Swift

I

"Cousin Swift, you will never be a poet." Words supposedly uttered by Dryden on the occasion of Swift's first publication, his Pindaric *Ode to the Athenian Society* (1692). If the story is an invention, we may well think it a happy one.

We have the four ungainly Odes, written to the sober norm of his patron and Covering Cherub Sir William Temple, and the two pentameter couplet poems: *To Congreve* and *On Temple's Illness*. The *To Congreve* is especially instructive—a creaky adulatory buttonholing, a supposed love affair with the encomiastic muse, a savage presumptive fancy of his own power and calling as a satirist. *Saeva indignatio* without much evidence that it has been earned. "How easy it is to call rogue and villain," Dryden was saying in this very year, 1693, "and that wittily! But how hard to make a man appear a fool, a blockhead, or a knave, without using any of those opprobrious terms!" Swift all his life would be a rebel to this rule, but he had not yet found an idiom which could make the defiance interesting.

This essay first appeared in *The Author in His Work: Essays on a Problem in Criticism,* ed. Louis L. Martz and Aubrey Williams, intro. by Patricia Meyer Spacks (New Haven and London: Yale University Press, 1978), pp. 229–44. Reprinted with permission.

We entertain the image of an obscure young country versifier, who, except for the external testimonies of authorship, we might well hesitate to identify with the man-about-town and political writer, aged about forty-six in 1713, who could produce, in tetrameter couplets, the darkly lustrous myth of dalliance *Cadenus and Vanessa,* or, in his later years and bereavement at Dublin, could contrive *Verses on the Death of Dr. Swift* (1731) and *On Poetry: A Rapsody* (1733).

II

Much earlier he had demonstrated, if only for a moment, a successful way of writing even the pentameter couplet, in his two London poems of 1709 and 1710, *A Description of the Morning* and *A Description of a City Shower.* These are witty burlesque poems, but it is worth saying that they are not written in witty couplets, not like Pope or Dryden.

> The Slipshod Prentice from his Masters Door,
> Had par'd the Dirt, and Sprinkled round the Floor.
> Now *Moll* had whirl'd her Mop with dext'rous Airs,
> Prepar'd to Scrub the Entry and the Stairs.
>
> (5–8)[1]

The sentences avoid rhetorical pointing. The structure is studiously flat—a sort of soft-mat photo texture. This is the quiet anti-poetic, the bathetic. This ineloquent mock-pastoral-aubade, as Claude Rawson[2] points out, invites definition by contrast with the vibratory ethos or personal projection of such romantic city poets as Baudelaire and Eliot. *Morning* is the flatter of the two poems. It is a *very* flat poem, and hence short. This style could not be sustained long. The *Shower* is more rhetorical.

> Here various Kinds by various Fortunes led,
> Commence Acquaintance underneath a Shed.
> Triumphant Tories, and desponding Whigs,
> Forget their Fewds, and join to save their Wigs.
>
> (39–42)

They said it was the best thing Swift "ever writ," and he too thought so. This city rainstorm, so elaborately derived from Dryden's Virgil, the First *Georgic* and the Second and Fourth *Aeneids,* is described ingeniously by Brendan O Hehir as "an oblique denunciation of cathartic doom upon the corruption of the city."[3] The closing triplet and alexandrine are *not* low burlesque, not a mere travesty of Dryden's style, despite Swift's much later note on the passage (1735) and his letter to a friend. As there is really nothing wrong with either a triplet or an alexandrine, nothing prevents us from reading these as the climax of the poem's high burlesque or mock-georgic-heroic, raising low matter to a focus of ample and pregnant realization.

> Sweepings from Butchers Stalls, Dung, Guts, and Blood,
> Drown'd Puppies, stinking Sprats, all drench'd in Mud,
> Dead Cats and Turnip-Tops come tumbling down the Flood.
>
> (61–63)

All the life of the farm, says Irvin Ehrenpreis, appears as decayed garbage, yet still in action.

III

But even earlier Swift had made another and even better discovery. If it was an accident that he found his true idiom, the tetrameter or short couplet, during his *Wanderjahre,* the ten years of his unsettlement, from 1699, shuttling between England and Ireland, yet it may be seen as an emblematic accident. The immediate and chief antecedent of Swift's anti-sublime and anti-pathetic idiom is usually and correctly enough placed in the short, harsh couplets in stringy sequences and the absurdly manufactured rhymes of Samuel Butler's *Hudibras* (a very long poem which Swift is *said* to have known by heart and which indeed is present here and there in his *Tale of a Tub*).[4] This spavined mock epic, however, has its own antecedents, in English and continental literature, and difficult as they may be to trace, we can say something about the overall view.

The long couplet as perfected by Dryden and Pope came from the classical Roman hexameter and elegiac couplet,[5] and its basic theoretical formula can be found in the figures of parallel, antithesis, metaphor, and turn described in book 3, chapters 9–11 of Aristotle's *Rhetoric*. Add only such refinements as zeugma (described with the other figures in Puttenham's *Arte of Poesie*, 1589), chiasmus, and the vernacular figures of accentual meter and rhyme. The Popean couplet, in which Swift was always to experience a relative discomfort, was Ovid with the impasto of rhyme. Marvell's short couplet, as in the *Coy Mistress* and *The Garden*, may be described in the same mainly classical terms. But the short couplet in its laughing mode was something broader and coarser, distinctly late Latin, vernacular, and anti-classical. It was a revolt against and a vagabond swerve away from the ancient decorum. Its genius may be illustrated characteristically, at one of its peaks, in the deviant Latin poets of the high Middle Ages—the *vagantes* (*vagi clerici*), refugees from Parisian discipline, irreverent, scoffers, ribalds, ironist, parodists: Golias, Primate, Bishop, Archpoet. We know that these poets, having flourished for their brief heyday, lay long out of sight, beneath the horizon for some six centuries. Even by Chaucer's time a Goliardeys was no better than a coarse jester, a jangler, the quarrelsome Miller of the Canterbury prologue. In the Victorian mid-nineteenth century, the antiquarians Thomas Wright and Andreas Schmeller were performing acts of resurrection when they brought out their editions of the poems ascribed to Walter Map (1841) and of the Benedictbeuern manuscript, *Carmina Burana* (1847). During Swift's lifetime, it is true, we find the *Historia Poetarum et Poematum Medii Aevi*, edited by the Helmstadt scholar Polycarp Leyser at Halle in 1721. And Pope in a satiric squib alludes to Blackmore as an ArchPoet. The tradition was no doubt carried all along in student drinking songs, such as the *Gaudeamus igitur*, which emerges in Germany during the later eighteenth century. But there is no likelihood that either Swift or Pope knew any Goliardic poetry.

I am speaking synchronically of poetic affinities. "Deep within I seethe with anger," confessed the twelfth-century Archpoet to his patron the Archchancellor of the Empire. "In my bitter mind I'm talking. . . . I'm like a dead leaf on the wind."

> Aestuans intrinsecus ira vehementi
> in amaritudine loquar meae menti:

factus de materia levis elementi
folio sum similis de quo ludunt venti.

The four-plus-three medieval Latin septenary and the trochaic tetrameter (*Dives eram et dilectus*) were contemporaries of the French octosyllabic, and the French was the model for the English. The Goliardic rhyming was the last expressive burst of Latin as a spoken language.[6] It is Latin hovering on the verge of vernacular: a verse written in clanging contrast to the quantitative measure of the classical tradition, and revelling in a verbal chime that is a barbaric opposite to the logical homoioteleuton of classical prose. Rhyme in the Goliardic-Skeltonic-Scarronian-Hudibrastic tradition is all that Gothic, rude, and beggarly jingle deplored by such civilized theorists as Campion, Milton, and Roscommon. In that short-couplet tradition Swift found his own voice, his characteristic freedom and crashing energy. Thwarted *Episcopus,* actual *Decanus,* Swift was an Augustan *Archipoeta Redivivus*—not a libertine singer of wine, woman, and song, nevertheless exuberant in the license of rhyming irreverence, "the sin of Wit, no venial crime."

> The Language *Billingsgate* excel
> The Sentiments resemble *Hell.*
> (*A Panegyric* [1729–30],
> ll. 108–09)

It is a familiar enough idea that Swift made poetry out of anti-poetic materials, or simply that he made poetry that was anti-poetry. I myself might prefer to say that the anti-poetry of that age was only the anti-classical, and that the paradox of the anti-poetic, in our own age of postexpressionism, has lost most of its force. After the cruelty, the blackness, the obscenity, the absurdity, the suicide, the zero level of our modern comic experience, Swift is no longer a radical instance of inversion as such. I proceed to some rhetorical observations, moving, perhaps unadventurously, within the established demonic frame of reference. Details, I believe, are likely to win against outline in any account of the episodic, spotty, staccato career of Swift in verse. Nevertheless, I have a central and fairly simple aim in this paper.

That is, to show some of the main ways in which the short couplet, rather than the long, emerged as his appointed expressive instrument.

IV

The long couplet in the classical tradition, and especially that couplet as it is refined by Swift's friend Alexander Pope, is a structure composed of *processed words,* words manipulated into new, momentary phrases—ellipses, compressions, inversions, zeugmas, extraordinary junctures, suspensions:

Where Wigs with Wigs, with Sword-knots Sword-knots strive.
Where *Nature moves,* and *Rapture warms* the Mind.
A hero perish, or a sparrow fall.
And now a bubble burst, and now a world.
The sot a hero, lunatic a king.[7]

Pope's unit of wit is the half-line. His rhymes depend very much on the very special syntactic mechanism which brings them into conjunction. "Each Atom by some other struck," Swift himself wrote in a poem to Pope, "All Turns and Motion tries; Till in a Lump together stuck, Behold a *Poem* rise!" (*Dr. Sw—— to Mr. P——e,* 1727). Even in Pope's use of the starkest everyday language, he arranges with atomic care; he maximizes in very exact, if excited and unusual, sequences.

Shut, shut the door, good *John!* fatigu'd I said,
Tye up the knocker, say I'm sick, I'm dead.
(*An Epistle to Dr. Arbuthnot,* 1–2)

The short couplet, a release and freedom for Swift, was a hobble for Pope. Swift did not think Pope imitated his couplet very well. He disparaged Pope's imitation of his style in supplying the episode of the town mouse and the country mouse to fill out the Horatian *Satire* 2.6. Probably we could not always, under any circumstances (that is, if not told the authorship in advance), be sure of seeing in Pope's lines something essentially different from the plainer and in a sense heavier phrasing of Swift.

Lines 9–28 of this poem are debated, the external evidence failing. But from line 133 on we are certain about Pope. And thus:

> O charming Noons! and Nights divine!
> Or when I sup, or when I dine,
> My Friends above, my Folks below,
> Chatting and laughing all-a-row,
> The Beans and Bacon set before 'em,
> The Grace-cup serv'd with all decorum:
> And even the very Dogs at ease!
> Which is the happier, or the wiser,
> A man of Merit, or a Miser?
> Whether we ought to chuse our Friends,
> For their own Worth, or our own Ends?
> *(Satire* 2.6.133–50)

The half-line chiming units and with them a certain buoyancy and sprightliness, a graceful soaring, fit conveniently with our knowledge on external evidence that these lines were written by Pope.[8]

V

The earliest surviving short-couplet poem by Swift, the *Verses Wrote in a Lady's Ivory Table Book* (1698?), is a sharp example of his peculiar love for what we can best, I think, call live *whole* phrases.

> Here you may read (*Dear Charming Saint*)
> Beneath (*A new Receit for Paint*)
> Here in Beau-spelling (*tru til deth*)
> There in her own (*far an el breth*)
> Here (*lovely Nymph pronounce my doom*)
> There (*A safe way to use Perfume*)
> Here, a Page fill'd with Billet Doux;
> On t'other side (*laid out for Shoes*)
> (*Madam, I dye without your Grace*)
> (Item, *for half a Yard of Lace.*)
> (7–16)

Add the following from the Horatian *Epistle* 1.7, to Lord Oxford, purporting to narrate Swift's first encounter with him:

> Swift, who could neither fly nor hide,
> Came sneaking to the Chariot-side,
> And offer'd many a lame Excuse;
> He never meant the least Abuse—
> *My Lord—The Honour you design'd—*
> *Extremely proud—but I had din'd—*
> *I'm sure I never shou'd neglect—*
> *No Man alive has more Respect—*.
> (*To Lord Oxford* [1713], ll. 63–70)

Swift's short couplets are composed, characteristically, of ready-made phrases, from the colloquial and stereotype repertory, pieces of stock language laid together in bundles, clattering parallels. He rattles the literal commonplaces, brandishes the living speech. We are close to the specimens of fatuity which he collected so lovingly in his *Polite Conversation* (in modern American parlance, *The Cliché Expert Takes the Stand*). The lines largely lack internal figural structure. The wit may come in the contrast between phrases drawn from different fonts, as that of the beau and that of the lady so systematically rhymed in the *Ivory Table Book*. Johnson said of Swift's prose (*The Conduct of the Allies*), "He had to count ten, and he has counted it right." Of Swift's verses, Johnson said, "there is not much upon which the critic can exercise his powers."

One may have felt the same kind of literalism, or fidelity to real speech, in the hexameter couplets of the greatest French comic writer, Molière. It is tempting to draw this proportion: as Pope, especially in his Homer, is to Racine, so Swift, in his short couplets, is to Molière.

VI

Swift found Berkeley's *Alciphron* "too speculative."[9] Swift was anti-metaphysical, anti-speculative. His orientation toward *things*—hard objects, such as can be set on a shelf, put in a box, or carried in pocket or hand (a "rhyming and chiming" universe,

yet how unlike the dappled cosmic vision of the poet Hopkins)—
reminds us of the philosophers in the Grand Academy of Lagado
who conceived the notion of carrying *things* about with them, to
use instead of words. One of Swift's most reliable poetic devices
(as we might expect in general from the author of *Gulliver*) is the
catalogue or "inventory" of miscellaneous physical things or of
verbal things: the *Furniture of a Woman's Mind* ("A Set of Phrases
learnt by Rote; A Passion for a Scarlet Coat"—[1727], 2.415);
the key literal items of millinery concern, *lace, stuff, yard, fan,* (in
rhyming positions), the samples of card-table talk, the cheats,
complaints, and accusations, all the splattering enumerations of
a cluttered life that make the *Journal of a Modern Lady* ("I but
transcribe, for not a Line/Of all the Satyre shall be mine. . . .
Unwilling Muse begin thy Lay,/The Annals of a Female Day"—
[1729], II.28–29, 34–35); the verbal trash that composes the
cliché mind of a *Grisette* (1730); the list of false parts removed
by *A Beautiful Young Nymph Going to Bed* (1731); the disgusting
clutter of a *Lady's Dressing Room* (1730): "Of all the Litter as it
lay; . . . An Inventory follows here."

> The various Combs for various Uses,
> Fill'd up with Dirt so closely fixt,
> No Brush could force a way betwixt.
> A Paste of Composition rare,
> Sweat, Dandriff, Powder, Lead and Hair.
> (8, 10, 20–24)

The imputation of slovenly vice or, at the mildest, of helter-skel-
ter frivolity conveyed in these catalogues represents a juncture
of couplet rhetoric and a certain kind of sexism which I am not
concerned to develop in this paper.

Such verbalized and inventoried objects are most conspicuous when they occur as rhymes. Rhyme is the most brilliantly
attractive feature of Swift's verse. "Rhyme," says Butler in *Hudibras,* "the rudder is of verses" (I.I.403). So much of Swift's line,
says Martin Price, "is absorbed into the rhyme."

In a cunning blend of prudence and artistry, Swift sometimes teases us with a rhyme word left blank—either a scatological word ("Celia, Celia, Celia——") or the name of some
dangerous political target.

How the Helm is rul'd by——
At whose Oars, like Slaves, they all pull.
(*To a Lady* [1733], ll. 159–60)

If we have any doubt how the music of that rhyme goes, we can consult its complement in another poem of about the same date.

But why wou'd he, except he *slobber'd*,
Offend our Patriot, Great Sir R——?
(*The Life and Character of Dean Swift*
[1733], ll. 107–08)

The first poem quoted just now, the *Epistle to a Lady, Who desired the Author to make Verses on Her, in the Heroick Stile*, exhibits, I believe, the most sustained instance of this unheroic device that Swift ever achieved.

I, WHO love to have a Fling,	
Both at Senate-House, and——	King
. . . .	
If I treat you like——	a crown'd Head
You have cheap enough compounded.	
Can you put in higher Claims,	
Than the Owners of *St. J*——*s*.	James
You are not so great a Grievance	
As the Hirelings of *St. St*——*s*.	Stephens
You are of a lower Class	
Than my Friend Sir *R*—— *Br*——*s*.	Robert Brass
	(221–22, 239–46)

That kind of rhyming is the complementary opposite of a French diversion described by Addison in *Spectator* 60, the game of *bouts-rimés*—where only the rhyme words are given, and the player is challenged to fill in the blank lines to his fancy. Swift's extraordinary rhymes sometimes seem to invite being extracted from his verse for use in that way too. A few of his most bravura passages might make almost manageable parlor games. What might we not make, for instance, of such a series of expressions as:

dupes us
Peri Hupsous,

> *Longinus,*
> outshine us.
> over-run ye,
> for love or money,
> translation,
> *Quotation.*

Words combined into makeshift rhymes play a large part here.
In many, perhaps in most, of Swift's comic two-syllable rhymes,
we find one makeshift (sometimes with forced accent, and better
if the first of the couplet) combined with one ready-made, the
excuse or occasion for the couplet. In the passage I have just
dismembered, we note, along with the excellent *Peri Hupsous* and
Longinus, the no less ready-made cliché or tag phrase "for love
or money." The closing couplet, formed on the Latinate *translation* and *Quotation,* may be said to take advantage of a very easy
linguistic opportunity.

> A forward critic often dupes us
> With sham quotations *Peri Hupsous*
> And if we have not read *Longinus,*
> Will magisterially outshine us.
> Then, lest with Greek he over-run ye,
> Procure the book for love or money,
> Translated from Boileau's translation,
> And quote *Quotation* on *Quotation.*
>
> > (*On Poetry: A Rapsody*
> > [1733], ll. 255–62)

A more minute rhetorical examination of this passage might
choose for special remark such a word as *magisterially,* unrolling
itself so magisterially that, although only one word of four, it
manages to usurp three of the line's four metrical ictuses; it
illustrates what we might have been suspecting, that Swift's apparently flat and plain bundles of simple phrases are susceptible
of very nice tilting within the metrical frame. The last couplet,
with its easy rhyme of *translation* and *quotation,* is fortified inter-
nally in each line by an anagnorisis or "turn" upon the rhyming
word.

It is difficult to make significant statistical statements about

Swift's rhyme. The most florid passages stand out in the memory and color the whole. Broaden the base for a moment and think of the English tradition, most notably Butler, Swift, and Byron. Swift, said Byron, "beats us all hollow, his rhymes are wonderful."[10] Byron shows himself a true Swiftian when he joins Aristotle with Longinus via the word *bottle*.

> —"Longinus o'er a Bottle,"
> Or, "Every Poet his *own* Aristotle."
> (*Don Juan*, I.204)

The English comic rhymes are poetic *objects trouvés*, a flotsam and jetsam, jumble and tumble, of miscellaneous prefabricated linguistic objects, conspicuous curiosities, bric-a-brac, trophies hauled in, a polyglot litter, gravels, seaweed, driftwood, of a language and culture—classical adjuncts, history, proper names, tags, quotation on quotation, a world of partial assimilations to the native English stock, a collage of newspaper scraps, a Table Book of the real and the verbal world, where the poet finds scrawled his heterogeneous chiming vocabulary. Think of Stephen Dedalus on the beach at Sandymount, meditating the "ineluctable modality of the visible." "Signatures of all things I am here to read. . . . Seaspawn and seawrack, the nearing tide, that rusty boat."

The homonyms of a language sometimes offer each other so much mutual support as hardly to be realized for the different words which they actually are. Thus *light* in weight and *light* in color. Or they clash and compete, and one of a pair may win, the other surviving only in some formalized and redundant phrase ("without *let* or hindrance") or in a classic quotation ("By heaven, I'll make a ghost of him that *lets* me"). The feat of rhyming verse is to find and focus a context where a clash of partially homonymous expressions is rendered harmonious—in illustration of the Jakobsonian rule that in poetry the axis of selection (the range of equivalence which is put to one side in straight prose) is projected onto the axis of combination, which in poetry is an axis of analogy. Swift's short-couplet rhymes are a maximum demonstration of this feat, not verbal music but paronomastic meaning. "Longinus" becomes a new signature; it reveals a latent aspect of its meaning as it evokes "outshine us." *Peri Hupsous* gives up a secret through its affinity for "dupes us."

VII

Swift persisted in experiment with varied verse forms throughout his career. He returned often enough to the pentameter couplet. He wrote anapests. He tried ballad stanzas, songs, Skeltonic
dimeters. He scored such successes as the breathless gabble meter of *The Humble Petition of Frances Harris* and *Mary the Cook Maid's
Letter to Dr. Sheridan,* or the squalid stanzas of the *Pastoral Dialogue*
of Dermot and Sheelah. But it is fair to say that the poetic virtues
which I am trying to celebrate are exerted at their maximum in
the jabbing four-stress couplet (sometimes trochaic, more often
iambic) which Swift made so specially his own voice.

One of the conveniences which he discovered through the
use of his couplet was speed. The extraordinary speed of which
this idiom was capable appears perhaps most strikingly in some
of his shorter narrative poems. *The Progress of Marriage* (1721–
22), for instance: how to begin a story

> Aetatis suae fifty two
> A rich Divine began to woo
> A handsome young imperious *Girl*
> Nearly related to an Earl.
>
> (1–4)

Or *The Progress of Love* (1719): how to execute a turn in the
middle of a story.

> Suppose all Partyes now agreed,
> The Writings drawn, the Lawyer fee'd,
> The Vicar and the Ring bespoke:
> Guess how could such a Match be broke.
> (Guess how! She had run off with John the butler.).
> For truly John was missing too:
> The Horse and Pillion both were gone
> Phillis, it seems, was fled with John.
>
> (21–24, 40–42)

Or the principle of metamorphosis. Parallels (or similars) in general make for similitude, analogies, puns, metaphors, even metamorphoses—and even the latter a speedy operation in the short
couplet. In an early couplet poem, *Baucis and Philemon* (1708–

99

09), the metamorphosis, as Ehrenpreis observes, is like a "series of answers to riddles. How is a cottage like a church? How is a kettle like a bell?"[11]

> The chimny widen'd and grew high'r,
> Became a Steeple with a Spire:
> The Kettle to the top was hoist
> And there stood fastn'd to a Joyst. . . .
> (95–98)

Or the disappearing trick. How to make two trees disappear, gradually yet completely, in six lines.

> Here *Baucis*, there *Philemon* grew.
> Till once, a Parson of our Town,
> To mend his Barn, cut *Baucis* down;
> At which, 'tis hard to be believ'd,
> How much the other Tree was griev'd,
> Grew Scrubby, dy'd a-top, was stunted:
> So, the next Parson stub'd and burnt it.
> (172–78)

One hazard of the short line, the short, straight syntax, is that this structure may produce too many antithetic reversals, parentheses that get out of hand, digressions, loquacity—a sort of scrappiness. Swift's lesser poems are often enough notable as paragraphic assortments rather than as continuous movements. But segmentation can also produce the radiantly disjunct concentrations, the movement as of a series of shrapnel bursts, in such passages of Swift as the opening paragraphs of the *Verses on the Death of Dr. Swift* (1731).

> Dear Honest *Ned* is in the Gout,
> Lies rackt with Pain, and you without:
> How patiently you hear him groan!
> How glad the Case is not your own!
>
> What Poet would not grieve to see,
> His brethren write as well as he?
> But rather than they should excel,
> He'd wish his Rivals all in Hell.
> (27–34)

A term used very frequently by appreciators of Swift—whether of his verse or of his prose—is "energy." Energy—in his short verse a kind of direct insistence, an urgent announcement, a raw shock. The diapason of disgusting energy, for instance, that permeates the group of poems in which Cassinus and Peter and Strephon and Chloe and Corinna and Celia pursue their malodorous adventures. Or the energy of smiling outrage, the art of "obliging Ridicule," as he himself termed it (*Poems*, I.216), which he found so congenial in his poems of compliment to the other sex.

> WHY, *Stella,* should you knit your Brow,
> If I compare you to the Cow?
> (21–22)[12]

Another term which the critics have favored and which applies very well to a somewhat different range of energy in Swift is "exuberance." A nearly equivalent word might be "bumptiousness." Under this head I present a concluding contrast between Swift and his kindred spirit Pope. *On Poetry: A Rapsody,* from which we have already quoted, shows Swift in a maximum parallel to Pope—to Pope in the Horatian *Epistle to Augustus,* of course, an apology for poetry, with satire on the contemporary scene and salute to a reigning dunce. Swift did not, like Pope, write a close imitation of Horace, but he clearly had the classic model in mind (*Poems,* 2.658). Swift's poem anticipated Pope's by four years (1733). Consider the end of each poem. Pope's so remarkable for innuendo and subtlety:

> But Verse alas! your Majesty disdains;
> And I'm not us'd to Panegyric strains:
> The Zeal of Fools offends at any time,
> But most of all, the Zeal of Fools in ryme.
> Besides, a fate attends on all I write,
> That when I aim at praise, they say I bite.
> A vile Encomium doubly ridicules;
> There's nothing blackens like the ink of fools.
> (*Epistle to Augustus,* 2.404–11)

(The poem, we know, was mistaken by some for a panegyric upon the administration.) Add a certain kind of literalness in

Pope which invites special illustration from another poem: "Three thousand Suns went down on *Welsted's* Lye" (*Epistle to Arbuthnot*, l. 375). Not exuberance! Pope means that more than ten years had passed before he answered Welsted in *The Dunciad.*

How different all that from the cheerfully over-obvious ironies of Swift! (The *Rapsody* on poetry deceived Queen Caroline. But several printers and publishers of the poem at Dublin were taken into custody; *Poems,* 2.640.)

> Say, Poet, in what other Nation,
> Shone ever such a Constellation.
> Attend ye *Popes,* and *Youngs,* and *Gays,*
> And tune your Harps, and strow your Bays.
> Your Panegyricks here provide,
> You cannot err on Flatt'ry's Side.
> Above the Stars exalt your Stile,
> You still are low ten thousand Mile.
> On *Lewis* all his Bards bestow'd
> Of Incense many a thousand Load;
> But *Europe* mortify'd his Pride,
> And swore the fawning Rascals ly'd:
> Yet what the World refus'd to *Lewis,*
> Apply'd to *George* exactly true is:
> Exactly true! Invidious Poet!
> 'Tis fifty thousand Times below it.[13]
>
> (2.656–57, ll. 465–80)

"Overshooting the mark," said Longinus, "ruins the hyperbole."[14] "Those hyperboles are best, in which the very fact that they are hyperboles escapes attention." But Swift's way was to invert all those rules enunciated by classical authorities on the heroic or the sublime. His finesses came by extravagance—inventive extravagance. It takes a genius to go so joyfully wrong. This is the open door into the sunlight of laughter which Swift discovered when he moved from the murky constraints of his pentameter metaphysics on the illness of Temple into the abandoned fun of the *Lady's Ivory Table Book.*

Notes

1. Swift's verse is quoted throughout my essay from *Swift's Poems,* ed. Harold Williams (Oxford, 1958), vols. 1, 2, 3.

2. It is a pleasure to acknowledge the kindness of Professor Rawson in allowing me to study an eloquent chapter on the poems, from his forthcoming book on Swift.

3. Brendan O Hehir, "Meaning of Swift's 'Description of a City Shower,'" *ELH* 27 (1960): 194–207 [reprinted in this volume]. Cf. David M. Vieth, "*Fiat Lux*: Logos versus Chaos in Swift's 'A Description of the Morning,'" *Papers on Language and Literature* 8 (1972): 302–07.

4. Laetitia Pilkington, *Memoirs* (London, 1748), 1: 136; Harold Williams, *Dean Swift's Library* (Cambridge, 1932), pp. 87–88.

5. William Bowman Piper, *The Heroic Couplet* (Cleveland, 1969), chaps. 2–3.

6. Jakob Schipper, *A History of English Versification* (Oxford, 1918), pp. 126, 182, 192; F. A. Wright and T. A. Sinclair, *A History of Later Latin Literature* (London, 1931), pp. 234, 296, 305–06, 319, 323, 324, 330; F. J. E. Raby, *A History of Secular Latin Poetry in the Middle Ages* (Oxford, 1957), 2: 173, 183, 278, 362; *The Oxford Book of Medieval Latin Verse,* ed. F. J. E. Raby (Oxford, 1959), pp. 251, 485, 486; *Psalterium Profanum, Weltliche Gedichte des lateinischen Mittelalters,* ed. Josef Eterle (Zurich, 1962), pp. 534–36, 579–81.

7. Pope is quoted from *The Twickenham Edition of The Poems of Alexander Pope* (London, 1939–69), vols. 1–11.

8. Pope's Horatian *Epistle* 1.7, "Imitated in the Manner of Dr. Swift," seems to betray his hand far less clearly. On the other hand, Pope, adding only ten scraps from another poem by Swift, transformed the conclusion of the *Verses on the Death of Dr. Swift* from a curiously straight and inflated (if in part ironic) panegyric of the Doctor to what has been described as a "rapid-fire" antithetic dialogue, on the Horatian and Popean model. See Arthur H. Scouten and Robert D. Hume, "Pope and Swift: Text and Interpretation of Swift's Verses on His Death," *PQ* 52 (April 1973): 207–08, 215. [Reprinted in this volume.]

9. *The Correspondence of Jonathan Swift,* ed. Harold Williams (Oxford, 1965): 1: 16.

10. E. J. Trelawney, *Recollections of the Last Days of Shelley and Byron* (Boston, 1858), 1: 37.

11. Another early poem, *Van Brug's House* (1703–06), executes some remarkable metamorphoses of poetry and heraldry into architecture.

12. With a burst of laughter, and in the presence of his victim (Lady Acheson, an "agreeable young Lady, but extremely lean"), Swift once boasted: "That Lady had rather be a *Daphne* drawn by me, than a *Sacharissa* by any other pencil" (*Poems,* 3: 902). His awareness of another

possible sensibility is expressed in an earlier poem censuring some freedom in raillery taken by his crony Sheridan.

> If what You said, I wish unspoke,
> 'Twill not suffice, it was a Joke.
> (*To Mr. Delany,*
> 1718, ll. 65–66)

13. Other examples of hyperbolic number in Swift: *On Censure*
(1727), l. 27; *Journal of a Modern Lady* (1729), l. 139; *Strephon and Chloe*
(1731), l. 99; *Apollo* (1731), l. 20.

14. *Peri Hupsous,* chap. 38. Translation of W. Rhys Roberts.

IV. The *Description* Poems

BRENDAN O HEHIR

Meaning of Swift's
"Description of a City Shower"

A paradox may be felt in the fact that Swift's "Description of a City Shower," while abiding the editors and anthologists of two and a half centuries, in effect at least continues to out-top the searching of critics. The text has been barnacled over with notes and comments—one almost certainly emanating from Swift himself—but critics seem reluctant to push inward from its surface, or even to suggest a meaning or a purpose for the whole. Maurice Johnson, acute in reading Swift, suggests of the "Shower" only that it is a parody—in the concluding triplet, specifically of Dryden; and Colin J. Horne judges only that "in manner it was perhaps intended as a burlesque imitation of Virgil's *Georgics,* or at any rate of Dryden's translation of them."[1] Neither of these hypotheses is original, for both are available in the scholia of the eighteenth-century source-annotators collected by Harold Williams in his excellent edition of Swift's poem,[2] but the lack of originality itself may be accepted as witness to a probable truth in both suggestions. Such suggestions nonetheless seem deficient, and the intent of this paper is to make plain an impressive meaning, even a serious moral, that I believe can be discerned in the poem as a whole. It will be attempted to make that meaning more clear, not by overthrowing the judgments of previous com-

This essay first appeared in *ELH* 27 (1960): 194–207. Reprinted with permission.

mentarists, but by methodically reviewing their testimony in the light of a rereading of the poem.

Swift was proud of his "Shower," and agreed with the opinion of the friends who told him it was "the best thing [he] ever writ," and "beyond any thing that has been written of the kind." Our appraisal of that opinion must depend upon our understanding of what the "kind" was that the poem so happily exemplified, and our understanding must arise from study both of the poem and of the commentary that has clustered around it. The literal manifest of the poem condenses into four statements: I. the behavior or condition of characteristic city phenomena indicates the imminence of a rainstorm (ll. 1–12); II. the rainstorm is implacable and destructive (13–30); III. during the storm citizens act in typical ways (31–52); IV. at the end of the storm all sorts of inanimate and indiscriminate filth are swept away by the flood (53–63). Additional less obvious notes, though still manifest, depend upon closer inspection of the text. To the manifest, which must remain the fundamental from which a successful interpretation cannot radically depart, the possibility continues of attaching (*qua* lexicographical information) insights into form or content offered by the comments added to the poem by editors from time to time.

The first readers of the "City Shower," when it appeared in the *Tatler* No. 238 (October 17, 1710), had, outside their own knowledge and sensibilities, nothing but a slightly misleading headnote to guide their interpretation of the poem. That headnote compared Swift's city shower to "Virgil's land-shower . . . a shower of consequence . . . bringing matters to a speedy conclusion between two potentates of different sexes"—an allusion to *Aeneid* IV. 160–168. Subsequent editors of Swift have not reprinted this headnote, perhaps on the ground that it seems to conflict with the more readily defensible thesis that the poem is essentially a mock georgic. The latter theory perhaps had its origin in Pope's judgment, if Swift himself is not directly responsible for the first occurrence (in the 1727 "Last" volume of Pope-Swift *Miscellanies*) of the frequently repeated subtitle, "In Imitation of Virgil's Georgicks." This is the basis for Horne's tentative theory, and the *Georgics* of Vergil in fact are by far the most important model for the form of the "City Shower," as well as for much of its meaning. But Swift's poem is a literary tar-baby, and the *Tatler* note, like others, cannot easily be pulled away from it.

As an analogue or literary source for the "City Shower," nothing in Vergil's *Georgics* could be more self-evident or more specific than the famous description of a storm in harvest (*Georgic* I.316–334 [431–458]).[3] In fact the entire first *Georgic*, from its turning-point at the description of the storm until its end, is the setting for most of the classical details imitated in Swift's poem. The famous storm itself—its sudden violent on-slaught of wind and rain upon the peaceful scene of a farmer hiring his harvesters, the rising deluge sweeping "out from the field and its ditches to the great river, out from the great river to the greater sea,"[4] and the consequent terror of men and beasts, and even of inanimate nature, at the power of Jove—serves both as general model for Swift's entire poem and as particular model for his storm's outbreak and for the consequent behavior of his citizens. The weather-signs described by Vergil in lines 351–463 [483–624] provide the model for the "Prognosticks" of Swift's first twelve lines, and the flooding of the Eridanus in lines 481–483 [649–652] anticipates the flood of Swift's terminal triplet. With rough but considerable accuracy each of the four parts of Swift's poem may be assigned to a source in *Georgic* I, and if on the basis of Williams' reminder that in point of composition the first part of the "Shower" was last,[5] we assume that the body of the poem, written first, began at line 13 ("Meanwhile the South rising with dabbled Wings"), certain parallels become more strik-ing. Whereas Swift's storm derives chiefly from Vergil's storm in *Georgic* I. 316–334, the "Prognosticks" of Swift's opening come from Vergil's subsequent 351–389 [483–534]—"Atque haec ut certis possemus discere signis"—so that Swift's order of com-position corresponds to Vergil's order of presentation.

But identification even of the prime model for the form of a poem yields only a dubious clue as to its meaning or intention. If the "City Shower" is a mock georgic, the inference is reason-able that its mockery has a target, the poem a satirical or moral aim. A non-mock georgic would have a similarly didactic end, for the genre itself falls, in Addison's words (*Essay on the Georgics*), "under that Class of Poetry, which consists in giving plain and

direct Instructions to the Reader; whether they be Moral Duties . . . or Philosophical Speculations . . . or Rules of Practice."
As we have seen, Dryden, or his translation of Vergil, has been
proposed as Swift's butt—not without reason. In a letter dated
12 April 1735, Swift boasted that "above twenty-four years ago"
he had been so enraged both at the triplet—"a vicious way of
rhyming, wherewith Dryden abounded"—and at the "Alexandrine verse at the end of the triplets"—"likewise brought in" by
Dryden—that he had "banished them all by one triplet, with an
Alexandrine, upon a very ridiculous subject."[6] A similar claim
appended in Faulkner's 1735 Dublin edition to the triplet at the
end of the "City Shower" leaves no doubt as to the occasion on
which Swift fancied he had struck that blow. Since Swift's contempt for Dryden, especially as a translator of Vergil, had already
been patent in A Tale of a Tub and in The Battle of the Books, the
possibility of interpreting the burlesque-Vergilian "City Shower"
as an attack on Dryden is inviting. But just as in those earlier
instances attacks on Dryden had been merely incidental to other
business, so it seems unlikely that the total purport of the "City
Shower" amounts to no more than that of the metrical parody
in its last three lines. Verbal parodies may with fair security be
guessed at in a few places, where Swift's "imitation" seems closer
to Dryden's translation than to Vergil's original, but it appears
doubtful that the echo could often be held to imply derogation.[7]
In short, whatever the extent of attack upon Dryden to be found
in the poem, it must be acknowledged to be intermittent at most,
and peripheral to some other intention.

Certain elements in the "City Shower" are clearly derived
from sources other than the *Georgics*. Williams' edition, for instance, accurately notes that the episode of Laocoon and the
Grecian horse reflected in Swift's "epic simile" (47–52) derives
from *Aeneid* II. The investigator's task is here complicated by the
fact that Dryden of course translated the *Aeneid* also, but the
immediate problem is to determine if possible how or why this
extraneous Vergilian matter has worked its way into Swift's
georgic. Some noteworthy objective links may be uncovered between the separate *loci* imitated by Swift. For one example, an
unusual phrase—"sata laeta boumque labores"—occurs twice
only in all Vergil: *Georgic* I. 325 [410], and *Aeneid* II. 306 [409–

410], also in depicting a storm and flood. The description in *Aeneid* II exists only as a simile for the flames that spread uncontrollably over Troy, but awareness of the verbal coincidence might have carried Swift along Vergil's path from the earlier context to the later. Whatever the cause, details of at least two passages in *Aeneid* II narrating the destruction of Troy (228–267, 40–53) [300–349, 52–69] are combined to furnish Swift's digression: "So when *Troy* Chair-men bore the Wooden Steed. . . ."

Consideration of Swift's use of these *Aeneid* passages will make evident the difficulty attendant on naming the exact "source" for any of his classical borrowings, and will caution against any tendency to assume without proof that "imitation" implies derogatory parody. The simile in "City Shower" 47–52, following the conventional *qualis-talis* formula, illustrates how a Beau, boxed in his chair during the storm, "trembles from within" (46); so, inside the Horse, "each imprison'd Hero quak'd for Fear" (52). The trembling of the Beau derives from Vergil's storm in *Georgic* I: "Terra tremit, fugere ferae, et mortalia corda/ per gentes humilis stravit pavor" (330–331) [448–452]; but that the Greeks in their horse "quak'd for Fear" is nowhere intimated by Vergil. Swift's supplement is justified by a separate tradition going back chiefly to *Odyssey* XI. 523–532, but whether he made the synthesis independently, or because Dryden's translation of *Aeneid* II. 52–53 reflects the same tradition, it is impossible to tell.[8] Similarly, if the *Tatler*'s supposition is correct, that Swift's shower is related to the rainstorm in *Aeneid* IV, Dryden's translation rather than the original may quite well be the model. There can be small doubt that the *Tatler*'s guess was stimulated by lines 39–40 of Swift's poem: "Here various Kinds by various Fortunes led,/Commence Acquaintance underneath a Shed." In this case Vergil's terse record of the junction of "two potentates of different sexes"—"Speluncam Dido dux et Troianus eamdem/ devenient" (124–125)—may seem to contrast sharply with Dryden's prolix speculation upon causes: "The queen and prince, as love or fortune guides,/One common cavern in her bosom hides" [239–240]. But again dogmatic conclusions from this probability may mislead.

Much less ambiguity seems to attend an imitation in the "City Shower" of the work of another contemporary. Faulkner in 1735 noted the indubitable fact that Swift's line 26 ("'Twas doubtful which was Rain, and which was Dust") is borrowed from a line in Sir Samuel Garth's *Dispensary* ("'Tis doubtful which is Sea, and which is Sky").[9] Burlesque can hardly have been the point of this borrowing—the *Dispensary* is itself a burlesque. Swift was dining occasionally with Garth during the weeks in which the "Shower" was written, and the echo might have conveyed a compliment, but even so the selection of one line rather than another must have had at least a cause if not also a purpose. It is not surprising to find that the context of Garth's line is also a description of "The liquid Volley of a missive Show'r" (v. 166)— this one discharged from the clysters and "levell'd Syringes" of embattled physicians: "Like Spouts in Southern Seas the Deluge broke,/And numbers sunk beneath th'impetuous Stroke." But it is enlightening to note that the same description continues in an epic simile strikingly reminiscent of the Vergilian passages imitated by Swift:

> Thus when some Storm its Chrystal Quarry rends,
> And Jove in rattling Showrs of Ice descends;
> Mount Athos shakes the Forests on his Brow,
> Whilst down his wounded Sides fresh Torrents flow
> And Leaves and Limbs of Trees o'er spread the Vale below.
>
> (*Dispensary* v. 184–188)

The mention of Mount Athos recalls especially *Georgic* I. 328–334:[10] "Ipse Pater . . . in nocte corusca/fulmina molitur dextra; quo maxima motu/terra tremit . . . ille flagranti . . . Athon . . . deiicit . . . nunc nemora ingenti vento, nunc litora plangunt." With this there seems to be some conflation of Swift's other model, *Aeneid* II.305–307: "rapidus montano flumine torrens . . . praecipitesque trahit silvas." Swift, if nothing else, appears attracted to the contexts of literary showers and floods, and exploration of these separate contexts reveals still further connections between them. Thereby perhaps hangs the unified meaning of his whole poem. In Addison's view of the georgic, ornaments and diversions should be "brought in aptly, and [be] something of a piece with the main Design. . . . For they ought to have a remote Alliance at least to the Subject, that so the whole Poem may be more uniform and agreeable in all its Parts. Addison's next sentence (if "Shower" be substituted for "Country") may seem to have foreshadowed Swift's practice: "We shou'd never lose Sight of the Country, tho' we are sometimes entertain'd with a distant Prospect of it."

Of the context of the rainstorm in *Aeneid* IV little need be said. That storm, as Dryden remarked ("Dedication of the Aeneis"), quoting Ovid, "brought Dido and Aeneas into a cave, and left them there not over honestly together." Vergil views the event in darker and more ominous terms: "Ille dies primus leti primusque malorum/causa fuit" (169–170); and Dryden's translation carries even stronger overtones of a primal fall:

> From this ill-omen'd hour in time arose
> Debate and death, and all succeeding woes.
> [245–246]

The context of the episodes from *Aeneid* II employed by Swift is even less debatable: it is the downfall of the city of Troy. Swift refers specifically to the treacherous contrivance of the Greeks and the vain effort of Laocoon to alert the Trojans to their peril—vain because, whether fated by the gods or by the perversity of men's minds (*Aeneid* II.54), the town was irrevocably doomed.

The context that requires most discussion is the entire second half of the first *Georgic*, the source of most of the Vergilian material in the "City Shower." Of this material, three major passages—those dealing with prognostication (351 ff.) [483 ff.], storm (316 ff.) [427 ff.], and flood (481 ff.) [649 ff.]—have each a special noteworthiness in classical literary history. Behind Vergil's literary treatment of weather-signs lay not only a considerable body of Greek scientific speculation, but also a poetic tradition having roots in Hesiod, Homer, and Pindar, and a vastness of living popular lore.[11] From earliest times, as might be expected, weather-prediction has often been contaminated with divination, for it was natural to see in storms and similar unpleasant tricks of weather—as in political tumult—sure signs of the deity's anger, and, through normal human pessimism, to identify the deity chiefly with the perpetration of malignant mischief. The Father was, to both Greeks and Romans, as to the Hebrews, at the same time Lord of the Storm-cloud and the fashioner of "bitter war." At the heart of Vergil's storm we find Jupiter, dealing his fiery bolts about, just as in Vergil's source and model, *Iliad* XVI.384–393,[12] we are told that the rain is poured down by Zeus when he is bitterly angry with men "who render by force crooked judgments . . . and drive out justice, not caring about the vengeance of the gods." Such moral concern is perhaps not always evident, but it is quite clear that Homer interpreted signs of storm as equivalently prophetic of war. Pindar and other poets after him did the same, so there is little to surprise in the facility with which Vergil's weather prognostics in *Georgic* I shift over into a review of the signs that foretold the civil wars in Rome and the assassination of Julius Caesar. Careful observers may foretell, by observing the sun, not merely when to dread a shower projected by the South, but when to expect "fierce tumults, hidden treasons, open wars" [627]:

> quid cogitet umidus Auster,
> Sol tibi signa dabit. Solem quis dicere falsum
> audeat? Ille etiam caecos instare tumultus
> saepe monet, fraudemque et operta tumescere bella.
> Ille etiam exstincto miseratus Caesare Romam.
>
> (462–466)

Dryden's translation expands considerably upon the last line of this: "He first the fate of Caesar did foretell,/And pitied Rome, when Rome in Caesar fell" [628–629]. It was among the omens of this fall of the City—a fall associated by Vergil with the fate of Troy: "sanguine nostro/Laomedonteae luimus periuria Troiae" (501–502)—that Swift found that flooding of the Eridanus he converted to his own use. *Georgic* I ends in an image of chaos, on a note of despair of the state and of civilization, and Dryden's rendering of the lines depicting the flood (481–483) sufficiently exemplifies the disorder of Nature:

> Then rising in his might, the king of floods
> Rush'd thro' the forests, tore the lofty woods;
> And, rolling onward, with a sweepy sway,
> Bore houses, herds, and lab'ring hinds away.
>
> [649–652]

In both classical and neo-classical literature the overflowing

114

of a river was often the portent of civil disorders or destruction.[13] The floods in *Georgic* I portended the death of Caesar and the dissolution of the state; the flood in *Aeneid* II. 305 ff. depicted the burning of Troy. Even Homer's flood in *Iliad* XVI described a military defeat of the Trojans. Troy had been doomed, and Vergil prayed that a like fate might be spared Rome, the new Troy. London—or Troynovant, or Romeville—believed itself the heir of both ancient cities, and with the pride went the prejudices: in Augustan London a "Greek," whether boxed in a chair or in a wooden horse, was still a sharper and a cheat. Swift, however, offers no prayers for the safety of the newest Troy, doomed like its predecessors: "the Flood comes down/Threat'ning with Deluge this *Devoted* Town" (31–32; italics Swift's).

London is "devoted"—set apart for destruction—for reasons suggested in Swift's poem. The city's corruption is betokened in the omens of rain—the stink of sewage (5–6), the throbbing of corns and toothache (9–10), the splenetic "Dulman" enacting the eponymy of his race (11–12)—but still more radically in the behavior of the citizens caught in the downpour. Hypocrisy, or falseseeming, is the essence of their natures. The "daggled Females" crowd the shops for shelter, "pretend" to bargain for goods, "but nothing buy" (33–34). The "Templer spruce . . . Stays till 'tis fair, yet *seems* to call a Coach" (35–36). Tories and Whigs, in face of the threatening deluge, discard their ostensibly principled differences and reveal their true common purpose, "to save their Wigs" (41–42). The Beau in his chair, "impatient," but "trembl[ing] from within" at the clatter of the rain (43–46), is an avatar of the Greeks inside "the Wooden Steed," who, though "impatient to be freed" (48), likewise "quak'd for Fear" (52). Like "those Bully Greeks," the "Modern" is both a deceptive coward and a deadly menace to the chair-men who carry him— as to the city that admits him (49–50).

In lines 39–40 ("Here various Kinds . . ./Commence Acquaintance . . ."), as the *Tatler* intimates, it is possible to see the "bringing [of] matters to a speedy conclusion between . . . different sexes." And there exist grounds for implicating in this "not over honest" conjunction both the Templar and the "tuck'd-up Sempstress" (37–38). A poem called "A Town Eclogue"—obviously parallel to a city georgic—published about six months after the "City Shower," and often also ascribed to Swift, apparently equates sempstresses with prostitutes, and unequivocally identifies "Templers spruce"[14] as the usual clientele for the Royal Exchange whores.

The tumultuous flood at the end of the "City Shower" offers impressive evidence of the city's physical corruption:

Filth of all Hues and Odours seem to tell
What Street they sail'd from, by their Sight and Smell.
They, as each Torrent drives, with rapid Force
From *Smithfield*, or St. *Pulchre*'s shape their Course,
And in huge Confluent join at *Snow-Hill* Ridge,
Fall from the *Conduit* prone to *Holborn-Bridge*.
Sweepings from Butchers Stalls, Dung, Guts, and Blood,
Drown'd Puppies, stinking Sprats, all drench'd in Mud,
Dead Cats and Turnip-Tops come tumbling down the Flood.
(ll. 55–63)

Only by extension is this a picture of "the teeming conduits of a thousand streets and alleys tumbling down to Holborn bridge"[15]—specifically named are no more than the streets leading from Smithfield and "St. Pulchre's." As Williams perceptively notes, "Swift . . . pictured the garbage and offal from the sheep and cattle pens, then standing to the west of West Smithfield, washing down to meet the overflow from the neighbourhood of St. Sepulchre's Church at Holborn Conduit, the junction of Snow Hill and Cow Lane, and thence falling into the Fleet at Holborn Bridge." But the two named wellsprings of the Flood have each stronger associations with moral than with physical corruption. "Smithfield," Pope tells us (*Dunciad* I.2,n.), "is the place where Bartholomew Fair was kept, whose shows, machines, and dramatical entertainments, [were] formerly agreeable only to the taste of the Rabble." From the year 1123 until its suppression as a nuisance in 1855, Bartholomew Fair was notorious for profligacy, insolent violation of the law, and obscene plays. In 1708 unsuccessful attempts were made to suppress the Fair, and it was legally restricted to the three days, August 23–25. Despite the law, it seems often to have run as long as six weeks.[16] For the area of St. Sepulchre's Church, unlike that of Smithfield, no special primacy at all as a source of physical filth can be indicated,

but on the other hand the church has always been closely associated with crime. Newgate Prison was directly across from the
church, to which it was connected both spiritually and physically
(a tunnel is thought at one time to have connected church and
prison). By reason of various pious bequests, the great bell of
St. Sepulchre's commenced to toll on execution days when the
procession left Newgate for Tyburn. Outside the church a nose-
gay was presented to each condemned criminal, and the cortege
then proceeded along precisely the route of Swift's torrent: from
St. Pulchre's down Snow Hill to its junction with Cock Lane and
Cow Lane—the site of Holborn Conduit (taken down in 1746)—
and thence to Holborn Bridge.[17] (From the Bridge, of course,
the route to Tyburn has no parallel in the "Shower.") The neighborhood of St. Sepulchre's is therefore also the neighborhood of
Newgate, and thence, as from Smithfield, the literal offal of society plunges toward Fleet Ditch, the notorious cloaca of eighteenth-century London. If the form of Swift's concluding lines
alludes to lax observance of the laws of verse, the content alludes
to abuses of the moral and the civil laws.

The second part of the "Description of a City Shower"—the
rising of the storm (13–30)—seems less well articulated than the
other three sections. The persons, and the relations among them,
are obscure, and though we may perhaps suspect the oblique
presence of Swift himself in the "needy Poet" whose distresses
occupy four lines (27–30), almost any further conjecture begins
at once to appear farfetched. (The resemblance, however, should
not be overlooked between Swift's implacable "Quean" and Jupiter at the center of a storm.) One couplet nonetheless surprises
by an excess that cannot be ignored:

> Not yet, the Dust had shun'd th'unequal Strife,
> But aided by the Wind, fought still for Life.
>
> (23–24)

Here dust is alive—though soon to be killed by the rain—and
sustained in its life by the wind. The wind as sustainer of life is
a concept Swift had played with before: "whether you please to
call the *Forma informans* of Man, by the Name of *Spiritus, Animus,
Afflatus,* or *Anima*; What are all these but several Appelations for
Wind? . . . what is Life itself, but as it is commonly call'd, the

Breath of our Nostrils" (*A Tale of a Tub,* viii). The latter question effectively identifies the ultimate source of this learned fooling in what is also an authentication and definition of living Dust: "And the Lord God formed man of the dust of the ground, and breathed into his nostrils the breath of Life; and man became a living soul" (Genesis ii.7). Even as a simple hyperbole Swift's couplet has an Old Testament reference, and therefore to some extent the wind-enlivened dust is mankind. To that same extent the threatening "Deluge" (32), or "Flood" (31,63), takes on the retributive coloring of its counterpart in Genesis. In Greek and Latin poetry storms always came from Zeus or Jupiter, and, at least in some cases, as a punishment for sin. But in the story of Jehovah's flood the tone of Hebrew morality is everywhere evident. That flood was provoked entirely by evil-doing—"all flesh had corrupted his way upon the earth" (Gen. vi.12)—and its consequences were far beyond the powers of either pagan deity: "all in whose nostrils was the breath of life . . . died (Gen. vi.22). At the end of Swift's poem no creature is left alive that comes "tumbling down the Flood."

To the literal manifest of "A Description of a City Shower" additional notes may now be attached: the omens, and the acts of the citizens, when not simply unedifying are corrupt; the town is explicitly said to be doomed ("Devoted"); and the primary associations of all the places named are with moral or physical corruption. In the subsidiary study of literary backgrounds, we find that all the traceable allusions in the poem come from a limited range of contexts—descriptions of divinely-ordained floods, and the falls of cities. Though the evidence bears out the eighteenth-century assumption that the over-all form of the "City Shower" is in some way that of a georgic, the case cannot be said to be proven for the further assumption that the main intention of the poem is to ridicule either the genre itself or its exemplars, whether Vergil's originals or Dryden's translations. The poem's import seems then to lie within its own terms, and to be primarily an oblique denunciation of cathartic doom upon the corruption of the city.

Such a way of reading the poem comports remarkably well with Addison's canons for the georgic, although the allusive and indirect didacticism this discussion has been extrapolating from the "City Shower" may appear to be nothing like "plain and direct Instructions." But Addison explicitly asserts that just such disguise of the moral import is what chiefly distinguishes Poetry from Prose: "Where the Prose-writer tells us plainly what ought to be done, the Poet often conceals the Precept in a Description." What might be criticized as factitious in this study's seeking of the moral direction of Swift's "Description" is specifically commended by Addison as one of the beauties proper to the georgic. In the light of certain of his remarks it is perhaps easy to understand the delight the "City Shower" aroused among its first readers:

> This way of Writing . . . is particularly practised by Virgil, who loves to suggest a Truth indirectly, and without giving us a full and open View of it: To let us see just so much as will naturally lead the Imagination into all the Parts that lie conceal'd. This is wonderfully diverting to the Understanding, thus to receive a Precept, that enters as it were thro' a By-way, and to apprehend an Idea that draws a whole Train after it. For here the Mind, which is always delighted with its own Discoveries, only takes the Hint from the Poet, and seems to work out the rest by the Strength of her own Faculties.

If the "Description of a City Shower" was the best thing "that has been written of the kind," its kind must be judged to be that anomalous thing, a city georgic. But a mock-georgic need not, any more than a mock-epic, lack an independent moral import: the mock-heroic tradition implies acceptance of the standards of the heroic tradition. It is perhaps significant that the English Augustan poets achieved no major successes in any of the classical "kinds" they upheld (other than satire), except in the form of parody or burlesque. Without a genuine Augustus to give moral coherence to society, genuine poets found themselves living in what to them was a mock-Augustan age.

The serious georgic in English, among first-rate poets, found embodiment only in the derivative form of "local poetry." Although many competent georgics were written by minor poets during the eighteenth century, *Windsor Forest,* roughly contemporary with the "City Shower," is the last poetically durable effort to engage in one discourse, according to something like the classical model, description of rural matters with political didacticism. Swift's urbanization of the georgic, that is, his absorption of the rural element into the political-didactic (thus in a sense emptying rural-descriptive poetry of concern with urban affairs), may be an unrecognized correlative of the growth of that contrary sensibility that found in the rural not an exemplum for the urban, but rather a sense sublime, if vague, of something far more deeply interfused.

Notes

1. Johnson, *The Sin of Wit: Jonathan Swift as a Poet* (Syracuse, 1950), pp. 84–89; Horne, ed., *Swift on His Age* (London, 1953), p. 224.

2. *The Poems of Jonathan Swift*, 2nd ed. (Oxford, 1958), I, 136–139. All reference in the present study to the text of Swift's poem is to this edition.

3. Numbers placed in square brackets throughout this paper identify the relevant lines in Dryden's translation of cited Vergilian texts, and refer to the Cambridge *Dryden* (1950), ed. Noyes.

The same sections of *Georgic* I identified in the text as models for the "City Shower" are recognized as those "parodied by Swift" in Dwight L. Durling, *Georgic Tradition in English Poetry* (New York, 1935), p. 40 n., and p. 230 n.

4. The description is that of R. S. Conway, *New Studies of a Great Inheritance* (London, 1921), p. 40.

5. On Oct. 12, 1710 Swift wrote to Stella, "I have finished my poem on the Shower, all but the beginning."

6. *Correspondence of Jonathan Swift*, ed. F. E. Ball (London, 1913), V, 162. In reproducing Faulkner's 1735 note to "City Shower" 61–63, Williams cites this letter as obvious evidence that "Swift's hand may be clearly seen" in the note.

7. Both the conflict of evidence and the inconclusiveness of this line of investigation may be demonstrated in Swift's "Brisk Susan" who "whips her linen from the Rope" (17) as the rainstorm begins. It may reasonably be accepted that she is a transformation of the mariners in *Georgic* I. 372–73 who furl their sails at an identical crisis. The "dropping sheets" [513] that Dryden has the sailors furl in his version— especially when it is recalled that his "dropping" meant our "dripping"—might seem peculiarly susceptible of metamorphosis in Swift's hands into the washing on Susan's line. But Vergil's "umida vela" in the same place might just as well have been Swift's provocation.

8. Dryden's "The sides, transpierc'd, return a rattling sound,/And

groans of Greeks inclos'd come issuing thro' the wound" [68–69], where Vergil had written "uteroque recusso/insonuere cavae gemitumque dedere cavernae," culminates a long process of syncretic translation, of which an earlier stage is reflected in John Ogilby's 1649–50 translation: "the hollow Caverns rung,/And dark Internals groan" (54–55).

9. Canto v.176. This is the line numbering of the early editions (1699 & shortly thereafter), but the numbering of later editions is variable. By a "ninth edition" of 1726 this line had become v.249.

10. Vergil mentions Mount Athos at one other place only (*Aen.* XII.701–703), whence Garth probably derived his "Ice" (unmentioned in *GeorgicI*), though not the details of the storm.

11. This fact has been noted from antiquity, and was remarked by Addison in the *Essay on the Georgic* he prefixed to Dryden's translation. For a modern discussion see W. E. Gillespie, *Vergil, Aratus and Others: the Weather-Sign as a Literary Subject* (Princeton, 1938).

12. This attribution is fairly common in seventeenth-century editions of Vergil; e.g., *P. Virgili Maronis Opera cum integris Notis Servii . . .* ed. Jacobi Emmenesii (Amstelodami, 1680), I, 273.

13. For a detailed examination of one use of this image (in Denham's *Cooper's Hill*), and other examples, see Earl R. Wasserman, *The Subtler Language* (Baltimore, 1959), pp. 80–81, esp. p. 80 n. 37.

14. The identity of phrase argues at the minimum a direct reflection of the earlier poem in the later; though there seems no convincing reason to doubt that Swift had at least a hand in the "Town Eclogue." See Williams, Swift's *Poems*, III, 1087.

15. Durling, *Georgic Tradition*, p. 36. Durling's lack of sympathy with "Swift's bludgeoning vulgarity" prevents him in other details also from reading accurately the "City Shower," which he calls "important only because it suggested Gay's *Trivia*."

16. See Henry A. Harben, *A Dictionary of London* (London, 1918), and William Kent, *An Encyclopedia of London* (New York, 1937). If the Fair ran its accustomed course in 1710, it was probably still running when Swift began his poem, about October 10.

Among the "dramatical entertainments" of Bartholomew Fair, appropriately enough, was Elkanah Settle's opera, *Siege of Troy*, especially adapted in 1707.

17. This route is difficult to trace on a map of modern London. Snow Hill did not follow the route of the present street of the same name except for two points of coincidence, St. Sepulchre's Church, and the junction with Cock Lane and Cow Lane (now Smithfield Street). From that point Snow Hill ran under the present Holborn Viaduct, to Holborn Bridge, which was roughly where Plumtree Court now opens off Farringdon Street.

ROGER SAVAGE

Swift's Fallen City
A Description of the Morning

*As to your Blank-verse, it hath too often fallen into
the same vile Hands of late. One* Thomson, *a* Scots-
Man, *has succeeded the best in that Way, in four
Poems he has writ on the four Seasons. Yet I am not
over-fond of them, because they are all Description,
and nothing is doing, whereas* Milton *engages me in
Actions of the highest Importance,* modo me Romae,
modo ponit Athenis.
     Swift to Charles Wogan, July 1732; Corr., IV, 53*

In 1709 Swift contributed a lean, unflorid poem to the ninth of
Richard Steele's *Tatlers*. He called it *A Description of the Morning*.
The title may strike us as prosaic, appropriately prosaic considering the bald way Swift treats his unromantic sunrise. But we
shall miss the point of the piece if we assume that Swift gave it
a plain name because plain names are aptest for lean poems. If
title underlines treatment here, it does so ironically, for the associations of 'description' in Augustan poetics were far from prosaic. In fact, *descriptio* was a respected ingredient of the Grand

This essay first appeared in *The World of Jonathan Swift: Essays for the Tercentenary*,
ed. Brian Vickers (Oxford: Basil Blackwell; Cambridge: Harvard University
Press, 1968), pp. 171–94, and is reprinted by permission of the Harvard University Press, © 1968 by Basil Blackwell.

Manner. Le Bossu has a chapter on it (VI.ii) in his *Traité du poème épique*—a book admired and mined extensively by Dryden, Addison and Pope—while Rymer chooses to spend half the preface to his version of Rapin's *Reflexions sur la poétique* analysing specimens of description from the *Argonautica*, the *Aeneid*, *The Conquest of Mexico* and so on. But the work best preserving the glamour of Augustan *descriptio* is a verse-essay with which Swift himself was closely connected only a few years after the *Morning* appeared. This was the ambitious *Essay on the Different Stiles of Poetry* which his Irish protégé Thomas Parnell published in 1713. The year before, Swift had generously appointed himself stage-manager of Parnell's reputation at Court, and decided that the half-finished *Essay* could play a vital part in his plan to give the unknown Irishman 'a little friendly forwarding'. He chivied Parnell into finishing it, helped him correct it, got him to add a eulogy of Lord Secretary Bolingbroke at its climax. And though Swift was chiefly interested in the poem as a device for putting his gifted friend in the way of some enviable Court patronage, it would be hard to believe under the circumstances that he strongly disapproved of its themes and arguments. Yet Parnell demonstrates in his *Essay* that proper *descriptio* is the reverse of lean and unflorid.[1]

The *Essay,* as its preface explains, is an allegory: 'Wit *is made to be* Pegasus, *and the* Poet *his* Rider, *who flies by several* Countries *where he must not touch, by which are meant so many vicious* Stiles, *and arrives at last at the* Sublime'. *En route* Parnell is much concerned with varieties of poetic Description and Narration, and when it comes to discussing them, as we might expect of someone soon to be an intimate of Pope's, he drops into the dialect of classicist idealism. For instance, one of the countries his Pegasus makes a point of avoiding is the land of lean literalism, where Description and Narration are skimped:

> Here flat *Narrations* fair Exploits debase,
> In Measures void of ev'ry shining Grace;
> Which never arm their *Hero* for the Field,
> Nor with *Prophetick Story* paint the Shield,
> Nor fix the Crest, or make the Feathers wave,
> Or with their Characters reward the Brave;

Undeck'd they stand, and unadorn'd with Praise,
And fail to profit while they fail to please.
(vv. 75–82)

The landscapes of 'forc'd *Description*' here are equally bare and unmemorable:

The liveless Trees may stand for ever bare,
And Rivers stop, for ought the Readers care.
(vv. 85–86)

But when at last we reach the Sublime, *narratio* comes into its own 'by boldly vent'ring to dilate in Praise', and so does *descriptio*—as an Italianate fresco-painter:

Above the Beauties, far above the Show
In which weak Nature dresses here below,
Stands the great *Palace* of the *Bright* and *Fine*,
Where fair Ideas in full Glory shine . . .
Here bold *Description* paints the Walls within,
Her Pencil touches, and the World is seen:
The Fields look beauteous in their flow'ry Pride,
The Mountains rear aloft, the Vales subside . . .
The Skies extended in an open View,
Appear a lofty distant Arch of *Blue*,
In which *Description* stains the painted Bow,
Or thickens Clouds, and feathers out the Snow,
Or mingles Blushes in the Morning ray,
Or gilds the Noon, or turns an Evening gray.
(vv. 189–192, 237–240, 247–252)

Parnell gives no details of the landscape produced when his *descriptio* 'mingles Blushes with the Morning ray', so we cannot compare her work directly with Swift's *Description of the Morning*. But we can be sure that her paintings are more like Claude's or Poussin's than Breughel's, for we know generally that her art heightens 'weak Nature', transcends mere appearances and idealises every beauty it touches. And beyond this we can assume that her techniques of making images of 'the *Bright* and *Fine*' are essentially those of just *narratio*. Just Narration's methods can be established by reversing the faults (already shown us) of *flat* Narration; and this makes her an out-and-out classicist. The arming of the hero, the roll-call of his companions, the recital of the legends carved on his shield: each of these shining graces has a sound pedigree in ancient poetry. It seems, then, that sublime presentation of superior nature (superior to that dull, weak, untidy reality which commonly passes for nature) will best be achieved through adaptation of the classics. What Goldsmith says sixty years later of Parnell's own poetic achievement can well be applied to the narrative-descriptive techniques recommended under the eye of Swift in the *Essay*:

> Parnell . . . appears to me to be the last of that great school that had modelled itself upon the ancients, and taught English poetry to resemble what the generality of mankind have allowed to excel. A studious and correct observer of antiquity, he set himself to consider nature in the lights it lent him; and he found that the more aid he borrowed from the one, the more delightfully he resembled the other. To copy nature is a task the most bungling workman is able to execute; to select such parts as contribute to delight, is reserved only for those whom accident has blest with uncommon talents, or such as have read the ancients with indefatigable industry.[2]

As Goldsmith suggests, Parnell's circle shared a belief—a belief they saw increasingly threatened—that imitation of the ancients was the modern artist's surest guide to *la belle nature*. In the spring of 1713, when his *Essay* appeared, Parnell was seeing more and more of Pope (it may well have been Parnell who introduced Pope to Swift about that time); and it was Pope who two years before had embodied the belief most memorably in his fable of the poetic education of Virgil:

> When first young *Maro* in his boundless Mind
> A Work t'outlast Immortal *Rome* design'd,
> Perhaps he seem'd *above* the Critick's Law,
> And but from *Nature's Fountains* scorn'd to draw:

But when t'examine ev'ry Part he came,
Nature and *Homer* were, he found, the *same*.
(*An Essay on Criticism*, vv. 130–135)

Nature at her worthiest = Homer. Parnell implies the same in his *Essay on the Different Stiles*. His *narratio* is an emulator of ancient epic ritual. His *descriptio* can be seen as an active connoisseur of classic landscape poetry.

But if Parnell only implies this about *descriptio,* John Hughes the following year makes it explicit. In the thirty-ninth *Lay Monk* (February 12th, 1714) he has an unsigned essay, reprinted in his collected works of 1735, on how the great poets have classicised their dawn-scenes. The essay is in the line started by Rymer with his discussion of night-scenes in the Rapin preface; but where Rymer is careful to save his highest praise for his most modern exhibit, Hughes puts the emphasis on the workings of tradition. 'There is no particular Description', he says, 'which the Writers of Heroick Poetry seem to have labour'd to vary so much as that of the *Morning*. This is a Topick on which they have drawn out all the Copiousness, and even the Luxury of their Fancies.' Description is copious and luxuriant, not lean and unflorid, and description of the morning especially so:

> The Morning is most frequently figur'd as a Goddess, or divine Person, flying in the Air, unbarring the Gates of Light, and opening the Day. She is drawn by *Homer* in a Saffron Garment, and with Rosy Hands (which is the Epithet he almost constantly bestows on her) sprinkling Light thro' the Earth. She arises out of the Waves of the Sea, leaves the Bed of *Tithon* her Lover, ascends the Heavens, appears to the Gods and to Men, and gives Notice of the Sun-Rising. . . . She is usher'd in by the Star which is her Harbinger, and which gives the Signal of the Morning's Approach.

Now though Hughes says at the outset that descriptions of the morning have been more varied than any others, we soon see that what has been treated in so many ways is an event in classic art, not an event in nature. Homer's Aurora is the common *datum*. 'On this, as a Ground, the Poets following *Homer,*

127

have run their Divisions of Fancy'. Their variations, such as the dawn-formula Virgil uses twice in the *Aeneid*—

> Now rose the ruddy morn from Tithon's bed,
> And with the dawns of day the skies o'erspread[3]

—are on a Homeric rather than a natural theme, *if* the two can be distinguished. But it seems they cannot, for Hughes, going on to quote some lines of Tasso to show 'how the same Images have been copy'd or diversify'd by the Moderns', adds significantly that 'our own *Spenser*, who excells in all Kinds of Imagery, following the same Originals, represents the Morning after the like manner'. Spenser excels in all kinds of imagery and is working in a descriptive mode friendly to copious fancy; yet still he sees imitation of the classics as the best imitation of ideal nature, representing morning as the Renaissance in general represented it by following the same originals. Nature's dawn and Homer's are, Spenser finds, the same.

The trouble with a demonstration like Hughes's, however high-minded its intentions, is that it gives the untalented modern poet rich scope for disguising his lack of talent. To copy nature delightfully, says Goldsmith apropos of Parnell's classicism, is 'reserved only for those whom accident has blest with uncommon talents, or such as have read the ancients with indefatigable industry'. The more the lineaments of ideal *descriptio* or *narratio* are vulgarised by analysis in *Lay Monks* or exhibition in commonplace-books, the less intense this industry will need to be, the more the Grub Street hack will be able to apply classical formulae mechanically in and out of season, and the more any 'uncommon talent' will be provoked into looking for an entirely different way of describing nature. It is significant that it should be an anonymous, faceless entry in one such commonplace-book—Edward Bysshe's *British Parnassus*, also published in 1714—which offers us the fullest Augustan embodiment of Hughes's dawn-topos. Day's harbinger, her aged lover's bed, the gates of day, the blushing sky and lingering stars: all the images are there in the lines quoted below, supplemented with fitting generalities from an Arcadian landscape. By the early eighteenth century, such cataloguing of landscape was as traditional as the Aurora-motifs themselves. In his chapter on *descriptio*, Le Bossu had recommended the 'fine *Description* of a Calm and quiet Night' in the *Aeneid* (IV, 522–528), where Virgil describes the repose of nature—woods, waves, stars, cattle, birds—and so 'renders the cruel Disturbances of *Dido* a great deal more moving, since they rob her of that Rest which all Nature enjoy'd, to the very vilest and most despicable Creatures'.[4] Le Bossu's recommendation was not lost on the Restoration dramatists. Not only sleepy night-catalogues but Arcadian dawn-catalogues too are reeled off by the soliloquists of Otway and Nathaniel Lee before they announce in Dido's vein that they alone of all creation know no rest or happiness. So the couplets which follow from Bysshe's *Parnassus* present the classical ideal—and the classical cliché—both in the invocation of a revered myth and in the segmentation of a picturesque landscape:

> —And now Aurora, Harbinger of Day,
> Rose from the Bed, where aged Tithon lay;
> Unbarr'd the Doors of Heav'n, and overspread
> The Path of Phoebus with a blushing Red.
> The starry Lights above are scarce expir'd;
> And scarce the Shade from open Plains retir'd;
> The tuneful Lark has hardly stretch'd her Wing;
> And warbling Linnets just begin to sing;
> Nor yet industrious Bees their Hives forsake;
> Nor skim the Fish the Surface of the Lake;
> Nor yet the Flow'rs disclose their various Hue;
> But fold their Leaves, oppress'd with hoary Dew;
> Blue Mists around conceal the neighb'ring Hills:
> And dusky Fogs hang o'er the murmuring Rills;
> While Zephyr faintly sighs among the Trees;
> And moves the Branches with a lazy Breeze.
> No jovial Pipe resounds along the Plains,
> Safe in their Hamlets sleep the drowzy Swains.[5]

When Parnell, Swift's protégé, presents Description 'mingling blushes in the morning ray', he has surely something like these eighteen lines in mind. We are to look over the poet's shoulder for a distant, harmonious, elevated landscape. But when Swift himself presents *A Description of the Morning* in eighteen lines, it is of quite another scene:

Now hardly here and there an Hackney-Coach
Appearing, show'd the Ruddy Morns Approach.
Now *Betty* from her Masters Bed had flown,
And softly stole to discompose her own.
The Slipshod Prentice from his Masters Door,
Had par'd the Dirt, and Sprinkled round the Floor.
Now *Moll* had whirl'd her Mop with dext'rous Airs,
Prepar'd to Scrub the Entry and the Stairs.
The Youth with Broomy stumps began to trace
The Kennel-Edge, where Wheels had worn the Place.
The Smallcoal-Man was heard with Cadence deep,
'Till drown'd in Shriller Notes of Chimney-Sweep,
Duns at his Lordships Gate began to meet,
And Brickdust *Moll* had Scream'd through half the Street.
The Turnkey now his Flock returning sees,
Duly let out a Nights to steal for Fees.
The watchful Bailiffs take their silent Stands,
And School-Boys lag with Satchels in their Hands.

(Poems, 124–5)

Unless we are aware of such Augustan stock-responses to Swift's title as those suggested above, we are not likely to achieve more than a partial reading of his poem. The *Description of the Morning* has often been seen as a piece of uncomplicated realism, vivid and assured or barren and pointless, according to the taste of the critic; but its realism is not simply the result of a walk through London at dawn with a camera. It is determined and moulded by what Swift has learned from the masters of the descriptive tradition and by the attitude to them he has come to adopt. The poem is basically mock-*descriptio*, a comic imitation of the classical ideal; and on this level it reads like a parody of the dawn-scene in Bysshe's *Parnassus*. Each begins with two mythological couplets which lead to seven of appropriate amplification from nature. Swift's nature, though, has no distancing or elevation: it is a world of scavengers and bailiffs, dirt and dust, scrubbing and screaming.[6] Warbling larks and tuneful linnets become coalmen and chimney-sweeps; the shepherd-swain about to wake and sound his jovial pipe becomes the turnkey counting his flock of thieves as they come in from night-pasture: and this because Swift's is a nature amplified from a mythology of hackney coaches and fallen Pamelas. The mythology is adapted daringly and wittily from the classical tradition, and the result is rich burlesque.

Apart from two couplets of morning-description in the 'tragical elegy' *Cassinus and Peter* (vv. 31–34), so perfunctory in themselves, so cruelly ironic in their context, Swift the poet only once allows himself to make significant use of the conventional dawn-myth. This is in the enthusiastic epistle *To Lord Harley on his Marriage* (1713), a tribute to the son of one of Swift's few modern heroes, Queen Anne's Lord Treasurer. Harley's bride, Lady Holles (whose unfashionable red hair may have provoked the comparison) is 'as Aurora bright':

> Thus the bright Empress of the Morn
> Chose, for her spouse, a mortal born . . .
> Tho' like a virgin of fifteen,
> She blushes when by mortals seen.
>
> (vv. 65–66 and 69–70)

The myth—which Spenser had kept alive in his *Fairie Queene* and Milton in his Latin Elegy *In Adventum Veris*, which Guercino and Agostino Carracci had both illustrated in Roman frescos[7]—celebrates an amorous, blushing dawn-goddess escaping from Tithonus, her domestic Struldbrugg, to drive her eager horses Lampos and Phaethon ahead of the sunrise. In Dryden's Virgil the 'ruddy morn' rises from 'Tithon's bed'; and in Hughes she is 'usher'd in by the Star which is her Harbinger, and which gives the Signal of the Morning's Approach'. In Swift's *Description* the myth is revised. Here the ruddy morn's approach is signalled by quite other harbingers and the dawn-spirit leaves the bed of a very different lover. Hackneys deputise for the stars (and perhaps for the Lampos and Phaethon too) of a conventional fresco, while Betty takes over the role of the Aurora. The pat symmetry of 'from her Masters Bed had flown—stole to discompose her own' persuades us to take it as a matter of course that when a *modern* Aurora is 'figur'd as a Goddess, or divine Person, flying in the Air' she will have something more pressing to do before the other folk are up than 'unbarring the Gates of Light, and opening the Day'. The low nature Swift presents makes a mockery of high art.

And a nature of sorts it certainly is, though an untidy and corrupt one, which makes the mockery. Swift here is not simply putting a moustache on the *Mona Lisa,* reducing outworn tradition to mere grotesque. Throughout the *Description* he is working from the jottings of an on-the-spot reporter in an average street, not very far from one described by his journalist contemporary, Tom Brown:

> Some carry, others are carried. 'Make way there,' says a gouty-legged chairman, that is carrying a punk of quality to a morning's exercise; or a Bartholomew babybeau, newly launched out of a chocolate-house, with his pockets as empty as his brains. 'Make room there,' says another fellow, driving a wheelbarrow of nuts, that spoil the lungs of the city 'prentices. . . . 'Stand up there, you blind dog,' says a carman, 'will you have the cart squeeze your guts out?' One tinker knocks, another bawls, 'Have you brass-pot, iron-pot, kettle, skillet or a frying-pan to mend?' . . . Here a poet scampers for't as fast as his legs will carry him, and at his heels a brace of bandog bailiffs, with open mouths ready to devour him and all the nine muses; and there an informer ready to spew up his false oaths at the sight of the common executioner.[8]

The tone is very different. Brown has a journalist's camera: Swift is working on a canvas prepared for formal *descriptio.* But their Londons are recognisably the same. Again, comparison with other mock-descriptions of the age will also show how positive the element of realism is in Swift's burlesque. We may take what another of his contemporaries, Francis Hutcheson, calls the 'fantastical imitation of the poetical imagery and similitudes of the morning' in Butler's *Hudibras,* a poem Swift himself admired immensely:

> The Sun, had long since in the Lap
> Of *Thetis,* taken out his *Nap,*
> And like a *Lobster* boyl'd, the *Morn*
> From *black* to *red* began to turn.[9]

The calculated vulgarity of 'taken out his *Nap*' is not unlike Swift's more potent shock-tactics with Aurora the chamber-maid (more potent because, with the names of his *dramatis personae* changed, Swift is able to preserve ideal epic dignity and mock it at the same time, while Butler's travesty can only coarsen). But the simile of the lobster has no counterpart in Swift. It is a metaphysical-farcical conceit, and its witty surrealism only intensifies by contrast the low-life naturalism of *A Description of the Morning*. Swift's imitation is not fantastical. And neither is it merely literary. Here a burlesque Description of the Night from the *Orpheus and Euridice* in William King's *Miscellanies* of 1707 is relevant:

> 'Twas Night, and Nature's self lay dead,
> Nodding upon a Feather-bed;
> The Mountains seem'd to bend their Tops,
> And Shutters clos'd the Mill'ners Shops,
> Excluding both the Punks and Fops.
> No ruffl'd Streams to Mill do come,
> The silent Fish were still more dumb;
> Look in the Chimney, not a Spark there,
> And Darkness did it self grow darker.

King's butt here is the Dryden purple passage from *The Conquest of Mexico* (III.ii):

> All things are hush'd, as Nature's self lay dead,
> The Mountains seem to nod their drowsie head

as Rymer quotes and praises it in his discussion of night-scenes. Dryden's solemnity and Rymer's connoisseur tone presumably make King uneasy. His reaction is good-natured, whimsical parody, with no holds barred. Deflation (mountain tops and milliners' shops), fantasy (night's feather-bed), low realism (the fops and punks), homely buttonholing (look in the chimney!), nonsense-hyperbole (darker darkness, dumber dumbness)—anything which can help ridicule the traditional descriptive mode is brought into play. And the indiscriminateness with which the weapons are chosen suggests that King's criticism of that mode is not a constructive one: that is to say, he has no directing awareness of a sordid actuality which demands to be presented. His *descriptio* is simply a pleasant literary joke. Swift's, on the other hand, is anchored to the Here and Now; and it is the tension between a positive and demanding poetic convention and a positive and demanding low reality which makes it more than a *jeu d'esprit*. Where King sees realism as one device among many useful to the parodist, Swift seems to be using burlesque of the formal *descriptio* just so that he can draw attention to the real, to common city nature. There is no place in his strategy for conceits *or* whimsies.

In this yoking of the poetic and the day-to-day, Swift stands closer to Samuel Garth in parts of *The Dispensary*. *The Dispensary*, which was published ten years before *A Description of the Morning*, is a baroque allegory satirising abuses among doctors. Its events are narrated in epic style, to give them enough significance to interest the layman and also to make a fitting framework for the personifications of Envy, Fortune, Health and so on which dominate the poem. But the abuses themselves and the stock-in-trade of the doctors who practise them are not at all sublime, and so the poem, for lack of any cohesive power on Garth's part, breaks up into an aimless alternation of epic and satiric paragraphs, with eulogies of the House of Nassau rubbing shoulders uneasily with indignant accounts of quacks' consulting-rooms. This uneasiness sometimes infects Garth's epic descriptions of evening, night and dawn. Most of these are perfectly lofty and well-behaved, like the evening scene in Canto IV, with its reeds and aspens, drowsy cattle and amorous birds. But some are tempted to visit the satiric-realist camp for the occasional detail, and the bathos which results must have appealed to Swift. For example, the Description of the Morning in Canto III, which begins

> With that, a Glance from mild *Aurora's* Eyes
> Shoots thro' the Chrystal Kingdoms of the Skies

could perfectly well go on like this without being untypical of *The Dispensary*:

> Now Trav'llers from their Eyes soft Slumbers shake,
> And for new Labour, Swains their Beds forsake.
> The roaming Lion, surfeited with Spoil,
> Comes to his Den fatigu'd with bloody Toil.

But in fact these two couplets come from a patriotic epic of Sir Richard Blackmore's; and what Garth actually writes here is

The Savage Kind in Forests cease to roam,
And Sots o'ercharg'd with nauseous Loads reel home.
Light's chearful Smiles o'er th' Azure Waste are spread,
And Miss from Inns o' Court bolts out unpaid.[10]

The relating of distant sky and jungle with furtive whoring and vomit on the pavement is certainly Swiftian, and yet Garth only makes a physical compound of these opposites where Swift's compound is chemical. In Garth, two pictures are put side by side. One belongs to the same world as the *Aurora* painted by Sir James Thornhill in 1715 for the Queen's Bedroom at Hampton Court: the goddess leaving Tithon and his starry mantle and rising on a cloud of Cupids to mount her golden coach. The other is closer to the urban morning scene of London in midwinter from Hogarth's *Four Times of Day,* with its very different heroine, the frosty *à-la-mode* spinster pointedly ignoring the Covent Garden whores at their work as she sails into Inigo Jones's church. In Swift, instead of alternating, the two pictures are superimposed.[11]

But it is symbolic that Thornhill was Hogarth's father-in-law, that Hogarth engraved high baroque illustrations for *Paradise Lost* as well as low realistic ones for *Hudibras,* and that when he was making studies for his portrait of the murderess Sarah Malcolm (a visual analogue to Fielding's Jonathan Wild, Gay's Macheath and Swift's own Clever Tom Clinch) his father-in-law was sketching beside him in the condemned cell.[12] Clearly the two men and the two manners, idealistic and naturalistic, found a *modus vivendi.* Is there a similar *modus* in A Description of the *Morning?* It is not enough just to say that in it Swift is using ironic imitation of the classical *belle nature* as an enabling device, as his means of rendering the immediate nature of contemporary London. Burlesque of this sort can hardly be neutral, cannot juxtapose two jarring natures without implying some sort of judgement. If low reality makes a mockery of high art in the *Morning,* with which does the blame lie?

According to the paragraph which introduces it in *Tatler* 9, we are to see the poem as a judgement against high art, a triumph of revolutionary realism over dead tradition. Swift, says the *Tatler,* 'has run into a Way perfectly New, and described Things exactly as they happen: He never forms Fields, or Nymphs, or Groves, where they are not, but makes the Incidents just as they really appear'. In other words, the Phoebus and Zephyr, open plains and drowsy swains of Bysshe's commonplace have been dismissed. Swift, we are to infer, has gone back to nature; her fountains are his true source. This praise of Swift in the *Tatler* strangely anticipates Joseph Warton's praise of James Thomson in his *Essay on the Genius and Writings of Pope.* Thomson, Warton says, has

> enriched poetry with a variety of new and original images which he painted from nature itself and from his own actual observations. His descriptions have, therefore, a distinctness and truth which are utterly wanting to those of poets who have only copied from each other and have never looked abroad on the objects themselves. Thomson was accustomed to wander away into the country for days ... while many a poet who has dwelt for years in the Strand has attempted to describe fields and rivers and generally succeeded accordingly. ... Hence that disgusting impropriety ·of introducing what may be called a set of hereditary images without proper regard to the age or climate or occasion in which they were formerly used.[13]

Swift has not wandered for days in the country, but his method—according to this reading—is the same as Thomson's. A poet of the Strand, he has drawn from nature's fountains by *describing* the Strand: his poem, the *Tatler* points out, is 'a Description of the Morning, but of the Morning in Town, nay, of the Morning at this End of the Town, where my Kinsman at present lodges'. Swift and Thomson both 'describe things exactly as they happen'; both scorn to draw on the 'set of hereditary images' offered them by art; both have 'a proper regard to age and climate'. In all this they recall one of the favourite Augustan images of Shakespeare, as the poet of direct realism, untutored and uninhibited. This is the Shakespeare who triumphed, according to Pope, by doing what Pope's own 'young *Maro*' was not allowed to

do, that is by taking his characters 'immediately from the fountains of nature', while those of all other dramatists 'have a constant resemblance which shows that they received them from one
another and were multipliers of the same image; each picture,
like a mock-rainbow, is but the reflection of a reflection'.[14] Swift,
interpreted in this way, is an unambiguous Shakespearian realist,
and we should ignore any slight hint of dusty traditions or hereditary images we may find in his poem as so much irrelevant
husk.

But this would be to assume too hastily that the analogy with
Shakespeare could tell us the whole truth about *A Description of
the Morning*. Actually it is a dangerous analogy for an Augustan
poet to draw, since a just unclassical imitation of nature could
only be a contradiction in terms after the revelation that Nature
and Homer were the same. In Shakespeare's time such a *mimesis*
had been possible because, as Pope put it, Elizabethan poets 'had
no thoughts of writing on the model for the ancients'.[15] But
things were different by 1709. Unclassical imitation by then
could only mean anticlassical imitation: which is to say that, in
spite of Swift's Shakespearian schoolboys with their satchels out
of *As You Like It*, the apparent naturalism of the *Description* is
really closer to the painter Caravaggio's than to Shakespeare's in
its relation to ideal antique tradition. Granted Caravaggio was
Shakespeare's contemporary, but their situations were different
in so far as the Italy of the 1600s had been fully exposed to the
learned enlightenment of the Renaissance, while England at the
time was still in outer darkness. Caravaggio's concern for 'mere'
appearances was held up as a terrible example by classicising
theorists. He was 'esteemed too natural', as Dryden puts it, trans-
lating from G. P. Bellori's *Vite de' Pittori* in his own *Parallel of
Poetry and Painting*, because 'he drew persons as they were'. The
sordid and anticlassical implications of this are brought out in
Bellori's life of the revolutionary Italian published in 1672. Caravaggio, he says,

> not only ignored the most excellent marbles of the an-
> cients and the famous paintings of Raphael, but he de-
> spised them, and nature alone became the object of his
> brush. Thus when the most famous statues of Phidias

and Glycon were pointed out to him as models for his painting, he gave no other reply than to extend his hand toward a crowd of men, indicating that nature had supplied him sufficiently with teachers. . . . With the majesty of art thus suppressed in Caravaggio, everyone did as he pleased, and soon the value of the beautiful was discounted. The antique lost all authority, as did Raphael. . . . Now began the representation of vile things; some artists began to look enthusiastically for filth and deformity. If they have to paint armour they choose the rustiest; if a vase, they do not make it complete but broken and without a spout. The costumes they paint are stockings, breeches and big caps and when they paint figures they give all of their attention to the wrinkles, the defects of the skin and the contours, depicting knotted fingers and limbs disfigured with disease.[16]

In the *Description* Swift too looks for the sordid. The crowd he points to is slipshod, raucous and none too clean; and there are obviously as many moral wrinkles and deformities as physical. Along with the brick-dust and coal, gutters and dirty doorsteps, there is Betty's whoring, his Lordship's profligacy, the prison system abused and the need for a secret police of watchful bailiffs. It is as though Swift, in his determination to avoid the sterilized purity of Phidias, Virgil and the rest, feels forced to insist that the fountains of true nature are dirty fountains; and it is apt that Goldsmith, when he characterises Swift's poetry later in the century, places the poet firmly in Caravaggio's camp:

> Dean Swift . . . perceived that there was a spirit of romance mixed with all the works of the poets who preceded him; or, in other words, that they had drawn nature on the most pleasing side. There still therefore was a place for him, who, careless of censure, should describe it just as it was, with all its deformities.[17]

'Persons as they were,' 'nature just as it was': Swift, like Caravaggio, makes a conscious rejection of antiquity and a conscious return to the fountains of nature, but with this difference in emphasis—that the consciousness of rejection is central to Swift's

poem. As a result, he does not dismiss Phidias absolutely in favour of the crowd. The antique has not lost *all* authority for
Swift. For all his low realism—and however ironically—he *is*
'writing on the model of the ancients'. When the *Tatler* announces
'a Description of the Morning, but of the Morning in Town', the
implication is that the poem does owe some sort of allegiance to
a *genre* with rules and hereditary images; while the assertion that
Swift 'never forms Fields, or Nymphs, or Groves, where they are
not' is only a half-truth. The gaoler's 'flock' return from burlesque fields; the chimney-sweeps and coalmen sing in makeshift
groves; Betty takes on the role of a classical nymph, however
degradedly she plays it. Swift is pointing to a crowd of men and
setting them beside the sculptures of Phidias and Glycon. In *News
from Parnassus*, a tribute to Swift written in 1721, his friend
Dr. Delany recalls the *Tatler's* phrase about Swift running into 'a
Way perfectly New'; but he makes a better balance than the *Tatler*
does between new and old. Swift for Delany is 'like *Virgil* correct,
with his own Native Ease'. Speaking in the *persona* of the verse-
god Apollo, he goes on to describe him as a poet

> Who admires the Ancients, and knows 'tis their due,
> Yet writes in a Manner entirely new;
> Tho' none with more Ease their Depths can explore,
> Yet whatever he wants he takes from my Store.
>
> (*Poems*, 269)

But even this is a little glib. Swift's exploration of ancient depths
cannot be sealed off entirely from his novel manner. He must
surely have been aware of the dilemma of being a modern among
ancients and an ancient among moderns. A similar dilemma
faced James Thornhill when commissioned to paint the momen-
tous landing of George I at Greenwich in 1714. Thornhill, as a
baroque idealist and as a servant of the Government, has to make
a sublime epiphany of the event. But as an honest observer, he
knows that the event was not at all sublime visually. For instance
(as he notes in the margin of one of his preliminary sketches),
'the king's own dress' was 'then not graceful, nor enough worthy
of him to be transmitted to posterity'. And who were the other
figures in the picture to be? 'If the real nobles that were there,
then some of them are in disgrace now and so will be so much

party in picture.' And worst of all, 'there was a vast crowd which to represent would be ugly, and not to represent would be false': ugly by the standards of classical beauty appropriate to a painting of the Golden Age Restored, false by the standards of naturalism appropriate to the literal transcription of a notable event.[18] The event in Swift, an ordinary morning, is less notable; but it is one haunted by potent poetic ghosts. However, Swift refuses to be 'false': he knows what morning at his end of the town is like, and will not compromise himself with mechanical goddesses or swains like a Grub-Street description-monger. One of the self-denying ordinances he puts into *Apollo's Edict,* the poem he sent Dr. Delany in reply to Delany's verses quoted above, covers this very point:

> No Simile shall be begun,
> With *rising* or with *setting* Sun . . .
> No Son of mine shall dare to say,
> *Aurora usher'd in the Day.*
>
> (vv. 12–13 and 20–21)

And yet Swift knows too that what he sees in the urban dawn is 'ugly'; and so he contrives to give his poem meaning and permanence by counterpointing this ugliness with elevated *descriptio.* Tradition is weighed in the balance with 'the representation of vile things', and it is the balance which animates the poem. Both sides have things to be said in their favour, but both are found wanting. The *Description* is at once a vigorous, no-nonsense parody of the sort of dawn-scene Bysshe would put into a commonplace book, and a classicist's mocking *exposé* of the corruption, triviality and untidiness of what passes for day-to-day reality in 1709. Swift both chafes at the classical ideal because it seems so little relevant to the reality he sees in the Strand, and is drily ironic about the reality he sees in the Strand because it will not live up to the standards set by the classical ideal.

A Description of the Morning was published in April, 1709. Two months later, Swift left London for Ireland. He came back to the capital in September, 1710, and found it a political chaos. 'We shall have a strange Winter here,' he reports to Stella, 'between the struggles of a cunning provoked discarded party, and the triumphs of one in power; of both which I shall be an indifferent spectator.' To be indifferent at such a time, or at least unpartisan, was certainly prudent. For instance, when Swift was on his way across London to visit Sir Godfrey Kneller's studio at the beginning of October, 'the rabble came about our coach, crying A Colt, a Stanhope, etc., we were afraid of a dead cat, or our glasses broken, and so were always of their side'. But Swift's private life was peaceful enough in those weeks, and this entry in the *Journal to Stella* is typical: 'we dined at the Chop-house with Will Pate, the learned woollen-draper: then we sauntered at china-shops and book-sellers.' And, for most of September at least, the sun shone: 'we have had a fortnight of the most glorious weather on earth, and still continues.' But the weather broke on September 27th; and between then and October 13th Swift wrote his companion-piece to the *Morning, A Description of a City Shower.* Coach-hire, saunterers in shops dining out, dead cats and the political crisis all feature in the poem, and in November, when it is already in print, Swift writes to Stella apropros of his London lodgings that 'I am almost st—k out of this with the sink, and it helps me to verses in my *Shower.*[19] 'The whole poem,' writes Sir Harold Williams, 'is built on scenes and incidents observed'— the scenes being presented so circumstantially that at one point a textual problem can be cleared up by 'reference to any good map of London in the eighteenth century'. (*Poems*, 137, 139). As with the *Morning*, Swift's subject is common city nature: coffee houses, whirling mops, dirty overcoats, stinking cesspools. Art could not mirror empirical life more closely. But at the same time, the mode in which Swift chooses to present London 'just as it is with all its deformities' announces that the crude actual is being weighed against a high style deeply involved with 'nature drawn on the most pleasing side'. The poem was in fact later subtitled '*In Imitation of* VIRGIL'S Georg.' More exactly it is the final section of the first *Georgic* which provides the counterpoise for Swift's low *mimesis* here; and reference to a good Augustan translation of Virgil—Dryden's is the obvious choice—is as important for a full reading of the *City Shower* as reference to a good map of London.

The 'Essay on Virgil's *Georgics*' which Addison wrote to preface Dryden's translation can help too. Addison brings out clearly what it was an Augustan critic expected from ideal description of weathers. 'A georgic', he explains,

> is some part of the science of husbandry put into a
> pleasing dress, and set off with all the beauties and
> embellishments of poetry. Now since the science of hus-
> bandry is of a very large extent, the poet shows his skill
> in singling out such precepts to proceed on as are useful
> and at the same time most capable of ornament. Virgil
> was so well acquainted with this secret that to set off his
> First Georgic he has run into a set of precepts which
> are almost foreign to his subject, in that beautiful ac-
> count he gives us of the signs of nature which precede
> the changes of the weather. . . . He delivers the meanest
> of his precepts with a kind of grandeur; he breaks the
> clods and tosses the dung with an air of gracefulness.
> His prognostications of the weather are taken out of
> Aratus, where we may see how judiciously he has picked
> out those that are the most proper for his husband-
> man's observation, how he has enforced the expression
> and heightened the images which he found in the orig-
> inal.[20]

Georgic *mimesis* demands a high antique decorum to turn raw
nature into *la belle nature,* a nature fit for sublime art. Mean
scientific fact must be embellished with beauty and grandeur;
image and expression must be heightened with ornament and
grace; all this being made very clear to the modern poet (the
poet planning the georgic description of a storm for instance)
by the inescapable presence of Virgil, supreme example and
judge of how it is to be done. The danger of course is that Virgil's
demands may be more than the modern poet's material is able
to bear. Thus Swift begins his account of the prognostics of a
storm grandly enough; but he soon finds that the Virgilian decorum of his style is at odds with the indecorousness of his subject, that the attempt to heighten and embellish a sublunary
London accurately observed has ironic consequences both for
London and for *la belle nature*:

> Careful Observers may fortel the Hour
> (By sure Prognosticks) when to dread a Show'r:

While Rain depends, the pensive Cat gives o'er
Her Frolicks, and pursues her Tail no more.
Returning Home at Night, you'll find the Sink
Strike your offended Sense with double Stink . . .
A coming Show'r your shooting Corns presage,
Old Aches throb, your hollow Tooth will rage. . . .

Compare Dryden's Virgil:

And that by certain signs we may presage
Of heats and rains, and wind's impetuous rage,
The sov'reign of the heav'ns has set on high
The moon, to mark the changes of the sky . . .
The crow with clam'rous cries the show'r demands,
And single stalks along the desart sands.
The nightly virgin, while her wheel she plies,
Forsees the storm impending in the skies,
When sparkling lamps their sputt'ring light advance,
And in the sockets oily bubbles dance.
(Georgics I, 483–486 and 533–538)[21]

An alley-cat for the austere crow, corns and toothache for the distant moon, a poor citizen with drain trouble for the virgin at her spinning-wheel; this is the poor best the city can offer, however orotund the language in which it is presented. And this is the theme of the *City Shower* throughout—the ludicrous attempt of an imperfect, trivial London to live up to classical dialects and situations.

As the storm gathers, the sky over the city makes a fine show of elemental grandeur:

Mean while the South rising with dabbled Wings,
A Sable Cloud a-thwart the Welkin flings . . .

And it is a grandeur closely linked with high art, witness its sinister echo of the biblical Flood in *Paradise Lost*:

Meanwhile the Southwind rose, and with black wings
Wide hovering, all the Clouds together drove
From under Heav'n; the Hills to their supplie

Vapour, and Exhalation dusk and moist,
Sent up amain.
(XI, 738–742)

But when Swift's storm breaks, the grandeur of the elements is
reduced to the level of the citizenry they drench, as London's
moist exhalations fill a sordid cloud

That swill'd more Liquor than it could contain,
And like a Drunkard gives it up again.

Again, the downpour itself is a fine Latinate one:

Now in contiguous Drops the Flood comes down,
Threat'ning with Deluge this *Devoted* Town . . .

but since the crowds in doomed London are too petty-minded
even to merit equation with Noah's wicked generation, the Lat-
inity has to be dropped:

To shops in Crouds the dagged Females fly,
Pretend to cheapen Goods, but nothing buy.

It is as though Swift's Miltonic Jehovah were too contemptuous
of the citizens to bother with any sublime retribution, verbal or
physical, just as Swift's Jove in *The Day of Judgement* twenty years
later will summon the sinful world to his judgement-seat only to
dismiss it again with the ultimate bathos:

"I to such Blockheads set my Wit!
I damn such Fools!—Go, go, you're bit."
(*Poems*, 579)

We have bathos of another sort at the climax of the *Description*, which presents the overflowing drains rushing the city's garbage down to Fleet Ditch and the Thames:

Now from all Parts the swelling Kennels flow,
And bear their Trophies with them as they go.

'Trophies' of course cries out to be undercut; but Swift's closing
triplet offers more than simple deflation:

Sweepings from Butchers Stalls, Dung, Guts and Blood;
Drown'd Puppies, stinking Sprats, all drench'd in Mud,
Dead Cats and Turnip-Tops come tumbling down the Flood.

No one could say that Swift tosses the dung about with an air of
gracefulness here; but it is less easy to say just what he *is* doing.
Clearly he cannot allow himself room for the hygienic storm-
scenes of the georgic tradition,

When the fleecy skies new clothe the wood,
And cakes of rustling ice come rolling down the flood.
                                    (Dryden's *Georgics* I, 417–418)

But why not exactly? Because they are fatuous in themselves, or
because modern London is not worthy of them, or because they
have been degraded by bad poets? What sort of weight should
we give Swift's own commentary on these lines? This is to be
found in a letter of 1735, as part of a general attack on the
triplet-form. Triplets, he writes, are 'a vicious way of rhyming,
wherewith Dryden abounded. . . . He was poor, and in great
haste to finish his plays, because by them he chiefly supported
his family, and this made him so very uncorrect; he likewise
brought in the Alexandrine verse at the end of the triplets. I was
so angry at these corruptions, that above twenty-four years ago
I banished them all by one triplet, with the Alexandrine, upon
a very ridiculous subject' (*Corr.*, IV, 321). Triplets with the Alexandrine certainly abound in Dryden's Virgil; and on this level
of ridicule, the dung, puppies, cats and turnips are to be seen
simply as aids to a destructive parody of Drydenisms like

The dykes are fill'd, and with a roaring sound
The rising rivers float the nether ground;
And rocks the bellowing voice of boiling seas rebound.
                                    (*Georgics* I, 441–443)

It is as though Swift were getting the 'needy Poet' he introduces
earlier in the *Description* to write the end of the poem for him.
And yet this is less than half the truth about Swift's triplet, for
to see no more in it than an angry stylistic joke is to ignore its
positive vitality, a vitality which is its own justification and which
has an effect transcending mere parody. Almost in spite of itself,

145

mockery of inept classicism here leads to a vivid rendering of modern nature.

Swift confronts modern with classical more openly in his treatment of the stranded beau earlier in the *Description*. The beau is puny enough in himself:

> Box'd in a Chair the Beau impatient sits,
> While Spouts run clatt'ring o'er the Roof by Fits;
> And ever and anon with frightful Din
> The Leather sounds, he trembles from within.

But his puniness is intensified when we see in him the city counterpart of Virgil's Earth Mother as she trembles at the din of Jupiter scattering his thunderbolts:

> The Father of the Gods his glory shrouds,
> Involv'd in tempests, and a night of clouds;
> And, from the middle darkness flashing out,
> By fits he deals his fiery bolts about.
> Earth feels the motions of her angry god;
> Her entrails tremble, and her mountains nod.
> (I, 444–449)

And as if it were not enough to place the impatient beau against Virgil's ideal natural world, Swift carries the shrinking process still further by dropping him into the ideal heroic world of the *Aeneid*:

> So when *Troy* Chair-men bore the Wooden Steed,
> Pregnant with *Greeks,* impatient to be freed,
> (Those Bully *Greeks,* who, as the Moderns do,
> Instead of paying Chair-men, run them thro'.)
> *Laoco'n* struck the Outside with his Spear,
> And each imprison'd Hero quak'd for Fear.

Swift's beau is to the Greeks in the Trojan horse as his Betty is to Aurora—here-and-now pettiness beside classic magnificence. The epic significance of the myth stresses the insignificance of the beau's world. The sedan chair imprisons one petulant fop where the horse is 'Pregnant with *Greeks*': Virgil's equivalent phrase in the *Aeneid* is *feta armis* (II, 238), which Dryden renders 'Big with destruction', the destruction of Troy which is in its turn the creation of Rome and western civilisation. Yet the beau's world, however insignificant, is inescapably our world; so the modern poet must allow it to cut the ancient myth down to size. In our world the heroic Trojans would be mere chairmen and the Greeks mere bullies, and so that is how they must be presented in an up-to-date Description. The Restoration poet John Oldham provides a similar case. He can write a *Praise of Homer* which makes the poet's work as sublime a fountain as nature's:

> Thou art the unexhausted Ocean, whence
> Sprung first, and still do flow th'eternal Rills of sense.
> To none but Thee our Art Divine we owe,
> From whom it had its Rise, and full Perfection too.

Yet when he has to put Homeric themes into a Restoration context, Oldham can describe Homer as

> He, who sung on *Phrygia's* Shore,
> The *Grecian* Bullies fighting for a Whore.[22]

Traditional ideal art, then, in the *Shower* as in the *Morning*, is at once a yard-stick and a dead letter, while the crude actual is both a source of vitality and a target for neoclassical irony. Swift's is certainly 'a Manner entirely new', but he is not suggesting that, because his immediate concerns must be with petulant fops and good-for-nothing chambermaids, the classical heroes and weather-gods are poetically irrelevant. Rather, there seems to be this sort of pattern in his assumptions: the classics embody a just and beautiful nature; the contemporary realities of a sordid Queen Anne London are no more than a travesty of true nature; so to copy these apparent realities (as I must if I am not to be quite out of touch with life as it is lived) is to travesty the classics. For an open-eyed city-dweller who knows that modern life does not live up to ancient art, the sublime second nature of young Maro's vision has a double function. It enables him to channel his explosive Hogarthian energies into burlesque; and at the same time it validates his hints that somewhere, however far away, order, decorum and nobility do really exist.

Swift had written as a committed Ancient in *The Battle of the Books*, some fifteen years before the *Descriptions*. He was to do so again in the third part of *Gulliver's Travels*, about fifteen years after them. Though it is never safe to assume that Gulliver's judgements in the *Travels* are identical with Swift's, the confrontation of ancient and modern seems to be one episode in which the hero does speak unequivocally for the author. Asking the wizards of Glubbdubdrib 'that the Senate of *Rome* might appear before me in one large Chamber, and a modern Representative, in Counterview, in another', Gulliver reports that 'the first seemed to be an Assembly of Heroes and Demy-Gods; the other a Knot of Pedlars, Pick-pockets, Highwaymen and Bullies'. (XI, 196). The *Descriptions* too set ancient demigods and modern bullies in counterview. But where the counterviewing in the Glubbdubdrib episode can be seen as sane and constructive—after all, it is in the power of a modern parliament to reform itself in emulation of a classical senate—there is a sound Swiftian reason for declaring the counterviews of the *Morning* and the *Shower* dangerously insane.

A favourite device of Swift's for satirising wrong-headed idealisms is to dramatise the madness which seizes the idealist when he is forced to face the facts of the real world. For example, Cassinus in *Cassinus and Peter* loses his wits on discovering that his adored Celia is not a disembodied goddess, and Strephon in *Strephon and Chloe* reacts to the same discovery by falling into a crazy bestiality. Both have let themselves be gulled into believing that the human creatures they worship are pure spirit, angels without bowels, etherial nymphs; and both pay the penalty. Similarly, Lemuel Gulliver comes to adore those ethical equivalents to etherial nymphs, the perfectly rational Houyhnhnms, and his disgust on returning to the world of men drives him mad. But is our description-writer any less sick than the Gulliver who brands all his fellow countrymen as Yahoos and hides in the sanctum of the stable-yard from the odious affections of his wife and children? Our *descriptor,* his mind clouded by the antique perfection of hero and demigod, can see nothing in contemporary London but pocket-picking, bullying and peddling. Granted that he exploits the counterviewing of ancient and modern brilliantly; but one wonders what he would have his fallen city do to redeem itself. Try to become another ancient Rome? The *Descriptions* nowhere imply this, and the *Satires* of Juvenal would have argued against it. Or try to transform itself into the English countryside of the early eighteenth century? Swift doubtless had as few illusions about *that* as a potential ideal as his friend Gay in *The Birth of the Squire* or *The Shepherd's Week*. Rather, the charade he forces his London to play is to disguise itself inadequately, grotesquely as Virgilian landscape and classical fresco. His basic grievance seems to be that Modern Town is not Ancient Country, which is as pointless as torturing oneself with the sad truth that the men one knows are not as virtuous as one's fantasy Houyhnhnm and the women not as antiseptic as one's fantasy Diana. We may accept that Augustan London is dirty, trivial and immoral; but can we honestly allow that our *descriptor* is any less deranged in his way than Strephon or Gulliver in theirs when he measures the facts of London life by the standards of Arcadian art and finds London odious as a result?

Perhaps Swift would agree with us. Perhaps the poker-faced, tight-lipped observer who speaks the *Descriptions* is an ironic *persona*, a dramatic creation not to be taken at his face-value. Perhaps the reader of this essay should substitute '*descriptor ridiculus*' for 'Swift' every time the name has been used in connection with the attitudes of the *Morning* and the *Shower*. But this would be to ignore not only Swift's declared allegiance to the Ancients but also the fact that, though arguments ultimately proving the madness of the *descriptor* may hold good by Swiftian logic, Swift himself never allows us time to apply such a logic. Both *Descriptions* are short considering the issues they bring up, and both are so busy with surface action that there is no room for *reductio ad absurdum*. Though it may be illuminating in one way to see the *Description of the Morning* as a fragment from a lost *Macheathiad*, in another it is as important to remember that Swift gave his poem no such context. Though here and in the *Shower* he pushes his ideas far enough to let them resonate with rich irony, in both poems he stops them far short of any *reductio*.

And even if it is a mad delusion to believe that Homer equals Nature, that decorum, nobility and order are vested uniquely in remote classic forms, and that our modern cities should aspire to the condition of Virgilian commonplaces, we may still find that the delusion has a positive use, just as the crazy fantasies of the rational horse and the sweatless goddess, though dangerous if taken in the wrong way, may do good if taken in the right one.

The heroes of *The Lady's Dressing Room* and *Strephon and Chloe* are partly figures of satiric fun because they should have known better than to idealise their mistresses in the first place; but they are also figures to sympathise with because their awakenings are unnecessarily traumatic: even as physical human creatures, their Celias and Chloes need not have been so filthy in their habits or so concerned to cover that filth with a gaudy veneer. Then Gulliver among the horses is stupidly wrong to make the glib equation of Yahoo with *homo sapiens,* but there are extenuating circumstances, for English *homo sapiens* in the eighteenth century has given Gulliver every provocation to make the equation: had his contemporaries been less single-mindedly vicious and less preoccupied with perverting their gift of reason to compound their vices, perhaps Gulliver would not have been gulled. A loved woman should try, as far as her limiting human condition allows, to deserve the praise of a Wholesome Nymph. And a civilised man should to the same degree try to emulate everything emulable which deserves emulation in the Good Horses. Similarly, the raillery of the *Descriptions,* however unsure its basis in logic or common sense, can serve usefully to deflate the complacency of the routine classicising poet or the routine citizen. These Houyhnhnm *Descriptions of the City of the Yahoos* may not be comprehensive photo-surveys of life in London, but their ludicrous gravity may provoke a few Londoners to look more intently at their neighbours, their drains, themselves. And to the irrelevant hack-classicist they may serve as eye-openers, as London's equivalent to the Laputian 'flapper', who is

> employed diligently to attend his Master in his Walks, and upon Occasion to give him a soft Flap on his Eyes; because he is always so wrapped up in Cogitation, that he is in manifest Danger . . . in the Streets, of jostling others, or being jostled himself into the Kennel. (XI, 159–60)

Notes

1. Quotations from the *Essay* are from the 1713 ed., with line-numberings from the modernised text in *Minor Poets of the Eighteenth Century*, ed. Fausset (London, 1930), pp. 185–197. For Swift's 'forwarding', see *Journal to Stella*, ed. H. Williams (Oxford, 1948), II, 586, 597, 611–612, 623, etc.

2. 'Life of Thomas Parnell', *Works*, ed. J. W. Gibbs (London, 1884–6), IV, 172.

3. IV, 584–585 and IX, 459-460 (Dryden's version of the latter).

4. *Monsieur Bossu's Treatise of the Epick Poem*, tr. 'W. J.' (1695), p. 240.

5. *The British Parnassus* (1714), II, 578–579. It seems, though the lay-out of his text is not clear at this point, that Bysshe ascribes these lines to Creech's translation of Lucretius; but I have not been able to find them there or elsewhere. For dawn-soliloquies, see Otway's *Orphan* IV.i.81–97 (*Works*, ed. J. C. Ghosh [Oxford, 1932], II, 54–55), and Lee's *Massacre of Paris* V.i.1–11 (*Works*, ed. Stroup and Cook [New Brunswick, 1954–5], II, 48).

6. Two other poems by Swift dating from the late 1700s show similar attitudes to *descriptio* and to the tension between town and country: *Baucis and Philemon*, vv. 163–164, and *In pity to the empty'ng Town*, vv. 5–16.

7. Spenser, *Faerie Queene* I.xi.51; Milton, *Elegia Quinta*, vv. 49–54; for the Carracci and Guercino paintings of Aurora, *inter alia*, see Irving Lavin, 'Cephalus and Procris', *Journal of the Warburg and Courtauld Institutes*, XVII (1954), plates 39 and 40.

8. *Amusements Serious and Comical*, ed. A. L. Hayward (London, 1927), pp. 11–12.

9. *Hudibras* II.ii.29–32; Hutcheson, *Dublin Journal* 10 (*Eighteenth Century Critical Essays*, ed. Scott Elledge [Ithaca, 1961], I, 378).

10. *The Dispensary*, 6th ed. (1706), p. 34; Blackmore, *Eliza* (1705), p. 22.

11. For the Thornhill, see F. Saxl and R. Wittkower, *British Art and the Mediterranean* (London, 1948), Section 50; for the Hogarth, see F. Antal, *Hogarth and his Place in European Art* (London, 1962), plate 58a.

12. Antal, *op. cit.*, p. 56.

13. *Essay*, I (1756), ii (Elledge, *op. cit.* [note 9], II, 730).

14. *Preface to Shakespeare* (1725), Elledge, *op. cit.*, I, 279.

15. *Ibid.*, I, 281.

16. *Vite de' Pittori* (1672), p. 5, tr. Dryden, *Essays*, ed. W. P. Ker (Oxford, 1900), II, 119; *Vite*, pp. 202–203 and 212–213, tr. Walter Friedlaender, *Caravaggio Studies* (Princeton, 1955), pp. 246 and 253.

17. 'History of England', *Works*, ed. J. W. Gibbs (London, 1884–6), V, 345.

18. Thornhill's notes are printed by Edgar Wind, 'The Revolution of History Painting', *Journal of the Warburg Institute*, II (1938), 123.

19. *Journal to Stella*, ed. H. Williams (Oxford, 1948), I, 24, 42, 43, 28 and 87.

20. Elledge, *op. cit.*, I, 2 and 6.

21. Dryden, *Poetical Works*, ed. G. R. Noyes, 2nd ed. (Cambridge [Mass.], 1950), pp. 450–451. (All quotations from Dryden's Virgil are taken from this edition, the line-numbers being those of the translation.)

22. *The Works of Mr. John Oldham* (1686), pt. ii, p. 63, and pt. iii, p. 167.

V. *Cadenus and Vanessa*

GARETH JONES

Swift's *Cadenus and Vanessa*
A Question of "Positives"

> *Though very individual [Swift] has still a represen-*
> *tative quality: lacking the Augustan politeness, he*
> *seems, with his dry force of presentment, both to make*
> *the Augustan positives—*
>
> > *That merit should be chiefly placed*
> > *In judgment, knowledge, wit and taste*
>
> *—look like negatives, and to give the characteristic*
> *Augustan lacks and disabilities a positive presence.*
> > (*F. R. Leavis,* Revaluation, *Chapter 4*)

I suggest that Dr. Leavis is wrong and wrong in an important way. The question does not seem to me a remote one. It concerns Swift's verse in the first instance: I think it necessary that people take another look at it, or at some of it. Certainly Dr. Leavis's objections can't be answered without giving the poems the kind of careful reading which they haven't, on the whole, received. But then the question also concerns our approach to Swift in general, and the way in which we fall so easily into using the term 'positives' as a handy interpretative and evaluative tool. I want to query the term's adequacy; and I want to argue from a particular case: the poem from which Dr. Leavis takes his illus-trative quotation, *Cadenus and Vanessa*. In my discussion (and I

This essay first appeared in *Essays in Criticism* 20 (1970): 424–40. Reprinted with permission.

apologise in advance to the reader for the detailed closeness of attention which my approach entails), I want also to look at what strikes me as a painstaking and carefully-argued article of its kind by an admirer of the poem, and to suggest that its kind will not do—will not do, paradoxically enough, for the reasons that Dr. Leavis's implied dismissal will not do. For *Cadenus and Vanessa* is not a 'comfortable' poem: like the other poems whose complexity has, I believe, been inadequately noted (*Verses on the Death of Dr. Swift* and *On Poetry: A Rapsody* come to mind), it resists in a high degree our attempts to whittle it down to the size of the moral commonplaces of its age. My contention, in short, is that *Cadenus and Vanessa* is a masterpiece of satiric counterpointing; and that Swift is far from resting on his positives with the immovable firmness which has been urged.

It will be as well first, however, to summarise the case for the other side. Let me quote some lines from the passage in which the elderly tutor Cadenus rejects the love of his pupil Vanessa:

> But Friendship in its greatest Height,
> A constant, rational Delight,
> On Virtue's Basis fix'd to last,
> When Love's Allurements long are past;
> Which gently warms, but cannot burn;
> He gladly offers in return:
> His want of Passion will redeem,
> With Gratitude, Respect, Esteem:
> With that Devotion we bestow,
> When Goddesses appear below.
>
> (ll. 780–789)[1]

There is, it may be alleged, no difficulty about those lines. In rejecting the chaotic irrationality of Vanessa's sexual passion in favour of a love/friendship based upon man's highest qualities, Swift (the case requires a certain blurring of the distinction between author and *persona*) was standing firmly within the framework of orthodox Christian opinion, and abundant evidence of his views may be found in the 'Stella' poems and in certain of his non-personal prose-pieces. In his *Letter to a Young Lady on her Marriage,* for example, he argues for a union founded, not upon sexual attraction, but upon 'true rational Love and Esteem.' He explains:

> You have but a very few Years to be young and hand-
> some in the Eyes of the World; and as few Months to
> be so in the Eyes of a Husband, who is not a Fool; for,
> I hope, you do not still dream of Charms and Raptures;
> which Marriage ever did, and ever will put a sudden
> End to. Besides, yours was a Match of Prudence, and
> common Good-liking, without any Mixture of that ri-
> diculous Passion which hath no Being, but in Play-
> Books and Romances.
>
> (IX, 89)

The young wife must therefore be at pains to 'improve [her] Mind,' to cultivate 'Modesty, and Gentleness of Nature' and 'Taste and Judgment.' While there is certainly no antipathy to sexual love, it occupies a peripheral position:

> ... cultivate your Mind; without which it is impossible
> to acquire or preserve the Friendship and Esteem of a
> wise Man, who soon grows weary of acting the Lover,
> and treating his Wife like a Mistress, but wants a rea-
> sonable Companion, and a true Friend through every
> Stage of his Life.
>
> (IX, 85–86)

It may then be argued that we have available in raw form, here and elsewhere, the terms in which to account for Cadenus/Swift's rejection of Vanessa's kind of love, and that we have hence the means to a satisfactory interpretation of the whole poem.

And this, essentially, is what is urged by Peter Ohlin in a well-documented essay.[3] Mr. Ohlin, having summarised (briefly, to his great credit) the autobiographical basis of *Cadenus and Vanessa*, explains that his interest will be directed towards 'the poem as poem,' which he considers 'a delicately executed dia-logue between reason and passion, utilising the conflict between those two principles as the controlling device.' Vanessa herself is flawless—the ideal blend of reason and passion. 'She conforms perfectly to Swift's understanding of what is admirable in a woman,' remarks Mr. Ohlin; and he brings abundant external evidence—including the *Letter to a Young Lady*—to support his contention. However, she permits her rational faculties to be swayed by her love for Cadenus, and so falls from grace. Cadenus, 'perfectly matched' to the Vanessa that was, rejects her passion and offers, not marriage, but friendship:

> ... the reasons for this are, again, to be found in the orthodox Christian views on the relationship between men and women

—which Mr. Ohlin duly cites. And so

> ... the poem becomes, in outlining the story of Vanessa, one long metaphor for the fall of man, leading into a presentation of the only love possible in the human situation.

A phrase like 'the human situation' comprehends, of course, the meanly particular cases of you and of me: I am trying to bring into prominence the question of Swift's alleged uncritical acceptance of that 'possibility'—of a rationally-guided-love—in terms of the actualities of living: those actualities which are a constant controlling presence in the major writings. Mr. Ohlin's method, as I have intimated, is to support his reading of the poem with considerable external evidence of Swift's orthodox and traditional attitude in the matters of sexual love and marriage. Some of this evidence may be disputable. For example, Mr. Ohlin quotes the well-known passage:

> *Reason* itself is true and just, but the *Reason* of every particular Man is weak and wavering, perpetually swayed and turned by his Interests, his Passions, and his Vices.
>
> (*On the Trinity*, IX, 166)

But he allows the characteristic and significant Swiftian distinction no clear place in his own argument. Yet it is not primarily upon the evidence—let us even suppose that we accept Mr. Ohlin's interpretation of it—but upon the *method* that doubt must centre itself. It is a method which, in the manner of its application, some readers may feel to be at odds with the professed interest in 'the poem as poem'; and they may feel so the more sharply when they are confronted, in Mr. Ohlin's conclusion, with such a comment as this:

> ... in 'Cadenus and Vanessa' Swift simply exhibits, in a slightly disguised and elegantly contrived form, the serious side of the same attitude [i.e., of antipathy towards the romantic cult of passionate love].

Mr. Ohlin, I must make clear, considers *Cadenus and Vanessa* a highly successful performance. His comment strikes one as expressive of a queerly limiting view of the possibilities of poetic expression. More pertinently, it is arguable that if *Cadenus and Vanessa*—a poem concerned to make a statement about 'the human situation'—does anything so 'simply' then it can hardly be worth more than a passing interest: hardly worth more, in fact, than Dr. Leavis's dismissal of it.

To neither critic, then, does the poem present any difficulties: its positives are portable. It is in their judgment of its value that they so violently differ. Yet if *Cadenus and Vanessa* is, as I believe, a poem, it is not one for Mr. Ohlin's reasons. It is a poem because it is a disconcertingly autonomous structure of words, offering us those 'positives' with a perverse life and wit of its own. For it is the wit and paradox of its counterpointed ironies which prevent the poem from being reducible to thesis—to easy affirmation. It is characteristic of Swift's poetic language to avoid bespoke resolution. In *Cadenus and Vanessa,* where success depends upon keeping the tension full and alive, easy resolution would amount to betrayal. The generalising abstraction would not be adequate to the multiple and baffling particularities of experience: those wild particularities which mock the ready answer, but which the intelligence must digest, order and judge if it is to survive. It is basic to an understanding of the poem's method to realise that Cadenus and Vanessa are comic figures, and a tribute to the distracting power of irrelevant data that anyone should have failed to realise the fact. Swift is concerned with 'is' before 'ought'; and though the first implies the second it also qualifies it and deters us from grasping at it too eagerly. *The Tribulations of Reason* might make a suitable sub-title for *Cadenus and Vanessa.*

A useful starting-point for a discussion of the poem would

be one of those paradoxical 'excrescences' which neither favour-
able nor adverse criticism has been at much pains to emphasise:
Vanessa's response to Cadenus' offer of a rationally-grounded
relationship 'Which gently warms, but cannot burn':

> While thus *Cadenus* entertains
> *Vanessa* in exalted Strains,
> The Nymph in sober Words intreats
> A Truce with all sublime Conceits.
> For why such Raptures, Flights, and Fancies,
> To her, who durst not read Romances;
> In lofty Style to make Replies,
> Which he had taught her to despise.
> But when her Tutor will affect
> Devotion, Duty, and Respect,
> He fairly abdicates his Throne,
> The Government is now her own;
> He has a Forfeiture incurr'd,
> She vows to take him at his Word,
> And hopes he will not think it strange
> If both shou'd now their Stations change.
> The Nymph will have her Turn, to be
> The Tutor; and the Pupil, he:
> Tho' she already can discern
> Her Scholar is not apt to learn;
> Or wants Capacity to reach
> The Science she designs to teach:
> Wherein his Genius was below
> The Skill of ev'ry common Beau;
> Who, tho' he cannot read, is wise
> Enough to read a Lady's Eyes;
> And will each accidental glance
> Interpret for a kind Advance
>
> (ll. 790–817)

The joke of assigning to Vanessa a sober, Royal Society factuality
and of imputing to Cadenus the half-baked exaltations of a
Grub-Street romantic comes as an alarming about-face, if we
have not been attentive to the tone of what has gone before.
Vanessa uses the language of fact because her passion is a fact,

and one which Cadenus' rationalisings have proved singularly inept at coming to grips with.

The admiring light in which Cadenus is first presented—

> Grown old in Politicks and Wit;
> Caress'd by Ministers of State,
> Of half Mankind the Dread and Hate
> And will each accidental glance
> (ll. 503–505)

—serves to enrich the beautifully modulated comedy of his obtuse reactions to his pupil's love. To Cadenus, love is a polite game:

> *Cadenus*, common Forms apart,
> In every Scene had kept his Heart;
> Had sigh'd and languish'd, vow'd and writ,
> For Pastime, or to shew his Wit;
> But Time, and Books, and State Affairs
> Had spoil'd his fashionable Airs.
> (ll. 540–545)

The social mockery implicit in the assumption that it is a gentlemanly accomplishment to fall in love occasionally goes with the delicious sense in which Cadenus *has* once been 'romantick' but has since got out of practice. The conventions of fashionable wit now reduce him to a gauche and floundering solemnity:

> Interpreting her Complaisance,
> Just as a Man *sans Consequence*.
> She railly'd well, he always knew,
> Her Manner now was something new. . . .
> (ll. 658–661)

But Vanessa's love is not a game; and his comic overthrow stems from what we have hardly been encouraged to consider a disability at all:

> This was a visionary Scheme,
> He wak'd, and found it but a Dream;
> A Project far above his Skill,
> For Nature must be Nature still.

161

> If he was bolder than became
> A Scholar to a Courtly Dame,
> She might excuse a Man of Letters;
> Thus Tutors often treat their Betters.
> And since his Talk offensive grew,
> He came to take his last Adieu.
>
> (ll. 584–593)

The exposure is subtly and economically done, the truisms ('For Nature must be Nature still') drawing their ironic charge from the total as well as the immediate context. His disregard of Vanessa's sexual attributes almost parallels that betrayed by the Goddess of Reason in the poem's first part (see ll. 198 ff.); but comic naivety passes imperceptibly into timid worldliness, as he comes to understand, not indeed the love itself, but the threat it constitutes to his own security:

> And ev'ry Beau wou'd have his Jokes,
> That Scholars were like other Folks:
> That when Platonick Flights were over,
> The Tutor turn'd a Mortal Lover.
> So tender of the Young and Fair?
> It shew'd a true Paternal Care. . . .
>
> (ll. 648–653)

—'That Scholars were like other Folks': Cadenus' human passions manifest themselves, however, in no such scandalous manner but, without prejudice to his dignity, in the subtler shape of self-love—

> Constr'ing the Passion she had shown,
> Much to her Praise, more to his Own.
>
> (ll. 764–765)

The comic insight of the passage (ll. 726–767) in which Cadenus, complacently conceiving himself to be still in the realm of logical discourse, reasons himself into a position which denies reason, has hardly had the attention it deserves. Cadenus, it's true, has misgivings:

> But tho' her Arguments were strong,
> At least, cou'd hardly wish them wrong.
> (ll. 746–747)

—By the end of the first line we are sure of the direction the sentence must take; by the end of the second that 'tho'' has quite lost its adverse force, the throat-clearing 'At least' covering a world of intellectual dishonesty, and the rhyme confirming the expiry of true reason. Drawing upon Vanessa's simile of the 'Book,' Cadenus is able to rationalise her physical passion into an astute piece of literary criticism—

> 'Tis Merit must with her prevail,
> He never knew her Judgment fail,
> She noted all she ever read,
> And had a most discerning Head
> (ll. 754–757)

—and thus to find his own excellence the inescapable consequence:

> Nature in him had Merit plac'd,
> In her, a most judicious Taste.
> (ll. 766–767)

The analysis of Cadenus' self-deception offers us a grotesque parody of the arguments for a rational and celibate love. The lines last cited invite comparison with that couplet—

> That, Merit should be chiefly plac'd
> In Judgment, Knowledge, Wit, and Taste
> (ll. 342–343)

—presented, so Dr. Leavis urges, for our uncritical approval with an inadvertently negating rawness. Whatever this may be, it is hardly complacency. 'Is' may be judged by 'ought' but 'ought' is judged by 'is' in its turn; and Cadenus' comedy is what befalls the ideal 'out there.' His humane learning and reason, admirable as they are, prove unequal to the crunch of the unknown and serve only to place him in moral jeopardy. Love—the fact of it—frightens him because it is chaotic and self-contradictory: something to be kept at a decent distance because it does not make common sense:

> *Love,* why do we one Passion call?
> When 'tis a Compound of them all;
> Where hot and cold, where sharp and sweet,
> In all their Equipages meet. . . .
> (ll. 772–775)

Such is the ironic context of Cadenus' offer of 'that Devotion we bestow,/When Goddesses appear below': a love noble, decent and manageable, because it involves limited commitment. With a splendid paradox, he offers a reasonable, passionless love for reasons of passion—of self-love and fear.

The point of Vanessa's angry response is now apparent. There is a sizeable element of actuality which Cadenus' fine qualities have unfitted him to comprehend. His words are 'sublime Conceits' (l. 793) because, like those of a hack novelist, their link with lived experience is tenuous. To promise 'Devotion, Duty, and Respect' (l. 799) must overthrow his pretensions in Vanessa's eyes because she is a complicated and demanding human being, not a simple, undemanding abstraction—a woman, not a 'Goddess.' Doctor Cadenus is a mere freshman in the Science of Love; indeed, the learned Vanessa can even slily taunt him—

> [He] wants Capacity to reach
> The Science she designs to teach
> (ll. 810–811)

—with impotence. The reader's support may be now enlisted. Vanessa, as advocate of tough reality, then throws her case into disrepute by citing the example of the 'common Beau;/Who, tho' he cannot spell, is wise/Enough to read a Lady's Eyes.' The absurdity is a disconcerting check: it becomes necessary to examine Vanessa's qualifications in 'The Science she designs to teach' not wholly in terms of her own valuation.

It is through Vanessa, of course, that Venus makes her supreme attempt to restore her declining power among men. Lavishly endowed in mind and body, she is to be a test-case, the success or failure of which, there can be no doubt, will be of archetypal significance. Her experiences will be a living commentary upon that ideal and classical love of which the mock-trial (ll. 1–141), where the poem's themes and pre-occupations are lightly rehearsed, offers us an explicit (and, one observes, routine) account:

> ... modern Love is no such Thing
> As what those ancients Poets sing;
> A Fire celestial, chaste, refin'd,
> Conceiv'd and kindled in the Mind,
> Which having found an equal Flame,
> Unites, and both become the same,
> In different Breasts together burn,
> Together both to Ashes turn.
>
> (ll. 28–34)

That concrete 'Experiment' (l. 139) is necessary, the conduct of the trial makes clear. It is an attempt, rendered the more grotesque by the legalistic jargon which so swiftly succeeds to that graceful pastoral opening, to reduce the wild question of love to reasonable proportions—to render it orderly, manageable and discussable by circumscribing it with precedents—'In *Virgil* (*vide Dido*'s Case') (l. 111)—and the rhetoric of logic. Significantly, the sixteen years' proliferation of argument settles nothing which is not commonplace, Venus, meanwhile, abandoning her 'Law-books' (l. 140) in her realisation that the difficulties can be resolved only by reference to the realities of human experience.

Vanessa's perfection—

> Offending Daughters oft wou'd hear
> *Vanessa*'s Praise rung in their Ear:
> Miss *Betty*, when she does a Fault,
> Lets fall her Knife, or spills the Salt,
> Will thus be by her Mother chid,
> "Tis what *Vanessa* never did
>
> (ll. 240–245)

—is hardly offered us with that solemn complacency which has repelled so many of the poem's critics. It is the 'good child's' perfection—untried and potential, its admirable components not yet run-in.

> Thro' Nature, and thro' Art she rang'd,
> And gracefully her Subject chang'd.
>
> (ll. 354–355)

—Our instinctive reaction to this (a Bronx cheer, perhaps) and to the accompanying instances of Vanessa's virtuosity, is, it turns out, the required response for the grasping of Swift's poetic design. Vanessa's sentiments are unimpeachable, save that—as they come from her lips—they are strictly without meaning, because rootless and notional instead of delicately and enrichingly controlled by living experience. They come from 'Books': the motif, whose appearances elsewhere have already been noted, becomes now the crucial emblem of an aloofness from a world chaotic in its banal and irreducible particularities, which is both splendid and perilous:

> The Goddess thus pronounc'd her Doom:
> When, lo! *Vanessa* in her Bloom,
> Advanc'd like *Atalanta*'s Star,
> But rarely seen, and seen from far:
> In a new World with Caution stept,
> Watch'd all the Company she kept,
> Well knowing from the Books she read
> What dangerous Paths young Virgins tread.
>
> (ll. 304–311)

Actuality, unhappily, is not card-indexed. Her paradoxical fate is peculiarly beautiful:

> *Vanessa*, tho' by *Pallas* taught,
> By *Love* invulnerable thought,
> Searching in Books for Wisdom's Aid,
> Was, in the very Search, betray'd
>
> (ll. 488–491)

—her choice of lover being as essentially capricious as that of any illiterate society belle: for it is Cupid, not Venus, who administers her love. She is 'betray'd,' then, by her reason and her education, as Cadenus, with differing results, is betrayed by his.

166

The implication is inescapable: try to despise the chaotic world of sense and passion, try to rely on naked reason as your guide—well; but you risk finishing like Gulliver in the muck of your stables, or like Vanessa in the muddle of hopeless infatuation, for actuality is liable to do dirt on you even more thoroughly. You will, moreover, remain in laughable ignorance of what is happening to you: your capacity for self-deception will even be increased. Thus, Vanessa can bring

> . . . weighty Arguments to prove
> That Reason was her Guide in Love
> (ll. 676–677)

—and we can only feel that, in a perverse sense, her claim is justified by the facts. Her reliance on reason continues unabated: reason can accommodate anything—even what enslaves it—without seeing anything for what it is. One is reminded, as Vanessa argues

> . . . as Philosophers, who find
> Some fav'rite System to their Mind,
> In ev'ry Point to make it fit,
> Will force all Nature to submit,
> (ll. 722–725)

of Swift's 'Stoics' and their 'Scheme of supplying our Wants, by lopping off our Desires.'[4] And with a perfection of irony, her faith in 'Books' stays with her to the last:

> If one short Volume cou'd comprise
> All that was witty, learn'd, and wise,
> How wou'd it be esteem'd, and read,
> Altho' the writer long were dead? . . .
> And this she takes to be her Case.
> *Cadenus* answers every End. . . .
> (ll. 696–699; ll. 703–704)

—A paper lover is as manageable as a 'Goddess.' Vanessa's comedy is just that she truly does believe that she can live out of 'one short Volume.' Her love is real; but it is not for her to lesson Cadenus in the realities.

Yet the full complexity of Swift's purpose has not been adequately suggested. We may feel a sense of frustration at that notorious 'conclusion' (ll. 818–827) which seems to conclude nothing; or at the poem's closing section in which Venus, losing patience with the Court of Love, leaves the world to her son's 'Discretion'—leaves it, that is, to return to the muddle of arbitrary passion. But the purpose is not to thwart and confuse, but to compel us, by tempting us ever and again to rest thankful in the easy certainties of judgment, and then subverting those certainties, not merely to contemplate but to live the difficulties of our predicament. The purpose is not to cheat, but to avoid cheating; not to escape commitment, but by a complex and rigorous counterpointing of one voice, one logic, one 'answer' against another, to show us, full and felt, the only possible commitment. The wonderfully done counterpointing of the follies of Cadenus and Vanessa holds out a continual invitation to us to cast our vote—for one, for the other. Vanessa's love—the point could hardly be more clearly made—is senseless; and so we throw in our lot with Cadenus, only to find ourselves interpreting his rejection of her love in terms which he himself would approve. Vanessa demonstrates the irrelevance of Cadenus' impressive protestations; then we are inclined to credit her with a grasp of the realities, which is, however, revealed to the nugatory. Or, resisting this temptation, we may accept another. The ignorance of Cadenus and Vanessa is not one which books can cure: it is, we should say, an ignorance of the world. But Swift is ready for us—

> (*To know the World!* a modern Phrase,
> For Visits, Ombre, Balls and Plays.)
> (ll. 430–431)

—and we are discomfited to be reminded of how close we have come to breathing the mental atmosphere of the *beau monde*.

That the absolute by which human action may be judged may itself be judged in the light of experience, and found wanting, is, as I have intimated, the poem's central paradox. We feel its force in the double-edged comparison of Vanessa with '*Atalanta*'s Star' ('But rarely seen, and seen from far'), and in the charged ambiguity of the comment upon her failure with the world:

> So Stars beyond a certain Height
> Give Mortals neither Heat nor Light.
> (ll. 442–443)

When Pallas demands,

> For how can Heav'nly Wisdom prove
> An Instrument of earthly Love?
> (ll. 294–295)

we must reply that the poem has contrived, apparently, both to substantiate and to refute her judgment. The refusal of the intelligent and cultivated Cadenus to fall in love with the Vanessa upon whom such gifts have been bestowed is clearly an archetypal failure for Venus—a portentous comment upon the achievable possibility of that love 'those antient Poets sing.' Vanessa, however, falls absurdly in love with Cadenus, giving us the giddy sense that 'Heav'nly Wisdom,' thrust into the hurly-burly of earthly existence, may indeed be indistinguishable from heavenly innocence. Yet the comic chaos with which *Cadenus and Vanessa* concludes implies, not the negation of hope, but, with the rigour and weight of the poem behind it, the affirmation of a hope that is substantial and honest and not abstracted from the paradoxical particularities to which it must apply. In this muddle, any simplification, any comfortable, excluding generalisation, is inadequate and dangerous. Without having earned the right to propound them, the poem's protagonists set forth their 'solutions.' But because their response to experience is reducible to the simplistic 'positive,' there is no need to suppose that Swift's should be.

The response, in Swift's best verse, is built up by the complex totality of the given poem. It cannot be adequately defined in any other way: there are no available terms save those which the poem, in its opposing ironies and paradoxes, itself lays down. Those octosyllabic generalisations, whose show of meagre finality tempts the critic to cite them out of context as evidence for the prosecution, or merely as handy digests of Swift's 'thought,' are not themselves definitions, but, in the transforming ironic structure, the means to definition. *Verses on the Death of Dr. Swift*, for example, might seem to have rather less, by way of 'quotable' extract, to offer the biographically-inclined critic, were its essential nature realised. The poem's burden does not lie in its explicit self-appraisals. *Verses on the Death* is a personal exploration: a search for the unassailable, because profoundly and inwardly true, personal statement which we in the end find it, in its totality, to be. It is an exploration which we ourselves must share and live through. What Dr. Leavis aptly characterises as Swift's 'dry force of presentment' continually seduces the unwary reader into accepting at face-value those self-estimations whose inadequacy the poem, in the fineness of its whole meaning, exposes.

> 'As for his Works in Verse and Prose,
> 'I own myself no Judge of those:
> 'Nor, can I tell what Cricks thought 'em;
> 'But, this I know, all People bought 'em;
> 'As with a moral View design'd
> 'To cure the Vices of Mankind:
> 'His Vein, ironically grave,
> 'Expos'd the Fool, and lash'd the Knave:
> 'To steal a Hint was never known,
> 'But what he writ was all his own.
>
> (ll. 308–318)[5]

(Others have noted the joke of that final couplet.) The poem's disconcerting power derives from one's growing sense that certainty—the assurance that the satiric forays are being launched, after all, from a firmly consolidated moral position—has ceased to exist: the satirist turns in upon himself, to question his own proceedings and prerogatives in a radical and disturbing way; and the reader is left in the wild, with only his own agility to save him from confirming the subtlety and efficacy of the snares of self-deception by falling into them himself. Reading the poem, though, is not merely a matter of inverting our expectation and then proceeding as before (the implication being that Swift has simply placed himself in the traditional position of victim or butt). For Swift is making demands, not so much upon our ingenuity, as upon our honesty: he is requiring us to be critically aware of our certainties, our habits of response—of our mental cliches. We are offered a series of statements so apparently impeccable, so unctuously ministering to our judicial certitudes, that we feel no temptation to pick them up and turn them over. But the counterpointed 'logic'—the subversive undervoice—insists that this is just what we must do; insists, not simply that the statements are absurd falsifications (for this too could minister to complacency), but that the kind of 'truth' which they embody will not suffice in any final way, because in taking account of too little it says too much. We are offered, then, an argument whose every step is both exploration and enactment of thesis. We are drawn into a restless dance where irony is itself 'placed' by further irony; and there can be no resolution, no 'giving over,' save in death:

> 'Meer Envy, Avarice, and Pride!
> 'He gave it all:—but first he dy'd.
> (ll. 159–160)

How Dr. Leavis was seduced into using such a term as 'positives,' and precisely what, in Swift, he was resisting, would make matter for another essay. My concern here is with the verse; and what I want, in as challenging a way as I can, to propose is that Swift is an exciting and valuable poet; and that to read him with attention is a lesson in the complexities involved in the true placing of a creative and original writer in his cultural context.

Notes

1. Line numbers refer to the poem as printed in *The Poems of Jonathan Swift*, ed. Harold Williams, 2nd ed., 3 vols. (Oxford, 1958), II, 686–714.
2. Volume and page numbers refer to *The Prose Works of Jonathan Swift*, ed. Herbert Davis, 13 (of 14) vols. published (Oxford, 1939–).
3. '"Cadenus and Vanessa": Reason and Passion,' *Studies in English Literature*, IV (1964), 485–496.
4. 'Thoughts on Various Subjects,' *Prose Works*, I, 244.
5. Line numbers refer to the poem as printed in *Poems*, II, 553–572.

VI. The Stella Poems

DAVID SHEEHAN

Swift, Voiture, and the Spectrum of Raillery

Jonathan Swift's biographers all agree that he had a genius for
raillery. Even in writing his own will, says Lord Orrery, Swift
could not help indulging in his peculiar manner of raillery and
jest, disposing of his three hats—his first, second, and third-best
beavers—"with an ironical solemnity, that render the bequests
ridiculous,"[1] and rallying his friends, the Grattan brothers, on
the poverty and wealth of their respective professions by
bequeathing "to the Reverend Mr. *Robert Grattan*, Prebendary of
St. *Audeon's*, . . . my strong Box, on Condition of his giving the
sole Use of the said Box to his Brother Dr. *James Grattan*, during
the Life of the said Doctor, who hath more Occasion for it."[2]
Some critical attention has been given to Swift's raillery.[3] But we
have still not entered all the way into what Letitia Pilkington aptly
termed Swift's "peculiar ironical strain."[4] Swift's raillery, we are
told, is a "good-mannered" kind, in which "the corrective truths
of satire have no place," and which "never aimed at discomforting its object."[5] This description does not fully accord with the
complicated raillery Swift actually uses in much of his poetry. In
the poems to Stella, with which this essay is ultimately concerned,
Swift sometimes employs a much sharper raillery in playing one
social verse game. Indeed we cannot fully appreciate Swift's ex-

This essay first appeared in *Papers on Language and Literature* 14 (1978): 171–88.
Reprinted with permission.

traordinary control of language and tone in his social verse unless we examine those poems which approach the fine line separating sharp from delicate raillery, precariously balancing praise and blame.

To study Swift's use of this complicated mode of raillery, we might follow his advice and turn first for instruction to the writings of Vincent Voiture, whom Swift recommended as a model for raillery.[6] Voiture was an immensely popular writer in the seventeenth century.[7] His influence on Swift's conception of raillery has been acknowledged, but not fully appreciated. This may be attributable to the current critical neglect of Voiture. The only modern study entirely devoted to his life and works is Emile Magne's *Voiture et L'Hôtel de Rambouillet*.[8] Although valuable for biographical material on Voiture and the other habitués of the Hôtel de Rambouillet, this study contains little critical discussion of Voiture's works. Antoine Adam devotes a few pages to Voiture in his standard *Histoire de la littérature française au XVIIe siècle*, but he rather patronizingly qualifies his recognition of Voiture's influential contribution of *la fine gallanterie* to seventeenth-century French literature by the assertion that Voiture was above all "a grand and eternal child."[9] Voiture receives more serious consideration in studies dealing with the larger phenomenon of précieux poetry,[10] but on the whole his writings have not received the critical attention they deserve. It is, therefore, not surprising that efforts to assess Voiture's importance in our understanding of Swift's raillery have tended to underestimate Voiture's achievement. While acknowledging "little doubt that Voiture was Swift's model," Timpe finds the debt limited, since Voiture's raillery was often "Clumsy," and his "Toadying, fawning, [and] sycophanting . . . must have been repulsive poses to the critical, proud, youthful Swift."[11] Bullitt is less disparaging, yet even he finds that Voiture's letters "rarely exhibit the strength of intellect or diversity of style that inform Swift's practice in the same vein of humor."[12] But the writer whose "Genius" Swift claims "first found out the Rule/For an obliging Ridicule" (1:216), and whose prose Swift recommends as the model for raillery, is a much more accomplished railleur than these estimates would have us believe.

Both Swift and Voiture were masters of a spectrum of rallying modes, ranging from simple praise-by-blame to a sharp raillery in which praise and blame coexist in a delicate balance, compliment poised on the edge of satire. In Voiture's letters a good example of the former end of the spectrum is his letter to Cardinal de la Valette, then in the midst of a successful military campaign across the Rhine. Voiture begins the letter by "blaming" the Cardinal for his inattention to literary matters: "Tell the truth, how long has it been since you pondered whether the four last books of the *Aeneid* are by Virgil or not, or if the *Phormio* is by Terence?"[13] But this "blame" is merely prelude to praise of the Cardinal's recent military success ("one of the greatest miracles ever seen in war") which has kept him from preoccupation with literary questions. The blame is in fact itself praise, for by evoking the Cardinal's neglect of intellectual questions, Voiture has drawn attention to what the Cardinal has sacrificed in order to fulfill his responsibility as a soldier. This is the simplest mode of raillery, in which praise is devoid of even a suggestion of ridicule or satire. Were we to learn that Voiture actually was disdainful of the Cardinal's learning or of his military accomplishments, we would surely read the raillery in the letter quite differently. But in fact, as Emile Magne says, the two men were kindred souls.[14] Although elevated to the dignity of a cardinal at the age of twenty-eight, and possessed of a certain wisdom, bravery, and liberality of character, the Cardinal was inclined towards epicureanism and the good life. The two men delighted in a light, elegant kind of raillery. Nevertheless, even in rallying La Valette, Voiture could move along the spectrum, putting a slight edge on his raillery.

In one letter to the Cardinal, then leading the French troops at La Rochelle, Voiture describes a beautiful evening-to-dawn excursion with some frequenters of the Hôtel de Rambouillet to La Barre, the country chateau of Madame du Vigean.[15] The scene Voiture describes stands in sharp contrast to the Cardinal's life in the camp of a besieging army. The floors of the chateau strewn with rose and orange blossoms, promenades across grand parterres and through great gardens, the sun setting in a cloud of gold and azure, niche-statues of goddesses which suddenly spring to life and dance around thundering fountains to the music of twenty-four violinists—all of this Voiture describes to the Cardinal away at war. This account of the elegant life he was

missing is at least potentially discomforting to the Cardinal, but
Voiture turns it into a witty compliment: "But what is strange,
Monseigneur, is that in the midst of such pleasures, which should
be so completely fulfilling, and raise the spirits of those enjoying
them, one never stopped thinking of you, and everyone said
something was missing from so much contentment, since you and
Madame de Rambouillet were not there." The letter then renews
the description of dinner and dancing in the chateau, again with
a discomforting observation. "At the beginning of dinner, no one
proposed a toast to your health, . . . nor at the end of dinner
either." Voiture apologizes for having to report this neglect of
the Cardinal, but says that he writes not to flatter, but, like a
faithful historian, "I report things just as they are." However, it
is also true, he continues, that far from being forgotten, "during
dinner everyone talked of you and the ladies especially wished
you were there." Thus the apparently disobliging detail of the
absence of a toast to the Cardinal's health is turned into the
clearly complimentary account of everyone talking warmly of the
Cardinal throughout dinner. The letter concludes with a description of the night of dancing suddenly ended by a spectacular
display of fireworks, and then the ride by torch-light back into
the still and empty streets of Paris in the predawn hours. In this
one letter alone we can see why Swift found Voiture's letters
entertaining and a model for raillery. The compliments are clear
and graceful, yet the raillery can be given an edge. A still sharper
raillery, which moves along the spectrum towards that raillery
which balances praise and ridicule, characterizes certain letters
Voiture wrote to the Duke of Anguien, the young leader of the
bande de petits maitres who gathered at the Hôtel de Rambouillet
at the time.

In his *Characteristics of Men, Manners, Opinions, Times,* Shaftesbury offers sensible advice on how to read Voiture's letters:
"It will be owned surely, by those who have learnt to judge of
elegancy and wit by the help merely of modern languages, that
we could have little relish of the best letters of a Balsac or Voiture, were we wholly ignorant of the characters of the principal
persons to whom those letters were actually written."[16] Swift may
have been correct when he wrote to Pope that "not only Voiture,
but likewise Tully and Pliny writ their letters for the publick view,

more than for the sake of their correspondents."[17] But recognition of the mode of raillery being used at a particular time depends on knowing the character of the person being rallied, and the relationship between that person and the railleur. An interesting case in point is the letter Voiture wrote to the Duke of Anguien, on the occasion of the Duke's successful crossing of the Rhine to link his troops with other French forces.[18] Before his departure from Paris, the Duke and Voiture, in the company of some lady friends, had played some games, particularly one called "fish," in which the Duke played a pike (*un brochet*) and Voiture a gold fish (*une carpe*). In this letter Voiture continues the fish game, sustaining from beginning to end the fiction of a goldfish writing to a pike. The roles seem merely playfully chosen: the warrior Duke of Anguien playing a large, extremely voracious fish armed with hundreds of sharp teeth, and the witty Voiture playing the sort of bright goldfish used to adorn pools and basins for the aesthetic pleasure of the wealthy and powerful. But when we consider the character of the person being rallied, and his relation to the railleur, the playful fiction takes on an added satiric dimension.

According to Emile Magne, the Duke's own contemporaries agreed in an unfavorable judgment on the Duke's character: "Cruel, treacherous, insolent, ambitious, proud, the young prince with an eagle's face illumined by fiery eyes showed little taste for speculations of the spirit."[19] Not surprisingly, says Magne, Voiture was no favorite of this *rude guerrier* preoccupied with war and love. The Duke "tolerated, but hardly loved Voiture. . . . The Duke reproached him with being too intelligent. The poet did not hesitate to underscore the faults of the prince, most notably his insolence and arrogance."[20] Given this character and relationship, the roles of pike and goldfish take on a measure of satiric significance. Whether or not Swift knew the Duke's character, and was thus in a position to feel the edge of satire in Voiture's raillery, is a question we can answer in the affirmative. Among the many seventeenth-century French memoirs listed in both the 1715 and 1745 catalogues of Swift's library is the *Memoires de la Minorité de Louis XIV*.[21] The Duke figures prominently in these memoirs, and, as the author of the preface to the volume says, the Duke is described as "a Captain invested with all the virtues, and all the vices, of an Alexander; a man extreme in everything, and who had nothing of the mediocre, either in spirit or in manner; in a word, a character so mingled that one could neither praise nor blame him too much."[22] The complications in the Duke's character are revealed most fully in the account of his actions immediately preceding and during the Fronde. After victories at Lens and Furnes in 1648, we are told, the Duke was generally admired, and seen as a moderating force between the Court and Parliament: "he was regarded by all the people with admiration. . . . and the two parties [Court and Parliament] considered him as their defender, or at least as the arbiter of their differences." But, according to the *Memoires*, the Duke's effectiveness as a moderator was seriously compromised by his character flaws. We are told, for example, that the Court urged an alliance between the Duke of Orleans and the Duke of Anguien, since the former had a more "temperate" nature than the latter, "who was incapable of any moderation."[23] Acceding to the arguments of the Queen, Mazarin, and others, the Duke agreed to join with Orleans in confronting the Parliament. The memoir's description of the Duke at this time is decidedly unflattering:

> . . . he closed his ears to all neutrality, without concerning himself about the loss of public goodwill. It is certain, that great geniuses, such as his, produce great virtues, but they also appear with great faults; and by an invincible immoderation, he ruined all the advantages which fortune had combined to the envy of all in him, and which were such that he would have surpassed the glory of the greatest men of past centuries, if piety, justice, and stability had corresponded to the supreme valour, the incredible firmness in adversity, and the brilliant spirit which one remarked in him. . . . At this moment he lost the affections of the Company [i.e., parliament], and when news of this action [silencing a speaker in parliament] had spread, the esteem which one had conceived for him because of his victories, changed into fear; and feelings of friendship into hate, not to say execration against his person. . . .[24]

With this account of the Duke's character in mind, we are

prepared to appreciate the very sharp raillery in a letter Voiture wrote to the Duke of Anguien on the occasion of the latter's success at the battle of Rocroy against the Spanish in 1643.[25] Voiture begins the letter by declaring his resolution to tell the Duke, at a distance, everything he has thought about saying, but dared not lest he should suffer the consequences he has seen others suffer who took the same liberty. You would be ashamed if you knew how everyone in Paris is gossiping about you, he tells the Duke, and you would be shocked to see with what little respect and fear of displeasing you everyone talks about what you have done. "Frankly," Voiture says,

> I don't know what you are thinking about: for it was, without dissembling, an excessive impudence, and an extreme violence for you, at your age [the Duke was twenty-two years old in 1643] to offend two or three old Captains, whom you ought to have respected, if only for their antiquity; to have killed the poor Comte de Fontaine, who was one of the finest men of Flanders, and whom the Prince of Orange never dared touch; to have taken sixteen cannons, belonging to a prince who is uncle to the king and confidant of the queen, with whom you have never had any quarrel; and to have thrown into disorder the best Spanish troops, who had let you pass by with such kindness. I do not know what Father Musnier has to say about it, but all of this is a violation of good manners, and offers, it seems to me, considerable material for confession.

Far from being "Clumsy" and barely able to "pass muster as raillery," indeed far from being an irony "sufficiently transparent to avoid misunderstanding,"[26] the raillery in this letter is complicated, and has moved towards the far end of raillery's spectrum, where praise and blame are held in the most delicate balance. Voiture's letter charges the Duke with the "faults" of impudence, extreme violence, insolence ('to have at your age"), cruelty, and pride—all faults the Duke's contemporaries did in fact attribute to him. Of course Voiture's letter is raillery, not satire. As Swift accurately puts it in "To Mr. Delany," "Fools would fancy he intends/A Satyr where he most commends"

(1:216). The "faults" as presented in Voiture's raillery are also virtues, the warrior virtues that had won for the Duke and France what Voiture called "the most beautiful and most important victory that we have seen in our century."[27] But we miss the perfectly controlled tension in Voiture's raillery here, and in some of Swift's poems, if we fail to recognize the delicate balance of praise and blame. The tension exists even in the direct praise of the Duke as a "true Caesar, in spirit and knowledge, a Caesar in diligence; in vigilance, in courage, a Caesar, *et per omnes casus Caesar*. . . . Receive the praises due you: and allow one to render unto Caesar that which belongs to Caesar."[28] Addressed to a powerful young man of twenty-two seen by his contemporaries as insolent and ambitious, cruel and proud, such praise flirts with blame. This is, indeed, a complicated mode of raillery, and to create and control it require consummate skill. By recognizing the complicated raillery in the works of his model, Voiture, we can avoid oversimplifying Swift's raillery into a single "delicate," "good humored," "good mannered" kind, in which "the corrective truths of satire have no place." Norman Knox helpfully clarifies the basic meanings of the word raillery to the Augustans by distinguishing three distinct senses: a sharp raillery, akin to ridicule and aimed at real faults; a delicate raillery, not motivated by contempt and not attacking real faults or intending to hurt; and a raillery in the general sense of jesting of any sort at all. But lest his three basic categories of meaning seem mutually exclusive, Knox stresses the spectrumlike quality of raillery: "Although the important distinctions between *railing* (#2) as angry invective, *raillery* (#1) as ridicule, and *raillery* (#2) as a harmless verbal gambit are not difficult to draw, it is obvious that even abstractly considered the one type of thing modulates into the next without any pause."[29] Despite Swift's several defenses of "delicate" raillery against those who misused it, both he and Voiture knew how to combine the sharp and delicate modes of raillery. In *An Essay Towards Fixing the True Standards of Wit, Humour, Raillery, Satire, and Ridicule* (1744), Corbyn Morris gives special attention to this complicated raillery, and, significantly, illustrates the mode with one of Voiture's letters:

It is also easy to apprehend, that the several Subjects of

> *Wit, Humour, Raillery, Satire,* and *Ridicule,* appear not
> only *singly* upon many Occasions, or *two* of them com-
> bined together, but are also frequently united in other
> Combinations, which are more *complicate*; An Instance
> of the Union together of *Humour, Raillery,* and *Ridicule,*
> I remember to have read somewhere in Voiture's Let-
> ters.[30]

The example is a passage in which Voiture draws a "humourous"
portrait of a ship's captain, against whom he directs ridicule
while also subjecting himself to raillery. "There are other Com-
binations of *Wit, Humour, Raillery, Satire,* and *Ridicule,*" Morris
says, "where *four* of them, or all *five,* are united in one Subject. . . .
But they are often so intimately mix'd, and blended together,
that it is difficult to separate them clearly, tho' they are all certainly felt in the same Piece."[31] As do Voiture's letters, Swift's
poems to Stella illustrate a spectrum of raillery, from the simplest
modes of praise-by-blame to the more complicated modes in
which praise and blame exist in fine balance.

Of the poems Swift wrote to Stella between 1719 and 1727,
four are poems of direct praise, untouched by the comic ironies
of raillery. These poems—"To Stella, Visiting me in my Sickness"
(1720), "To Stella on her Birth-day" (1722), "To Stella" (1724),
and "Stella's Birth-day" (1727)—are nonetheless important in
appreciating Swift's raillery, since the feelings expressed in these
poems are a part of the amicable context in which the sometimes
sharp lines of raillery in other poems to Stella were received. As
in the letters of Voiture, so in the poetry of Swift, direct praise
is the complement of raillery. In "Stella at Wood-Park" (1725),
we see Swift enter into the spectrum of raillery at that end where
the blame is most simply transformed into praise. From April to
the first week of October 1723, Stella and her companion, Re-
becca Dingley, visited with Charles Ford at his country home of
Woodpark. Swift was gone on his "long Southern journey" during much of this time, but was with his friends at Woodpark
twice briefly during the early part of their visit, and perhaps
again towards the very end of their stay late in September. For
most of its length, "Stella at Wood-Park" is apparent ridicule of
Stella, first for her purportedly demanding and domineering

manner while a guest at Woodpark:

> In half a Week the Dame grew nice,
> Got all things at the highest Price.
> Now at the Table-Head she sits,
> Presented with the nicest Bits:
> She look'd on Patridges with scorn,
> Except they tasted of the Corn:
> A Haunch of Ven'son made her sweat,
> Unless it had the right *Fumette*.
>
> [2:749–50]

How fastidious Stella had become: "Through Candle-Light she view'd the Wine,/To see that ev'ry Glass was fine." Having described Stella as "grown prouder than the D——l,/With feeding high, and Treatment civil," Swift then describes her irritable and ill-tempered return home to Ormond Key:

> The Coachman stopt, she lookt, and swore
> The Rascal had mistook the Door:
> At coming in you saw her stoop;
> The Entry brusht against her Hoop:
> Each Moment rising in her Airs,
> She curst the narrow winding Stairs.
>
> [2:751]

The final twenty lines of the poem, however, seem totally to transform this blame into praise:

> Thus, far in jest. Though now I fear
> You think my jesting too severe:
> But Poets when a Hint is new
> Regard not whether false or true:
> Yet Raillery gives no Offence,
> Where Truth has not the least Pretence;
> Nor can be more securely plac't
> Than on a Nymph of *Stella*'s Taste.
>
> [2:751–52]

In his *Remarks on the Life and Character of Dr. Jonathan Swift*, Orrery offered a rather picturesque image of how Swift's raillery should be interpreted:

Even in some of his highest scenes of benevolence his expressions are delivered in such a manner, as to seem rather the effects of haughtiness than of good nature: but you must never look upon him as a traveller in the common road. He must be viewed by a *camera oscura* that turns all objects the contrary way. When he appears most angry, he is most pleased; when most humble, he is most assuming. Such was the man, and in such variegated colours he must be painted.[32]

The final lines of "Stella at Wood-Park" indicate that this is precisely the mode of this poem. From the mere "Hint" of Stella's perfectly understandable regret and "sigh to leave *Wood-Park*," Swift projected this character of a domineering and irritable Stella. Perhaps we should not be too quick to allow for a perfect *camera oscura* reversal, for Swift does resharpen the ridicule: "I must confess, your Wine and Vittle/I was too hard upon *a little*" (Swift's emphasis). And in the manuscript version of the poem Swift had continued, "And you must know in what I writ/I had Some Anger in my Wit."[33] But the printed poem is ultimately and clearly fine praise of Stella, and, simultaneously, of Charles Ford's generosity and of the elegance of his country home entertaining. The poem's four concluding lines are a simple and graceful expression not only of Stella's special powers, but also of Woodpark's function as an ideal:

> We think you quite mistake the Case;
> The Virtue lies not in the Place:
> For though my Raillery were true,
> A Cottage is *Wood-Park* with you.
>
> [2:752]

How simple it would be if we could view all of Swift's poems of raillery as through a *camera oscura,* and merely reverse details and assertions in these poems in order to see the truth. But Swift's poems to Stella are too complex to be read according to a principle of simple reversal. Indeed, a main source of pleasure in these poems of raillery lies in attempting to distinguish truth from fiction, praise from blame, even though, as Corbyn Morris said about complicated mixtures of wit, humour, raillery, ridicule, and satire, "they are often so intimately mix'd, and blended together, that it is difficult to separate them cearly, tho' they are all certainly felt in the same Piece."[34]

In the earliest of the birthday poems which has come down to us, Swift moves along the spectrum towards a more complicated mode of raillery. "On Stella's Birth-day Written AD. 1718–[19]" is couched in near ridicule with the opening blunt declaration of the lady's age, and the repeated references to her size throughout the poem:

> Stella this Day is thirty four,
> (We won't dispute a Year or more)
> However Stella, be not troubled,
> Although thy Size and Years are doubled,
> Since first I saw Thee at Sixteen
> The brightest Virgin of the Green,
> So little is thy Form declin'd
> Made up so largely in thy Mind.
> Oh, would it please the Gods to split
> Thy Beauty, Size, and Years, and Wit,
> No Age could furnish out a Pair
> Of Nymphs so gracefull, Wise and fair
> With half the Lustre of Your Eyes,
> With half thy Wit, thy Years and Size:
> And then before it grew too late,
> How should I beg of gentle Fate,
> (That either Nymph might have her Swain,)
> To split my Worship too in twain.
>
> [2:721–22]

What are we—indeed, what was Stella—to make of a "compliment" which asserts she is twice as old and twice the size she was at sixteen? First, in the social situation of her birthday gathering, Stella had every reason to be confident of the affection and esteem with which she was regarded by her company of friends. As Dean Swift later wrote, "her politeness and her wit so engaged the attention of the learned, that she became universally admired by all those among the Doctor's acquaintance who had any pretensions to either."[35] Secondly, Swift lessens the chance that his raillery might be misunderstood by using direct praise as the companion to raillery. But what of the reference to her doubled size: is it sharp or delicate raillery, referring to a real or a non-existent fault?

Reliable descriptions of Stella's appearance at that time do not exist. After studying various paintings and engravings said to be portraits of Stella, Henry Mangan concludes that "we are left in doubt," because none of the portraits can be identified with any certainty as Stella.[36] In the account he wrote at her death, Swift says that Stella "was sickly from her childhood until about the age of fifteen: But then grew into perfect health, and was looked upon as one of the most beautiful, graceful, and agreeable young women in London, only a little too fat."[37] Stella's health remained generally good until 1722, but declined the following year, beginning the period of "continual ill-health" which ended only with her death in 1728.[38] In February 1723 Swift writes in a letter that "Mrs. Johnson eats an ounce a week, which frights me from dining with her," and in 1725 Swift writes to Ford twice within ten days to the effect that "Mrs. Johnson is as usuall, unless rather worse, for she eats now but a mouthfull a day" and "I am in pain about her."[39] Thus in her last years, as in her early ones, Stella's ill-health was marked by thinness. The references to her size in "On Stella's Birth-day," while touching (perhaps "a little mercilessly," as one biographer put it[40]) upon a "real fault" in Stella, are also references to her general good health in those years, specifically contrasted to her poor health through her fifteenth year. Swift's rallying, although glancing at a fault in Stella, playfully compliments her, and probably elicited from her other friends assurances of how fine she looked and what good health she enjoyed. So, too, the repeated references to her years as well as her size having doubled, and the opening line's deliberate understatement of her age, followed immediately by an acknowledgment of an error of "a Year or More," would have teased laughter both from Stella and her friends. Stella's age is the subject of similar joking in Swift's letter to Sheridan (22 December 1722): "We have new Plays and new Libels, and nothing valuable is old but *Stella,* whose Bones she recommends to you."[41] The finely balanced raillery in "On Stella's Birth-day," accompanying the implicitly serious themes of transience and permanence which Ronald Paulson has discerned in the poems to Stella,[42] produces a festive, warm, and comic compliment to Stella, and a highly successful piece of social verse.

However, in reading this and some of the other poems to Stella, one thinks of Swift's objections to the raillery written by his friend Thomas Sheridan, who "Not allways judges what is fit," and "sometimes walks beyond his Bounds," and certain of whose writings were "out of all the Rules of Raillery, I ever understood."[43] Indeed in a later poem Swift acknowledges about himself that "there are persons who complain/There's too much satire in my vein,/That I am often found exceeding/The rules of raillery and breeding" (2:489). In "Stella's Birth-day" (1722), for example, Swift compares Stella's face to a decayed and weathered inn-sign; in "Stella's Birth-Day" (1725) she is described as greying and wrinkled, an unfit subject for poetry; and in "A Receipt to Restore Stella's Youth" (1725) she is compared to a meager, lank, and famished cow (2:734, 756, 758). But in each of these poems Swift avoids transgressing the rules of raillery. In the birthday poems of 1722 and 1725 Swift's raillery of Stella's physical deterioration is not aimed at real faults, since a main assertion of the poems is the superiority of virtues of the mind over physical appearance. And in each of these two poems Swift exercises discretion and judgment by including lines of direct praise to insure proper understanding of the ultimate intention of praise. "A Receipt to Restore Stella's Youth" is a different matter. As we saw in the preceding paragraph, Stella's health during these years was declining. Unlike other poems to Stella designed to praise and to please her, "A Receipt to Restore Stella's Youth" uses blame akin to ridicule in order to persuade Stella to take steps to restore her health:

> Why, *Stella*, should you knit your Brow,
> If I compare you to the Cow?
> 'Tis just the Case: For you have fasted
> So long till all your Flesh is wasted,
> And must against the warmer Days
> Be sent to Quilca down to graze;
> Where Mirth, and Exercise, and Air,
> Will soon your Appetite repair.
>
> [2:759]

Swift has pushed to the far end of raillery's spectrum: the ridicule is sharp and clearly intended to discomfort Stella, in order to prompt action. But even here Swift manages through playful exaggeration and lines of direct praise to keep the poem within the bounds of raillery. Despite its sharp ridicule, the poem is a skillful piece of social verse designed to affect Stella's behavior, and to express Swift's serious concern and affection for her.

But among all of Swift's poems to Stella, the one depending on the most complicated and precarious balancing of praise and blame is "To Stella, Who Collected and Transcribed his Poems" (1720). Swift's usual pattern in poems of raillery is to begin with the blame, and then to introduce lines of direct praise. In this poem, he reverses the pattern. The first section of the poem (2:727–28, ll. 1–24) could stand alone as one of the poems of direct praise. He gives to Stella "The Merit and the Praise" for any approval posterity might grant "this Pile of scatter'd Rhymes" which she collected and transcribed. He specifically eschews the "*Cupid*'s Darts," "killing Eyes" and "bleeding Hearts" kind of love, as he describes himself "With Friendship and Esteem possesst." And he concludes this first section by describing man's seemingly unending search for the best by asserting, "But his Pursuits are at an End,/Whom *Stella* chuses for a *Friend*."

The second section of the poem (ll. 25–82) is essentially a discourse on the poetry of praise, and raises the question of the truth of a poet's fiction. The Grub Street poet, "starving in a Garret,/Conning old Topicks like a Parrot," substitutes rhetorical commonplaces for the truth. His poetic "Goddesses" are in reality trollops, "Whose Scoundrel Fathers would not know 'em,/If they should meet 'em in a Poem." True poets, on the other hand, describe not the ephemeral and accidental details of physical appearance, but the enduring and defining qualities of moral virtue. And, most importantly, the true poet is a master of blame as well as of praise:

> True Poets can depress and raise;
> Are Lords of Infamy and Praise:
> They are not scurrilous in Satire,
> Nor will in Panegyrick flatter.
> Unjustly Poets we asperse;

> Truth shines the brighter, clad in Verse;
> And all the Fictions they pursue
> Do but insinuate what is true.
>
> [2:729]

The final section of the poem (ll. 83–144) then takes an unusual turn:

> *Stella,* when you these Lines transcribe,
> Lest you should take them for a Bribe,
> Resolv'd to mortify your Pride,
> I'll here expose your weaker Side.
>
> [2:730]

For the next almost sixty lines, Swift accuses Stella of a variety of faults, all generated by the main fault of being unable to accept constructive criticism from friends:

> Your Spirits kindle to a Flame,
> Mov'd with the lightest Touch of Blame,
> And when a Friend in Kindness tries
> To shew you where your Error lies,
> Conviction does but more incense;
> Perverseness is your whole Defence:
> Truth, Judgment, Wit, give Place to Spite,
> Regardless both of Wrong and Right.
>
> [2:730]

These lines of reproach appear devoid of irony. Swift tells Stella that he is attempting "to mortify your Pride" lest she take the earlier lines of praise "for a Bribe." If so, his main charge of hypersensitivity to criticism, and the attendant charges of perverseness, unreasonableness, abuse of friends, and hypocrisy, provide mortification enough. But was Stella in fact guilty of either the main or attendant faults? No evidence available outside this poem indicates that she was. We could, as Lord Orrery suggested, view Swift "by a *camera oscura* that turns all objects the contrary way," and regard the main fault with which Stella is charged as the very opposite of the truth. As we have seen, this simple mode of raillery was Swift's express method in "Stella at Wood-Park." Also in support of this simple reversal are Swift's

190

comments in the prose portrait of Stella he wrote on the evening of her death and the days following: "She never mistook the understanding of others; nor ever said a severe word, but where a much severer was deserved. . . . She was never positive in arguing, and she usually treated those who were so, in a manner which well enough gratified that unhappy disposition; yet in such a sort as made it very contemptible, and at the same time did some hurt to the owners."[44]

But given the absence of unexceptionable outside evidence, we must also consider the possibility that Stella was indeed guilty of overreacting to friendly criticism, and that, having devoted the first section of the poem to direct praise, Swift devoted the last section to Stella's "weaker Side," thus placing himself among those "True Poets [who] can depress and raise;/Are Lords of Infamy and Praise." But in a poem addressed in appreciation to Stella, why would the section of reproach be more than twice as long as the section of direct praise? The answer lies, I think, in the description Swift wrote of Voiture in "To Mr. Delany":

> He flatters with peculiar Air
> The Brave, the Witty, and the Fair;
> And Fools would fancy he intends
> A Satyr where he most commends.
>
> [1:216]

The lines of blame in "To Stella, Who Collected and Transcribed his Poems" are an excellent example of "obliging Ridicule," of praise and blame precariously balanced. The assertion of Stella's weakness is cushioned by statements that it is her "only Fau't," and "a Fault we often find/Mix'd in a noble generous Mind." The good attending the fault is described by comparing it to a volcano which elicits admiration as well as fear and to the sun which burns but also ripens. Even the refutation of Stella's alleged rationalization for her fault is presented in the complimentary form of "for once you reason wrong."

It is the final verse paragraph, however, that most wittily transforms the blame into praise:

> Say, *Stella*, when you copy next,
> Will you keep strictly to the Text?
> Dare you let these Reproaches stand,

And to your Failing set your Hand?
Or if these Lines your Anger fire,
Shall they in baser Flames expire?
Whene'er they burn, if burn they must,
They'll prove my Accusation just.

[2:732]

Regardless of the reality outside of the poem, within the poem's fiction these final lines clearly place in Stella's hands the preservation or destruction of these "Reproaches." According to Swift's definition in this poem of true poets, "all the Fictions they pursue/Do but insinuate what is true." Within its own fiction, this poem's very existence demonstrates that Stella has in fact corrected her "only Fau't," and overcome her aversion to "the lightest Touch of Blame." "To Stella, Who Collected and Transcribed his Poems" shows Swift as railleur at his finest. In an essay on the "Ode to Sancroft," Edward W. Rosenheim, Jr. has observed that Swift's "love for his friends and even for Stella openly embraces their frailties together with their virtues; few if any mortals are ever urged on us as models."[45] In the poems to Stella, Swift's control of a spectrum of raillery, paralleled in the works of his model Vincent Voiture, allowed him to express his perception of the invariable mixture of frailties and virtues even in one so fine as Stella. Swift's raillery in these poems is thus not just one social verse game, but a perspective on human nature. What Swift says about "True Poets" applies to the poems to Stella: "And all the Fictions they pursue/Do but insinuate what is true."

Notes

1. John Boyle, Earl of Orrery, *Remarks on the Life and Writings of Dr. Jonathan Swift* (London, 1752), pp. 244–45. For other references to Swift's raillery by his early biographers see Patrick Delany, *Observations Upon Lord Orrery's Remarks on the Life and Writings of Dr. Jonathan Swift* (London, 1754), p. 16; Thomas Sheridan, Introduction to *The Life of the Rev. Dr. Jonathan Swift* (Dublin, 1785), p. 2; and *Memoirs of Mrs. Letitia Pilkington*, ed. Iris Barry (New York, 1928), p. 53.

2. *The Prose Works of Jonathan Swift*, ed. Herbert Davis, 14 vols. (Oxford, 1964), 13:155.

3. See especially Eugene F. Timpe, "Swift as Railleur," *Journal of*

English and Germanic Philology 69 (1970): 41–49; and John M. Bullitt, "Swift's 'Rules of Raillery,'" in *Veins of Humor*, ed. Harry Levin, Harvard English Studies, vol. 3 (Cambridge, Mass., 1972), pp. 93–108. Also see Norman Knox's discussion of Swift's raillery in *The Word Irony and Its Context, 1500–1755* (Durham, N.C., 1961), pp. 187–208; Herbert Davis, *Jonathan Swift: Essays on His Satire and Other Studies* (1931; rpt. New York, 1964), p. 54; and Oliver Ferguson, "'Nature and Friendship': The Personal Letters of Jonathan Swift," in *The Familiar Letter in the Eighteenth Century*, ed. Howard Anderson, Philip B. Daghlian, and Irvin Ehrenpreis (Lawrence, Kans., 1968), pp. 14–33.

4. *Memoirs*, p. 53.

5. Bullitt, p. 105.

6. See "To Mr. Delany," *The Poems of Jonathan Swift*, ed. Harold Williams, 2d ed., 3 vols. (Oxford, 1958), 1:214–19. Subsequent references will be to this edition of Swift's poems and will be cited in the text by volume and page. According to both the 1715 and 1745 catalogues of his library, Swift owned two editions of Voiture's *Oeuvres* (Paris, 1652 and Brussels, 1695). See T. P. LeFanu, "Catalogue of Dean Swift's Library in 1715, With an Inventory of his Personal Property in 1742." *Proceedings of the Royal Irish Academy* 37 (1927), sect. C., 263–75; and for the 1745 catalogue see Harold Williams's *Dean Swift's Library* (Cambridge, 1932), items 116, 353.

7. Timpe's statement (p. 41) that Voiture's writings had been published twice by 1697 is misleading. Thirty-four editions of his works had been published between his death in 1649 and the end of the century, with another nine editions in the first half of the eighteenth century; see Voiture's *Poésies*, ed. Henri Lafay (Paris, 1971), 1:xxii–xxxi.

8. 2 vols., rev. ed. (Paris, 1929–30).

9. "Voiture," in *L'Epoque d'Henri IV et de Louis XII*, vol. 1, *Histoire de la littérature française au XVIIe siècle* (Paris, 1948), p. 388.

10. See George Mongrédien, *La Vie littéraire au XVIIe siècle* (Paris, 1947); Réné Bray, *La Préciosité et les Précieux* (Paris, 1948); Odette de Mourgues, *Metaphysical, Baroque & Précieux Poetry* (1953; rpt. Oxford, 1969); and Roger Lathuillère, *La Préciosité: Étude historique et linguistique* (Geneva, 1966).

11. P. 42.

12. P. 99.

13. Letter 66, *Les oeuvres de monsieur de Voiture*, 5th ed. (Paris, 1656), p. 232 (hereafter cited as *Les oeuvres*). All translations from French in this essay are mine.

14. 1:116–20.

15. Letter 10, *Les oeuvres*, pp. 31–37.

16. Anthony, Earl of Shaftesbury, in "Treatise VI: Miscellaneous Reflections on the preceding Treatises, etc.," in *Characteristics*, 2 vols. in one, ed. John M. Robertson (Indianapolis, 1964), 2:168.

17. *The Correspondence of Jonathan Swift*, ed. Harold Williams, 5 vols. (Oxford, 1963), 4:408.

18. Letter 144, *Les oeuvres*, pp. 446–49.

19. 2:159.

20. 2:240–41.

21. The full title is *Memoires de M. Le Duc de la Rochefoucault et de M. de la Chastre. Contenant L'Histoire de la Minorité de Louis XIV* (Villefranche, 1690). I use the edition of 1700, and hereafter refer to the book as *Memoires*.

22. Préface, unnumbered page 13.

23. Pp. 133–34, 143.

24. Pp. 145–46.

25. Letter 141, *Les oeuvres*, pp. 439–41.

26. Timpe, p. 42; Bullitt, p. 100. Bullitt mistakenly understands the Duke to have been "a modest man who despised flattery" (p. 100).

27. Letter 141, *Les oeuvres*, p. 440.

28. Ibid., pp. 440–41.

29. Pp. 192–202.

30. *Augustan Reprint Society* no. 10 (November 1947): 47–48.

31. Pp. 49–50.

32. Pp. 234–35.

33. 2:747. Swift's "Anger" in this manuscript version is because Stella's complaining about "this odious Town" of Dublin simply encourages their friend Ford to leave them and Ireland for life in London.

34. P. 50.

35. *An Essay upon the Life, Writings, and Character of Dr. Jonathan Swift* (London, 1755), p. 91. For similar praises of Stella see Orrery, p. 23; Thomas Sheridan, p. 265; Swift's prose portrait of Stella, *Prose Works*, 5:227–38; and even Swift's letter to the Reverend Tisdal (20 April 1704), *Correspondence*, 1:44–46.

36. Appendix 7, "Portraits of Stella and Vanessa," in *Journal to Stella*, ed. Harold Williams, 2:687–703.

37. *Prose Works*, 5:227.

38. *Prose Works*, 5:228; Appendix 14, "Stella and Her History," *Correspondence*, 5:239.

39. *Correspondence*, 2:450, 3:52, 53.

40. Stephen Gwynn, *The Life and Friendships of Dean Swift* (New York, 1933), p. 270.

41. *Correspondence*, 2:441.

42. "Swift, Stella, and Permanance," *ELH* 27 (1960): 298–314.

43. *Poems*, 1:218; *Correspondence*, 2:301.

44. *Prose Works*, 5:229, 235. That Swift did not reserve this prose portrait of Stella just for praise is illustrated by his disapproval of her "folly" in handling money as a young woman (pp. 231–32).

45. "Swift's *Ode to Sancroft*: Another Look," *Modern Philology* 73 (1976): S38–S39.

VII. *A Satirical Elegy*

CHARLES PEAKE

Swift's "Satirical Elegy on a Late Famous General"

'I have been only a man of rhymes,' Swift told Charles Wogan
in 1732, 'and that upon trifles, never having written serious couplets in my life, yet never any without a moral view.' Although
Swift was here partly concerned to excuse himself from the task
of correcting the verses Wogan had sent him, there is other evidence that he did not rate himself highly as a poet. In 1732 most
of his verse had been occasional, provoked by political struggles
or events, or contributed to the pastimes and celebrations of his
friends; the moral purpose was personal or local and contemporary, not universal, and therefore not 'serious' in the sense in
which true poetry was serious.

Yet poets notoriously err in judging their own work, and
Swift's self-depreciation has to be measured against his standards
for judging poetry and poets. For him the title of 'poet' was often
claimed but rarely deserved:

> Say *Britain,* cou'd you ever boast,—
> Three *Poets* in an Age at most?
> Our chilling Climate hardly bears
> A *Sprig* of Bays in Fifty Years
> (p. 640)[1]

and the art of poetry was of incomparable difficulty:

This essay first appeared in *A Review of English Literature,* vol. 3, no. 3 (July 1962):
80–89. Reprinted with permission.

Not *Empire* to the Rising-Sun,
By Valour, Conduct, Fortune won;
Nor highest *Wisdom* in Debates
For framing Laws to govern States;
Nor Skill in Sciences profound,
So large to grasp the Circle round;
Such heavenly Influence require,
As how to strike the *Muses Lyre.*

(p. 641)

If the name of 'poet' was to be reserved for the Miltons, Drydens,
and Popes, then Swift's disclaimer is not so humble as at first
appears. It is more expressive of the pride of a man who would
decline to compete where he could not triumph. He would not
be a mediocre poet: he could not equal Pope; and so he would
renounce all claims to the poet's name. But few readers will demand of every poet that he be the equal of Pope; and in any
case the question of competition does not arise. At its best, Swift's
poetry has its own peculiar excellencies.

A Satirical Elegy on the Death of a late Famous General, for instance, is far more than the work of 'a man of rhymes'; it is a
poem of great emotional power controlled by taut and precise
language and by firm poetic organisation.

His Grace! impossible! what dead!
Of old age too, and in his bed!
And could that Mighty Warrior fall?
And so inglorious, after all!
Well, since he's gone, no matter how,
The last loud trump must wake him now:
And, trust me, as the noise grows stronger,
He'd wish to sleep a little longer.
And could he be indeed so old
As by the news-papers we're told?
Threescore, I think, is pretty high;
'Twas time in conscience he should die.
This world he cumber'd long enough;
He burnt his candle to the snuff;
And that's the reason, some folks think,
He left behind *so great a stink.*

Behold his funeral appears,
Nor widow's sighs, nor orphan's tears,
Wont at such times each heart to pierce,
Attend the progress of his herse.
But what of that, his friends may say,
He had those honours in his day.
True to his profit and his pride,
He made them weep before he dy'd.

Come hither, all ye empty things,
Ye bubbles rais'd by breath of Kings;
Who float upon the tide of state,
Come hither, and behold your fate.
Let pride be taught by this rebuke,
How very mean a thing's a Duke;
From all his ill-got honours flung,
Turn'd to that dirt from whence he sprung.

(pp. 296–97)

The poem has all the Swiftian characteristics which have induced critics to accept him at his own valuation, when they did not turn away in genteel disgust: colloquial diction (no poet uses the 'real language of men' more consistently); outspoken, unmerciful judgement; emotional reinforcement of the satirical point by words and images designedly repellent. The violence of the expression suggests a man moved by hatred rather than moral indignation, and this perhaps accounts for Sir Harold Williams's dismissal of the *Satirical Elegy* as an 'ungenerous attack on Marlborough.'

Whether or not Swift hated Marlborough, the emotion so powerfully expressed in this poem is moral indignation. There are passing references to Marlborough's greed and pride and to his origins, but the chief crime with which Marlborough is charged is that he was one of those great men who for their own gain or glory have brought misery on the rest of mankind. Rightly or wrongly Swift believed that Marlborough had tried to prolong the war with France, and, as Gulliver's conversations in Brobdingnag and Houyhnhnmland show, warfare was to Swift the final expression of human wickedness. The fact that the title of the poem reads 'a late famous General'—not 'the late Duke

199

of Marlborough'—may suggest that its moral condemnation will apply to more than one particular military leader. (The poem was not published in Swift's lifetime, so the avoidance of Marlborough's name was not merely an attempt to escape prosecution.)

Can satire, however morally indignant, legitimately attack the newly dead? Is this poem compatible with Swift's claim that

> His Satyr points at no Defect,
> But what all Mortals may correct?
>
> (p. 571)

By dying, a man puts himself beyond the reach of a satirist's correction. But although the satirist may sometimes claim to be teaching his victims the errors of their ways, more frequently he makes an example of the foolish and the vicious in order to dissuade or deter others from following their example. For Swift this satirical function was far more important than any convention of respect for the dead. In *An Answer to a Paper, called 'A Memorial of the Poor Inhabitants, Tradesmen, and Labourers of the Kingdom of Ireland,'* where he attacks his old enemy, Lord Chief Justice Whitshed, he considers the objection that Whitshed is dead.

> What an encouragement to vice is this! If an ill man be alive, and in power, we dare not attack him; and if he be weary of the world, or of his own villainies, he has nothing to do but die, and then his reputation is safe. For these excellent casuists know just Latin enough to have heard a most foolish precept, that *de mortuis nil nisi bonum*; so that if Socrates, and Anytus his accuser, had happened to die together, the charity of survivors must either have obliged them to hold their peace, or to fix the same character on both. The only crime of charging the dead is, when the least doubt remains whether the accusation be true; but when men are openly abandoned, and lost to all shame, they have no reason to think it hard if their memory be reproached. . . . Such creatures are not to be reformed, neither is it prudence or safety to attempt a reformation.

> Yet, although their memories will rot, there may be
> some benefit for their survivors to smell it while it is
> rotting.

This passage not only offers a justification for such a poem as
the *Satirical Elegy* and for its right to be regarded as useful satire
rather than mere vilification, it also recalls the poem's manner
of proceeding; and this brings us from considering the legiti-
macy of Swift's moral position to the question of whether his
indignation has been expressed in the form and language of a
poem.

Far from being a mere outburst of vituperation the poem
is complexly ordered. The basic pattern displays in the first
twenty-four lines the rapid decay of the Duke's reputation, and
in the last eight lines holds up this rotting memory to the nostrils
of those surviving 'empty things' who might benefit from smell-
ing it. Superimposed on this division of the poem is a chronological or processional order of the same kind as that so familiar
in the epithalamium, where the wedding day is followed from
the bride's rising to the bridal bed. In the epithalamium the
ordered sequence of events reflects the ceremonial of the wedding, and a similar sequence may reflect the ceremonial of a
funeral. It does so, for instance, in Tennyson's *Ode on the Death
of the Duke of Wellington,* and there is a suggestion of it in Pope's
Elegy to the Memory of an Unfortunate Lady, where there are successive references to the closing of the eyes of the dead, the
laying-out, the mourners, the grave, and finally a kind of epitaph
in the lines beginning 'So peaceful rests, without a stone, a name.'

In the *Satirical Elegy* the succession of events, though not
quite the usual succession, is clearly marked and fundamental to
the poem's structure and significance. In the first eight lines we
hear the rumour of the Duke's death circulating the town; in the
next eight the confirmatory detail of the newspapers' obituary
notices, and the comments arising from them; we see the funeral
cortège pass, unattended by tears. Then, in the words 'Come
hither, all ye empty things,' we hear the funeral sermon (with
echoes of the voice of the Preacher crying 'Vanity of vanities; all
is vanity'); and finally in the last line comes a distorted reminiscence of the burial service, as the priest casts earth on to the
coffin and says, 'Earth to earth, ashes to ashes, dust to dust.'

As I have suggested, this funeral procedure in the poem is not only entirely appropriate but an essential part of the meaning. It would be as absurd to read the opening lines of the poem as though Swift were indulging in 'ungenerous' sarcasm, as to read the chatter of the town in *Verses on the Death of Dr. Swift* (where a similar chronological sequence is used) as expressive of Swift's own views on the subject. The first sixteen lines of the *Satirical Elegy* are palpably in the rhythms and language of town gossip. The central theme of the poem is that ill-got fame is a bubble pricked by death. No sooner is the great man dead than the foolish idolaters and lickspittles, who refer to him as 'His Grace' and 'that Mighty Warrior' and who find it inconceivable that he should share the common vulnerability to age and death, first shrug their shoulders—'Well, since he's gone, no matter how'; then hint their dislike—'He'd wish to sleep a little longer' assume a bolder frankness—''Twas time in conscience he should die'; and finally come down to downright abuse of one who, at least as 'some folks think,' has left only a stink behind. The back-biting voice is not Swift's: it is more to his purpose to show that Marlborough's reputation will quickly be destroyed by the very men who praised him while he was alive and powerful.

With the appearance of the funeral the tone darkens; scurrility gives way to an indictment delivered with much greater subtlety, and with a bitter irony which treats the tears of widows and orphans as battle-honours. Yet even here the accusation is not levelled directly by Swift: Marlborough is convicted on the testimony, so the pretence is, of his friends.

It is only in the concluding apostrophe that Swift passes judgement in his own person, and holds up the putrefaction of Marlborough's memory as an example. And here the last two lines draw together the images and tones of the first part of the poem. We have already been given an indication of what the Duke's 'ill-got honours' involved in human misery, and the simple conversion of the neutral and traditional 'dust' to the unexpected and shocking 'dirt' recalls the earlier 'stink.'

In these ways the organisation of the poem reinforces and contributes to its total significance, and the figurative language employed is similarly functional. It was a stock criticism of Swift's writings in the eighteenth century that he was unusually sparing in his use of metaphorical language, and there is some truth in the charge, in that he is not given to using ornamental figures. 'His few metaphors,' said Johnson in his *Life of Swift,* 'seem to be received rather by necessity than choice.' Yet in the *Satirical Elegy* the deflating purpose of the poem would be hindered rather than helped by striking and original metaphor, over and above the structural metaphor of the funeral procession, which I have described. Swift solves his problem by a device which he had practised frequently ever since he wrote *A Tale of a Tub.* He takes the stock figures of speech associated with death and turns them to his own ends. The empty pomp of the line 'And could that Mighty Warrior fall,' with its suggestion of heroic death in battle, is destroyed by placing it immediately after the information that Marlborough died in bed. The elevated but hackneyed image of 'the last loud trump' is reduced to humbler terms by presenting the Duke as a man unwilling to leave his bed in the morning. The familiar metaphor for a man who has led a full life—'He burnt his candle to the end'—is deflated by the substitution of the low word 'snuff,' and by the extension of the image to include the consequent stink.

In every case Swift, instead of creating a new metaphor, has taken a tarnished one, commonly used with reference to the dead, and made it serve his own purposes by exposing its absurdity, or by giving it a low interpretation, or by extending it in an unexpected way. This deflation of the stock figures of the obituary notice is a use of metaphorical language very typical of Swift, and entirely appropriate to his theme.

But with the increasing seriousness of tone as the funeral passes, the figurative language becomes more complex. The absence of a grieving widow or child from the funeral cortège at first suggests that the Duke was so unlovable a man that even his own family did not honour him with their tears. But in the defence of his 'friends,' the widows and orphans are multiplied into the families of those for whose deaths Marlborough was responsible; while the 'honours' are no longer tears shed as a mark of respect, but a kind of battle-honour won from those over whom he has triumphed. Moreover, Marlborough's preference for the latter type of 'honour' is seen as symptomatic of his pride and greed, requiring even the debt of tears to be paid while he was still alive to enjoy them. The elements of the image—the weeping family, the battle-honours—are still drawn from the common ingredients of a military funeral, but they are twisted to present Swift's main indictment of the Duke's personality and career.

In the conclusion of the poem Swift uses again conventional metaphors, but very differently. The comparison of man's life to a bubble is in the tradition of the funeral sermon, and for Swift's purpose nothing represents more precisely the creatures of a king than glittering, transient, empty, drifting bubbles. The phrase 'rais'd by breath of Kings' recalls significantly the story of the Creation:

And the Lord God formed man of the dust of the
ground, and breathed into his nostrils the breath of life;
and man became a living soul.

These words of *Genesis* lie behind the words of the Preacher, "All go unto one place; all are of the dust, and all turn to dust again,' as well as behind the words of the priest at the burial of the dead, 'Earth to earth, ashes to ashes, dust to dust.'

But these refer to the death of those into whose dust God has breathed the breath of life. Men like Marlborough, the bubbles of state, are formed by the breath of kings breathed not into dust, but into dirt.

In a sense, then, these concluding lines repeat the manœuvre of the earlier lines, in giving to conventional or traditional metaphors an entirely unexpected application. Yet the solemn religious associations lift the reversal of these metaphors to a plane of intensity and passion neither attempted nor desired at the beginning of the poem.

The inflation and deflation of the theme and the imagery are repeated in the diction and versification. There is a constant up and down movement between dignified words and phrases like 'Warrior' and 'Attend the progress,' and the colloquial 'Well' or 'pretty high.' Even the constructions vary from the formal 'Behold,' 'Come hither,' 'Let pride be taught' to the casual 'after all,' 'that's the reason.' The octosyllabics too are handled with great variation of pace and metre, from slow, heavily stressed lines like:

> Nor widow's sighs, nor orphan's tears,
> Wont at such times each heart to pierce,

to a hasty, lightly stressed line like:

> And so inglorious, after all.

Everything in the poem has been shaped, either by conscious art or by the force of Swift's passion, to echo and repeat in its own way his theme. The poem is a practical demonstration of 'proper words in proper places.'

All this is thoroughly characteristic of Swift's poetry. Compared with Pope's it is more energetic, less supple in its movement; the transitions and variations of pace are more abrupt; language and imagery are less sensitively, but perhaps more forcefully, handled. Swift is a great master of language but lacks some of Pope's sensuous relish of it; the beauty of his verse is athletic, functional; it is less rich in connotation and ornament. A comparison such as this may seeem impressionistic and old-fashioned. But for exact discussion of those very aspects of poetry in which Swift excels we may still lack adequate critical tools. The old Latinate techniques for examining the rhythm of a poem are discredited, but they have not been replaced: consequently, although we may notice that initial stresses are rare at the beginning of the poem but occur in nearly three out of four lines after halfway, and may perceive how this helps to convey the mounting emotional pitch, beyond that kind of observation our methods of scansion hardly help. We may suggest that the crispness and precision of the language is partly due to the very high proportion of monosyllables (about five-sixths of the total number of words) and to the way in which clashing consonants are juxtaposed at the ends and beginnings of words to make the mouth of the reader bite off, as it were, each word separately— as in 'Wont at such times each heart to pierce,' 'Let pride be taught by this rebuke,' or 'Turn'd to that dirt from whence he sprung': but such observations only emphasise how limited are our means of investigating one of the crucial qualities of a poem—how it goes.

It is, however, possible to identify some elements which contribute to Swift's peculiar poetic style. For instance, although it is easy to find in his verse examples of alliteration producing the familiar local effects of onomatopoeia, emphasis, or epigrammatic neatness, it more characteristically extends over a dozen or more lines and rings the changes on some five or six consonants (occurring in any part of a word)—as in the interweaving of b's, p's, t's, and d's of the second half of the *Satirical Elegy*, which comes to a climax in the last line. Certainly this device, probably as much instinctive as deliberate, helps to give the verse briskness and liveliness, and, like so much else in Swift's verse which eludes the critic, speaks directly to the ear of the reader.

The *Satirical Elegy* seems a good test-piece. It has emotional power, wit, a compact and logical structure, appropriate and unified imagery and tone, controlled variation of diction and movement—and a wholeness in conception and execution not unworthy of a great writer like Swift. Even his few popular poems, like the *Verses on the Death of Dr. Swift*, deserve more critical attention than they have received. For Swift may be a minor poet, but he is minor in the best sense of the word. It is not that he did well what others did superlatively well, but that, like Peacock among novelists, he did superlatively well certain things which, as much as we may value them, we do not place on the highest rank in the hierarchy of literary kinds.

Note

1. The page references given in parentheses throughout this article are to *Swift. Poems,* 2nd edition, ed. by Harold Williams (Oxford, 1958), 3 vols.

VIII.   The "Scatological" Poems

JOHN M. ADEN

Corinna and the Sterner
Muse of Swift

Despite much recent progress in the rehabilitation of Swift's
Muse, it must be admitted that we have not yet attained to an
adequate appraisal of that lady, and certainly not of her most
celebrated offspring, "Corinna, Pride of Drury-Lane."[1] More
than any other of his poetic compositions, if we may judge by its
criticism, Swift's *Beautiful Young Nymph* frustrates the appreciation of Swift as a serious poet, for it is with her, apparently, that
even the most resolute efforts to accommodate to his Muse finally
break down. As Ehrenpreis says, the *Nymph Going to Bed* represents, for most readers, Swift "at his most damnable . . ."[2]

Orwell regarded the poem as a prime example of how Swift
"falsifies his picture of the world by refusing to see anything in
human life except dirt, folly and wickedness."[3] And Middleton
Murry has outdone Huxley and Lawrence in their rather frenetic
appraisal of the "unprintable" poems:

> Lust is natural and wholesome compared to the feeling
> Swift arouses. Moreover, the horror of such a 'poem' as
> *A Beautiful Young Nymph going to Bed* is not confined to
> the nausea evoked by the hideous detail; it proceeds
> equally from the writer's total lack of charity, his cold

This essay first appeared in *English Language Notes* 4 (1966): 23–31. Reprinted
with permission.

brutality, towards the wretched woman who is anatom-
ized. It is utterly inhuman.[4]

Clearly such an indictment of the poem and its author must be
set aside if the case for Swift's sterner Muse is not to prove hopeless. The effort has been made, but not very successfully, by both
Maurice Johnson and Irvin Ehrenpreis, neither of whom, despite
valuable contributions, has really met the issue head-on or themselves quite perceived the true nature of the poem. Johnson has
reminded us of its witty dimension, Ehrenpreis of its biographical provocations and of its burlesque relation to the conventions
of Petrarchan and Cavalier amatory verse.[5] But Johnson will finally conclude that in the poem Swift "describes the wages of sin
as effectively as a preacher shouting hell-fire and brimstone, or
the photographs in a medical treatise, or the scenes drawn by
Hogarth for 'A Harlot's Progress.'"

> The rather obtrusive moral [he continues] affixed to
> Moll Hackabout's disintegration and punishment as Ho-
> garth draws her, when she is revealed as a hopelessly
> miserable creature in miserable surroundings, is the
> moral Swift affixes to the picture of Corinna going to
> bed.[6]

The analogy of Hogarthian realism is useful, but the emphasis
upon preaching, the wages of sin, and moralizing is not, for it
not only obscures the distinction between Swift the churchman
and Swift the poet, but it fails to see the difference between Swift
and Hogarth (despite the likenesses, "Corinna" is not a "progress" poem) and, what is more crucial, it fails to comprehend the
Swiftian view of reality.

Ehrenpreis does little to improve upon this. True, he provides the important perspective of comparable satires and ana-
tomies,[7] but he too finally rests his case in an intentional and
moralistic, rather than poetic, argument: "Why should Swift
dwell on the domestic exercises of a courtesan? The simplest
answer is that as a conscientious priest he wished to discourage
fornication. Some critics [he adds prophetically] would snort
magnificently at this suggestion. But . . . ." and he goes on. Swift
was a serious priest, he was "old fashioned," "Conservative"; he

"took a traditional view of vice." He was "continuing the medieval Christian tradition of flaying the fornicator . . ."[8] Now Swift was indeed all that Ehrenpreis declares he was, but he was also a poet, and though the traits that Ehrenpreis invokes unquestionably figured in the making of the poem, neither they nor the burlesque tradition can quite account for the finished product, which is a poem, not a sermon, and which is earnest and poignant for all its spoofing.

The trouble with so much Swift criticism is that it assumes Swift wears only one mask, the *satyr's*. What it has generally failed to perceive is that he really carries two, a tragic as well as comic mask, and that in some way peculiar to his genius he usually displays them together, so that his satire keens while it carps and carps while it keens, that it finds the two moods, in reality, difficult to distinguish or keep apart. It may be said, in fact, that the unique mark of Swift as a satirist is that his mouth tends to turn down and up at the same time.

I can illustrate this point briefly, as it relates to "Corinna," with the following couplet, occurring early in the poem:

> Never did *Covent Garden* boast
> So bright a batter'd, strolling Toast[.]

Oxymoron brings *bright* and *batter'd*, *stroll* and *toast* into a composite of absurdity and pathos contrastingly descriptive of this modern nymph. For *batter'd* (as the context confirms) is a grim circumstance as well as tawdry image, and *toast* almost certainly carries, along with its more obvious meaning, the submerged scatological denotation of Dryden's "Morning Toast" in *Mac-Flecknoe*. It is, in short, in addition to being the other half of an oxymoron, a *double entendre* in itself, and so concentrates in one word the effect that also plays throughout the line—and throughout the poem—an effect of double perspective, tragic and comic, or ridiculous and pathetic.[9]

The very presence and use of parody itself has this same effect, of course, for parody works by juxtaposing disparities. This is no doubt why Swift found it so congenial to his satiric expression. It may also explain why he put it to subtler use than most parodists, for it was rarely for him a mere literary exercise, or witty allusion, but a vehicle of, and key to, the heightened realism that constitutes his peculiar satiric insight, the realism that reflects the coexistence of comic and tragic aspects in all significant human experience. That as a satirist he characteristically approaches this reality from the comic angle should not prevent us from perceiving the pathetic angle implicit in it, or actually co-present with it.

Before we turn to the poem, it will be useful to cut a fresh path through some of the terrain surrounding it. Orwell was at least right in recognizing the poem as one of Swift's "most characteristic works," though not for the reasons he advanced. The *Nymph* exhibits very nearly all the features we associate with Swift's verse satire: complete frankness, stubborn realism, irreverence for the shams of romantic convention (hence too its parodic reflex), impatience of false delicacy, and what I shall call, in keeping with my thesis, an instinctive or intuitive sense of humor (or comedy) in the pursuit of ultimately serious purpose. "Corinna, Pride of *Drury-Lane*" pictures the modern nymph, a fallen creature and a painful cry from her Olympian sisters. Swift is weary with the persistence of make-believe in the face of so much fact, and is annoyed that men continue to prate about nymphs when it is pathetically obvious that there are no such things anymore—if indeed there ever were. He is particularly irritated by the failure to discriminate between nymphs and slatterns, of whatever degree, high or low. If we must sing of nymphs, he seems to say, let us at least observe the breed more closely and cast off the fancy that makes us ready to believe any wench or hussy worthy of the epithet. If we would do that, we might indeed recover dignity to nymphdom, as we never will the way of romantic self-delusion and flattery.

But though Swift will paint her lot "As Truth will paint it, and as bards will not," he does not hate Corinna, or women. He does hate the pride and self-deceit, the lust and laziness, that permits them (and men too) to be less than they might be, if they were true to themselves and one another. He hates the shabbiness that so often lurks beneath the paltry, foolish, painted face, and the shallowness and stupidity of male judgment that is content with "being well deceived." As for himself, though he knows and loves a Stella, last week he saw a woman flayed, and you will hardly believe how much it altered her person for the worse.

The idealistic aspect of Swift's outlook has long been recognized. He is, in terms of the consideration in hand, profoundly more idealistic than the flock of nymphophiles who traffic in the ready-made idealism of romantic love. Swift's idealism is of a different and trustier mold: one that defines itself by the fact instead of the fancy. It is for that reason that it does not express itself sentimentally, but through the medium of candor. Out of the honest gaze and scornful laughter of *A Beautiful Young Nymph* emerges, not something pitiless or perverse, but something ultimately pathetic, an image of failure. Stark, to be sure, ugly and sordid, even comic (as it must be), but failure all the same. And since you cannot have failure without faith, Swift's poem is not "inhuman" at all, but very human indeed. Let us look at it again.

Like everything of Swift's, it is an intensely concentrated thing, its little over three score and ten lines falling into four concise parts: the picture of Corinna removing for the night all the false supports of her ravaged beauty (parodic of many a fine romantic disrobing); the account of her nightmarish dreams of prisons, transportation, constables, and duns (cf. Dido's dream in the *Aeneis*); the spectacle of her awakening to find her miserable props in further ruin from the accidents of a garret night (cf. Belinda's awakening); and a coda, or epilogue, declaring that all the same Corinna must "her Limbs unite" and "recollect [her] scatter'd Parts" again (a mock arming of the heroine) to fare forth once more upon the town. The odyssey of her night has been grotesquely comic, but also pitiful. Still her faring forth the morning after brings no sentimental relief, no poetic justice: the "strolling Toast" refuses to change into a Cinderella, but is still there, unwholesome as ever.

> *Corinna* in the Morning dizen'd,
> Who sees, will spew; who smells, be poison'd.[10]

A "bashful Muse," had she ventured upon such a scene, would have averted the eye at last, or taken refuge in the easement of tears. Not so Swift's, whose vision remains steady and clear: Corinna is still a drab, and always will be, along with the underworld she inhabits. Swift will not blink at that and lose his poem, or drain off its terrible impact, what he called *saeva indignatio*, what we might call *fierce sympathy*.

In examining the poem at close range I will show how, first structurally and then locally, Swift exhibits the two faces—comic and pathetic—of his subject. Except that in the final analysis he holds the two points of view in stubborn equilibrium, his poem tends to move in alternating scenes of grotesque and pathetic emphasis. It begins with a mocking tone, parodic at once of the literary and the meretricious imposture:

> Corinna, Pride of *Drury-Lane*,
> For whom no Shepherd sighs in vain.
> Never did *Covent Garden* boast
> So bright a batter'd, strolling Toast.

We have already remarked how the last verse insinuates and epitomizes the double perspective to follow. This emerges in full strength, and with arresting suddenness, in the verses immediately following, which disclose the hollowness beneath the pastoral and the forlornness beneath the harlot's facade:

> No drunken Rake to pick her up,
> No Cellar where on Tick to sup;
> Returning at the Midnight Hour;
> Four Stories climbing to her Bow'r.

Next, with a casualness indicative of the thin line that separates its two perspectives, the poem moves to a scene of unrelieved ugly detail, but which, though primarily mocking, is intermittently melancholy as well:

> Then, seated on a three-legg'd Chair,
> Takes off her artificial Hair:
> Now, picking out a Crystal Eye,
> She wipes it clean, and lays it by.
> Her Eye-Brows from a Mouse's Hyde,
> Stuck on with Art on either Side,
> Pulls off with Care, and first displays 'em,
> Then in a Play-Book smoothly lays 'em.

The last line is an especially poignant moment in the ludicrous

catalogue of the failure of beauty and dignity that goes relent-
lessly on through plumpers, dental wires, dug rags, sores, cosmetic greases, and sleeping pills. Her dismemberment
accomplished, Corinna crawls between two blankets to await a
sleep that affords no respite of the "Pains of Love" that rack her
in the interval.

The scene which follows—the dream—juxtaposes and mingles the pathetic and comic perspectives. Its first part is essentially a tonal reprieve of the scene preceding, though the
sombreness now more nearly overbalances the parody and mockery:

> Of *Bridewell* and the *Compter* [she] dreams,
> And feels the Lash, and faintly screams;
> Or, by a faithless Bully drawn,
> At some Hedge-Tavern lies in Pawn;
> Or to *Jamaica* seems transported,
> Alone, and by no Planter courted.

As the dream proceeds the comic aspect takes ascendancy and
the pathetic recedes, though it does not disappear:

> Or, near *Fleet-Ditch's* oozy Brinks,
> Surrounded with a Hundred Stinks,
> Belated, seems on watch to lye,
> And snap some Cully passing by;
> Or, struck with Fear, her Fancy runs
> On Watchmen, Constables and Duns
> From whom she meets with frequent Rubs;
> But, never from Religious Clubs;
> Whose Favour she is sure to find,
> Because she pays 'em all in Kind.

What is here, in the dream, a mixture of grimness and mockery
is now modulated to wry comedy in the next scene, the morning
after:

> Behold the ruins of the Night!
> A wicked Rat her Plaister stole,
> Half eat, and dragg'd it to his Hole.
> The Crystal Eye, alas, was miss't;

And *Puss* had on her Plumpers p—st.
A Pigeon pick'd her Issue-Peas;
And Shock [cf. Belinda!] her Tresses fill'd with Fleas.

This scene suspends, as it were, in its more playful way, the stricter comic-pathetic ebb and flow of the earlier scenes, preparatory to its resumption in the epilogue, where, however, the two moods become almost indistinguishable:

The Nymph, tho' in this mangled Plight,
Must ev'ry Morn her Limbs unite.
But how shall I describe her Arts
To recollect the scatter'd Parts?
Or shew the Anguish, Toil, and Pain,
Of gath'ring up herself again?
The bashful Muse will never bear
In such a Scene to interfere.
Corinna in the Morning dizen'd,
Who sees, will spew; who smells, be poison'd.

The foregoing has already disclosed the presence of certain local indicants of the pathetic angle of view in the poem, images, allusions, and ironies that express a rueful as well as risible point of view: Corinna's dependence on drunks and tick for bob and board; the relentless monotony of her return each night to her "Bow'r," a garret, four stories up, and of her painstaking dismemberment, as hapless as it is ridiculous; and lastly the scream-provoking dreams, threatening the lash, the jilt, and final abandonment. To which we must add the whole vocabulary of ruin and agony (ironically intensified by a "contrapuntal" vocabulary of romantic sentiment), language like *batter'd, contriv'd, flabby* (Those are dugs that were her breasts), *sad Disaster, Pains, tormented, Stinks, Fear,* and *Issue-Peas.*[11] And with this vocabulary, images and actions equally dismal: the three-legg'd Chair, the ritual of the crystal eye, the "hollow Jaws" and "Shankers, Issues, running Sores"; the *Bolus* indispensable to sleep (that will not here knit up the ravel'd sleeve of care); the blankets she creeps between; and the shambles made by rat, cat, and dog of her plaster, plumpers, and wig.

Such effects as these become especially keen in what I have

called the epilogue, where one should not overlook the pathetic force of such expressions as *mangled*, or *Anguish, Toil*, and *Pain*; or of such observations as "Must *ev'ry* Morn her Limbs unite"; the ambivalence of the word *recollect* (". . . recollect the scatter'd Parts"), where the idea of *remember* haunts the more obvious meaning of *reassemble*; or, finally, the two ways of reading the penultimate couplet (about the "bashful Muse").

But there is that final couplet that won't go away, that triumphant couplet which has apparently broken, though it makes, the poem:

> *Corinna* in the Morning dizen'd,
> Who sees, will spew; who smells, be poison'd.

It is this which has proved so far the point of no return for the common and uncommon reader alike, Swift's refusal to relent at last. But that refusal is the penalty of hard fact, not of hard heart, and is the unimpeachable token of Swift's worthiness of the Muse. Swift cannot alter the facts of Corinna's life; he can only (at least he will only) show them and let them witness whatever the pity of it is, the pity she's a whore. Nor in doing so does he make fun of the "wretched" creature: her way of life makes fun of itself, and that is part of its pity. Corinna is, as I have said, a parody of herself. And Swift will not repress that fact— the absurdity in this miserable spectacle—anymore than he will repress the ugliness and dreariness that complete its definition. He will instead exert his talent and his art to bring them both forth, the comic as well as the pathetic edge of truth, and in so doing create a remarkable testament of the power of shaped reality to plead its own case and excite its own due measure of sympathy.

A Beautiful Young Nymph is not a pretty poem; it is, as all have protested, an ugly one. But its ugliness touches while it offends, touches because it offends, because it offended Swift in the first place, who was poet enough to take the measure of the offence and secure it, in all its complexity, in his satire—a stern, harsh and mocking performance; but, as I hope I have also shown, profoundly understanding, eloquent, and solemn in the best sense of the word. It is eminently Swiftian, and it is very nearly a great poem.

Notes

1. "A Beautiful Young Nymph Going to Bed. Written for the Honour of the Fair Sex," published, with "Strephon and Chloe" and "Cassinus and Peter," in 1734; composed perhaps as early as 1731. See *The Poems of Jonathan Swift*, ed. Harold Williams (Oxford, 1958), II, 581. All quotations from the poem are from this edition.

2. Irvin Ehrenpreis, *The Personality of Jonathan Swift* (London, 1958), p. 33.

3. George Orwell, "Politics vs. Literature: An Examination of Gulliver's Travels," in *Shooting an Elephant* (London, 1950), p. 81.

4. Middleton Murry, *Jonathan Swift* (London, 1954), p. 439.

5. Joseph Horrell (*Collected Poems of Jonathan Swift*, Harvard, 1958) and Herbert Davis (*Jonathan Swift: Essays on His Satire and Other Studies*, New York, 1964) have also contributed to a better understanding of Swift's satiric poetry. Horrell may be the best judge of it to date.

6. Maurice Johnson, *The Sin of Wit* (Syracuse, 1950), p. 115.

7. Ehrenpreis, pp. 43–48.

8. Ibid., pp. 39–41. Ehrenpreis's *courtesan* is a token of his failure to comprehend the poem. Corinna is no *courtesan*, but a common whore. Her affairs are not so "fortunate" as a court, but are confined to the brutality of rakes and bullies.

9. I use the term *pathetic* throughout this paper in the Aristotelian sense, as signifying *pain* or *suffering*, and as tragic, not sentimental, in significance.

10. In quoting Swift, I alter last-line punctuation where convenient.

11. These words, like those of the pastoral vocabulary, function comically and pathetically at once. As I have said, ultimately Swift carries both views together.

DONALD GREENE

On Swift's "Scatological" Poems

> Any reader of Jonathan Swift knows that in his anal-
> ysis of human nature there is an emphasis on, and
> attitude toward, the anal function that is unique in
> Western literature. . . . The most scandalous pieces
> of Swiftian scatology are three of his later poems—
> *The Lady's Dressing Room, Strephon and Chloe, Cassinus
> and Peter*—which are all variations on the theme, 'Oh!
> Cælia, Cælia, Cælia—.'

So Norman O. Brown in his *Life against Death* (1959) begins the
latest comprehensive discussion of what he and others have
termed Swift's "excremental vision." Brown traces the history of
this reading of Swift back through Middleton Murry and others
to Aldous Huxley's essay of 1929—to Huxley belongs "the credit
for recognizing the central importance of the excremental theme
in Swift." Although praising Huxley and Murry for dealing with
the "theme" as fully as they have, and rebuking more academic
critics like Ricardo Quintana for neglecting it, Brown feels that
even Huxley and Murry have not given it the weight it deserves.
They are shocked by it and regard it as the product of Swift's
perverse idiosyncrasy: instead, they should have applauded
Swift's astuteness in discerning its paramount importance in any

This essay first appeared in the *Sewanee Review* 75 (1967): 672–89, © 1967 by
the University of the South. It is reprinted by permission of the author and of
the *Sewanee Review*'s editor.

sound analysis of the human condition. In this, Swift anticipated the great twentieth-century authority on human nature:

> The peculiar Swiftian twist to the theme that Cælia — is the notion that there is some absolute contradiction between the state of being in love and an awareness of the excremental function of the beloved. Before we dismiss this idea as the fantasy of a diseased mind, we had better remember that Freud said the same thing. In an essay written in 1912 surveying the disorder in the sexual life of man, he finally concludes that the deepest trouble is an unresolved ambivalence in the human attitude toward anality. . . .

and Brown quotes two longish passages from Freud which comment somberly on the deplorable but inescapable fact that we are born "*inter urinas et faeces.*"

Brown uses the "scatological" poems as his point of departure for a study of the "excremental vision" in Swift's works generally, going on to a consideration of *Gulliver's Travels, A Tale of a Tub,* and *The Mechanical Operation of the Spirit* in that light. There is not space in a short paper to deal with this larger question, but it may be useful to look again at the three poems, since they seem to have provided the initial impulse for this way of viewing Swift. Brown sees them as exhibiting a progression in Swift's treatment of the subject (though in fact their relative dating is impossible to determine). At first, in "The Lady's Dressing Room," Swift manages to cope with the "ultimate horror" of the facts by advising Strephon that "sublimation is still possible"— "Should I the Queen of Love refuse,/Because she rose from stinking Ooze?"—and that "Strephon should reconcile himself to 'Such Order from Confusion sprung,/Such gaudy Tulips rais'd from Dung.'"

> But in *Strephon and Chloe* (1731) sublimation and awareness of the excremental function are presented as mutually exclusive, and the conclusion is drawn that sublimation must be cultivated at all costs, even at the cost of repression. . . . In *Cassinus and Peter,* the last of these poems, even this solution is exploded because the

excremental vision cannot be repressed. . . . Cassinus explains the trauma which is killing him: 'Nor wonder how I lost my Wits;/Oh! *Cælia, Cælia, Cælia sh——.'*

"Any reader of Jonathan Swift knows. . . ." Brown's complacent opening may awaken in the cautious student some uneasiness about the foundations of this imposing structure of interpretation, erected on Huxley's "insight" of 1929, and a feeling that we ought to be quite certain of just what it is that we "know" about these three "scandalous" pieces of Swiftian "scatology." Perhaps it is time that we actually turned to them and read them through.

Since it is in "Cassinus and Peter" that Brown finds Swift's final realization of the "ultimate horror . . . at the thought that sublimation—that is to say, all civilized behavior—is a lie and cannot survive confrontation with the truth," we may as well begin by looking at it, and learn the worst. It is a story about "Two College Sophs of *Cambridge* Growth,/Both special Wits, and Lovers both." That is, they are not merely ordinary representatives of "civilized behavior": they are something "special," and acutely conscious of the fact; members of the undergraduate intelligentsia, the enlightened minority. They read and write poetry—or at least talk a great deal about it, "Conferring as they us'd to meet,/On Love and Books in Rapture sweet." They are experts on these two matters: they pride themselves on the fineness of their sensibilities in both literary and emotional criticism. They are still with us, on the campuses of not only the older but the newer Cambridge, probably wearing beards and quoting their *clichés* from Eliot—and Freud—instead of Ovid, and continuing to have sexual difficulties like Cassinus's, and for the same reason.

One morning Peter pays a call on Cassinus in his college room. Swift, not without significance, begins by giving us a detailed picture of the scene, whose realism anyone familiar with the squalor of male dormitory life will appreciate:

> One greasy Stocking round his Head,
> The t'other he sat down to darn
> With Threads of diff'rent colour'd Yarn.
> His Breeches torn exposing wide

A ragged Shirt, and tawny Hyde.
Scorcht were his Shins, his Legs were bare,
But, well Embrown'd with Dirt and Hair.
A Rug was o'er his Shoulders thrown;
A Rug; for Night-gown he had none.
His Jordan stood in Manner fitting
Between his Legs, to spew or spit in.
His antient Pipe in Sable dy'd,
And half unsmoakt, lay by his Side.

Let us keep the stink of Cassinus's foul pipe and jordan in mind as we read on.

Peter finds Cassinus suffering from "Spleen" ("the Hypps," "the Dumps"); as we should say, "in a state of severe depression." He greets him in their accustomed poetic idiom:

What makes thee lie a-bed so late?
The Finch, the Linnet and the Thrush,
Their Mattins chant in ev'ry Bush:
And, I have heard thee oft salute
Aurora with thy early Flute.

The boys are also "pre-Romantics," it seems. But there are to be no linnet songs for Cassinus this morning. He groans "Cælia!" thrice, and sighs the rest. Peter asks in alarm, "Is Cælia dead?" "How happy I, were that the worst!" "Has she played the whore? Has she contracted the small or greater pox? Has she had an affair with the barber's boy?" The order of these disasters is significant, ascending from the least evil—in the eyes of Peter and Cassinus—Cælia's death, to the greatest, the mortifying betrayal of Cassinus with someone as low in the social scale as the barber's boy. "Oh, no—it is a crime that shocks all human kind: a deed unknown to female race, at which the sun should hide his face." Cassinus's imminent death from psychological trauma gives him an opportunity for much fine rhetoric from his poetry books—

And on the Marble grave these Rhimes,
A Monument to after-Times:
"Here *Cassy* lies, by *Cælia* slain,
And dying, never told his Pain."

> Vain empty World farewel. But hark,
> The loud *Cerberian* triple Bark—

and so on, with Alecto, Charon, Medusa, and the rest. At last, after much pleading by Peter, and swearings to secrecy by Cassinus, the "ultimate horror" of "*Cælia*'s foul Disgrace" is revealed: "Nor wonder how I lost my Wits;/Oh, *Cælia, Cælia Cælia* sh——." So concludes the "Tragical Elegy," as Swift subtitles it.

Brown comments, unkindly but justly enough, that Middleton Murry "like Strephon and the other unfortunate men in the poems, loses his wits when he discovers that Cælia——." But is Brown himself immune? Surely it will take more than solemn citations from "Karpman (1942): 'It is submitted . . . that Swift was a neurotic who exhibited psychosexual infantilism, with a particular showing of coprophilia, associated with misogyny, misanthropy, mysophilia, and mysophobia'" to keep the literate reader from seeing that the poem is a devastating satirical *attack* on those who, like Cassinus, place a high estimate on the importance of "the anal function" and find the "ultimate horror" of the human situation ("Vain empty World farewel"!) in the fact that women as well as men excrete. And Swift makes the source of Cassinus's neurosis (*not* Swift's!) perfectly clear. Obviously Cassinus has nothing against excretion and stinks in themselves—witness his jordan and smelly pipe and unbathed skin. But while one side of his divided mind is perfectly content with fetor and squalor, the other entertains an inflated "image" of himself, drawn from his readings in romantic poetry, which nothing less than a completely ethereal Cælia will suffice. It is this preposterous arrogance, the blind enslavement to an ego-bolstering illusion—products of the human sin of pride—that Swift, a perfectly orthodox Christian moralist, discerns and condemns here as in so many other places.

In "The Lady's Dressing Room," we find another romantic young man, Strephon, "in love" with the glamorous Cælia—at least, with her "image": and we may suspect, as with Cassinus, that it is the prestige that accrues to Strephon's own "image" from the association that is the attraction. At any rate, one evening after she has finished putting on her glamor, he takes an "Inventory" of her dressing room and finds what might be expected. What is important is Swift's commentary on all this:

> But Vengeance, Goddess never sleeping
> Soon punish'd *Strephon* for his Peeping;
> His foul Imagination links
> Each Dame he sees with all her Stinks:
> And, if unsav'ry Odours fly,
> Conceives a Lady standing by:
> All Women his Description fits,
> And both Idea's jump like wits:
> By vicious Fancy coupled fast,
> And still appearing in Contrast.

Swift's point is perfectly clear: Strephon (who, like Cassinus, presumably goes on producing his own share of the world's stinks) is the victim of his "foul Imagination" and "vicious Fancy," which in the first place demanded for his inflated ego a superhuman partner, then deluded itself that in Cælia he had obtained the paragon he felt himself entitled to, and now, when his fantasy world collapses, makes him see in every woman *only* her excretory functions. (Something like this happens to Gulliver too, when *his* fantasy about the excellence of the race he represents is punctured.) *This* is madness; this is obsession; this is "the excremental vision," which makes a fetish of the routine, trivial, and harmless fact of human excretion; and this is what the poem pillories.

How odd that Huxley and the rest attribute the "foul Imagination" and "vicious Fancy" to the writer who is engaged in vigorously satirizing them! But of course it is one of the oldest and most persistent critical fallacies to ascribe to a writer sentiments which he puts into the mouth of a character in order to condemn them—the fallacy which made Bernard Shaw deplore Shakespeare's "fatalism," because Shakespeare gives a "fatalistic" speech ("Tomorrow and tomorrow and tomorrow") even to so unsympathetic a character as Macbeth; and in turn, made good Victorian souls condemn Shaw as immoral because his Mrs. Warren ran a house of prostitution, even though Shaw emphatically indicates that he is not writing the play in order to advocate the operation of houses of prostitution.

The point Shaw is trying to make, of course, is that the mere physical fact of prostitution is not so important as the economic, social, and psychological evils associated with it, and that these will not be rectified by pursuing a hush-hush policy about it. But his censors, irrationally obsessed with the idea that the physical fact of prostitution is the "ultimate horror," do not understand that there can be any other way of looking at it, or any other set of values than their own; and so the play is banned, and Shaw condemned as a dirty old man who revels in bringing prostitutes on the stage. Is not Swift's a parallel case? Perhaps Swift "revels" in presenting images of excretion to try to convince us that it is *not* in itself a particularly important matter—certainly not so important as the psychological damage to Strephon and Cælia of a relationship that consists only of pretence and illusion. But Huxley and the rest (strongly reinforced in their attitude by the teachings of Freud) cannot conceive of anyone adopting so un-heard-of a position as to *discount* the importance of *"urinas et faeces,"* and they notice nothing in the poem but Swift's appalling "excremental vision." (Brown, to be sure, finds it an admirable vision, but this is like praising Shaw for his frank recognition of the immutable necessity of prostitution.)

Like Shaw, Swift *tries* to make his point of view clear. "I *pity* wretched Strephon," he continues, "blind/To all the Charms of Female Kind;/Should I the Queen of Love refuse,/Because she rose from stinking Ooze?" Had Joyce written this—as, in effect, he did when he concluded Molly Bloom's magnificent soliloquy, punctuated by the use of the chamber pot, with a resounding "yes"—we should be told of Joyce's great paean of affirmation and acceptance of life. (Interestingly, there was a time when the main critical "fact" about Joyce was that he too had an excre-mental and sexual obsession; but intelligent criticism disposed of that long ago.) How these perfectly plain statements by Swift can be read in any other sense is hard to see. To be sure, Swift then resumes a mildly ironic tone:

> To him that looks behind the Scene,
> *Statira's* but some pocky Quean.
> When *Cælia* in her Glory shows,
> If *Strephon* would but stop his Nose . . .
> He soon would learn to think like me. . . .

225

Brown contends that what Swift is arguing here is that "subli-mation is still possible." Is Swift really laying it down as a general principle of morality, "Let us be careful never to look behind the scene, never to stop holding our noses"? In view of the straight-forward advocacy of accepting things as they are that precedes and follows this passage, I cannot think so. He is merely poking fun at the Strephons and Cassinuses: if their excessive "sensibil-ity," or rather egotism, will be satisfied with nothing less than a flawless Statira or an odorless Cælia, then let them stop their noses; only temporarily, one hopes, until they acquire more sense.

In the following lines, Brown says that Swift is advising Stre-phon to "reconcile himself to"

> Such Order from Confusion sprung,
> Such gaudy Tulips rais'd from Dung.

("Gaudy," again, is mild satire at the expense of Cælia, who has to deck herself out so ornately to satisfy the expectations of a Strephon.) But Brown, in his anxiety to establish Swift's Freud-ianism, omits the line which precedes this couplet. The whole concluding passage of the poem actually reads:

> He soon would learn to think like me,
> And *bless his ravisht Sight to see*
> Such Order from Confusion sprung,
> Such gaudy Tulips rais'd from Dung.

There is a tremendous difference between "blessing one's rav-ished sight to see" such beauty as there is in the world, and merely "reconciling oneself to it": it is the difference between Swift's Christianity and Freud's Stoicism. If one wanted to be theological about it, one might argue that Swift, as a serious and instructed Christian, knows very well that the creation of order out of chaos, the prime work of God Himself, is a proper object for blessing, and for nothing less than blessing; so is the raising of beauty—of spirit, if not of dress—through God's love and grace, out of the dung of man's soul sunk in original sin (which is the sin of pride). Or if one wanted to be "archetypal," one could praise Swift's awareness—in the parallel illustration of Ve-nus, symbol of human love and warmth and the continuity of the human species, rising from the Mediterranean slime—of the great eternal facts of the human condition. In these passages, Swift indeed sounds more like a robust Irish Molly Bloom in clerical garb than the hyperromantic male spinster with the agonizing neurosis that Huxley sees. And when one thinks of the self-conscious, fine-drawn, over-civilized Aldous Huxley, the end product of late nineteenth-century romanticism, always titillatingly attracted to the "savage" and always, in the end, shrinking back from it, one realizes with a start that what Huxley has managed to find in Swift is only Huxley himself.

"Strephon and Chloe" is a more forceful elaboration of "The Lady's Dressing Room," again describing first an irrational state of illusion, and then the equally irrational state of despair when the illusion collapses. As with "Cassinus and Peter," its important opening section is generally neglected. Swift devotes the first quarter of the poem to telling us in detail about the engagement and marriage of Chloe, of whom (so the poem begins) "all the Town has rung;/By ev'ry size of Poets sung." That is, she has acquired a marvelous "public image," which brings the desired results: "Think what a Case all Men are now in,/What ogling, sighing, toasting, vowing!" With such a build-up, the product proves eminently marketable—it is natural to drop into Madison Avenue terminology; indeed, Swift points out that Chloe is "spoiling the Trade" of Venus herself. Of the many bids for this desirable offering, Strephon's is the highest: "He blew a Settlement along:/And, bravely drove his Rivals down/With Coach and Six, and House in Town./The bashful Nymph no more withstands,/Because her dear Papa commands." The wedding is described with all the lush paraphernalia of pagan mythology or, perhaps more precisely, the *clichés* of Grub Street, the Madison Avenue of the time: Apollo, Mercury "with Silver Tongue" (the patron of advertising men), Hebe, Juno, and the rest are in attendance. Perhaps Swift is making the point that it is emphatically not a Christian marriage, for all that the setting seems to be eighteenth-century "Christian" London.

The most notable gimmick in constructing the public Chloe, "so nice, and so genteel," has been to stress her physical ethereality. She is guaranteed ninety-nine and forty-four one-hundredths per cent pure: "Such Cleanliness from Head to Heel:/

No Humours gross, or frowzy Steams;/. . . You'd swear, that so divine a Creature/Felt no Necessities of Nature." (Indeed, modern Chloes, at the instigation of Madison Avenue, spend many millions of dollars a year on preparations designed to perpetuate this same image.) The campaign has been so successful that Strephon himself, as he crawls into the marriage-bed, is overawed by what he has acquired, like the modern purchaser of a much-touted luxury automobile when he takes delivery; scrubbing himself solemnly, he wonders if he will be able to live up to his new status-symbol. Then comes the debacle: Chloe turns out not to be as advertised—she has an excretory system after all (you *can* hear the sound of the engine above the ticking of the dashboard clock!). The couple's world crashes about their ears, and they fall into unrelieved despair and defeatism, living in utter squalor, excreting as publicly as animals (since the steering wheel turns out to be not solid gold but only plated, there is nothing for it but to use the vehicle as a garbage truck).

What readers like Huxley have seized on as the significant part of the poem—the evidence of Swift's "excremental vision"— is the elaborate description of excretion in the second section of it. Actually, if one has carefully read the first section, the glowing, rapturous account of Chloe's sanitary charms, the starry-eyed enchantment of the young men-about-town, the too too delightful wedding, the second section provides a curiously satisfying aesthetic balance. It is a relief; it is at least honest, like a rowdy hockey game following an interminable syrupy television commercial. It is *less* nauseating than the earlier section. Should we not (Swift might ask) be far more scandalized at the details in the first part of the poem, at the perversion of marriage into the business of advertising and marketing an image? Is not that the truly shocking part of the work? That, and the devastating effect that involvement in such systematized pretence has on the psychology and future happiness of those who, like Strephon and Chloe, are brought up knowing nothing else? As with Cassinus and the other Strephon (and Gulliver, for a time at least) the consequence of living in a falsely prettified world is retreat, when truth breaks in, into despair and an equally false, blackened picture of it. Is not a description of the physiology of human excretion a trivial matter by comparison with the anatomy of such vicious self-deception and negation of life?

Swift's commentary on these events is long and complex, running to almost a hundred lines at the end of the poem; but his strategy in it, I think, is similar to that employed in the commentary at the end of "The Lady's Dressing Room": part of it is ironic "good practical advice" addressed to those in the grip of the illusion or perverted value that Swift is attacking, and part of it is straightforward statement of his own views. Here, the commentary divides fairly neatly into two sections, the first of which (lines 219–292) consists mostly of good advice, essentially ironic, about "decency." It begins with an address to "Fair *Decency*, celestial Maid,/Descend from Heav'n to Beauty's Aid"— the mock pomposity of this invocation hardly encourages us to take very seriously what Swift is going to say to Decency—

> Though Beauty may beget Desire,
> 'Tis thou must fan the Lover's Fire;
> For, Beauty, like supreme Dominion,
> Is best supported by Opinion;
> If Decency brings no Supplies,
> Opinion falls, and Beauty dies.

Is all this *Swift's* definition of the necessary terms of marriage— that it is to be based on "desire," which in turn is based on "beauty," which is completely contingent on "opinion" (Chloe is beautiful to Strephon only because everyone else in his circle says that she is desirable), and therefore the function of "decency" is to support "opinion" (the "image") and so preserve "beauty" and hence "desire"? Surely not. It is the philosophy of the advertising man (whose job is to create and maintain the "desirability" of a product), and of Strephon and Chloe—and, alas, it would seem of some Freudians as well. What Swift thinks of it is revealed by the advice he goes on to give: beware of being taken in by the advertising man's picture of the "radiant Nymph" as "some Goddess from the Sky/Descended, ready cut and dry"; for "fine Ideas vanish fast,/While all the gross and filthy last," as indeed happened to Strephon (but surely Swift's *real* advice to us in the poem is not to let our minds work at all in the way

Strephon's works!). Check the product carefully against the advertiser's claims for it (take the car out for a road test, without the salesman). What Strephon should have done was to begin by viewing Chloe "on her House of Ease": then he would forever have been immune to the salesman's wiles: had he done so, his "Heart had been as whole as mine." Strephon then would never have married a Chloe; and, given Strephon's conception of marriage, that would have been a good thing for everyone.

All this is complexly ironic. Certainly Swift (the serious Swift) is not opposed to "decency" and "prudence" and "practicality" and the rest of such virtues. But here he commends them to the Strephons and Chloes of the world in the only terms they can understand: since they are entirely governed by "ideas"—"images"—either "fine ones" or "foul ones," then let them take care to conceal the "foul ones," as indeed "authorities both old and recent" direct. The authorities Swift refers to are no doubt those disseminators of worldly wisdom represented in our day by syndicated female newspaper columnists and writers of manuals of good advice to teen-agers about how to "get a man" and "keep him." Swift goes on in the vein of such a counselor for a time, but the irony is transparent—

> Unjustly all our Nymphs complain . . .
> For, if they keep not what they caught,
> It is entirely their own Fault.

If marriage is conceived of, as Strephon and Chloe conceive of it, merely as the business of "catching" a desirable spouse (made desirable by "opinion") and then "keeping" him, of course a great deal of effort spent on concealment is necessary. But "decency" in the service of such an enterprise does not seem a very attractive virtue. And even in the midst of this, the ironic mask drops for a moment while Swift pillories some of the ways in which the fashionable woman catches her man—

> Some try to learn polite Behaviour,
> By reading Books against their Saviour;
> Some call it witty to reflect
> On ev'ry natural Defect. . . .

In the last twenty-two lines of the poem, however, Swift

abandons the pose of the "prudent counselor," advising his hearers to employ concealment or "repression" in order to preserve a marriage whose terms are those of catching and keeping, and gives a serious and straightforward sermon such as he might give to a young couple asking him to marry them. Swift was, after all, a Christian priest, who presumably solemnized for his parishioners the rite of Holy Matrimony according to the Anglican order, in which no doctrine of "sublimation" or "repression" is to be found. Swift's advice is no longer "Save the surface and you save everything," but is concerned with what is beneath the surface: this is the true prudence—

> A prudent Builder should forecast
> How long the Stuff is like to last. . . .
> Rash Mortals, e'er you take a Wife,
> Contrive your Pile to last for Life;
> Since Beauty scarce endures a Day,
> And Youth so swiftly glides away;
> Why will you make yourself a Bubble
> To build on Sand with Hay and Stubble?
> On Sense and Wit your Passion found—

not on "desire" and "beauty" and their master, "opinion"—

> By Decency cemented round;
> Let Prudence with Good Nature strive,
> To keep Esteem and Love alive.
> Then come old Age whene'er it will,
> Your Friendship shall continue still:
> And thus a mutual gentle Fire,
> Shall never but with Life expire.

Again, this seems perfectly straightforward: it is the traditional Christian conception of marriage (and that of some modern marriage counselors and post-Freudian psychologists as well), in which there is no place and no need for "sublimation" and "repression." To be sure, the repetition of the word "decency" from the earlier section may be misleading. But here it has very different overtones from its earlier use in the mouth of the ironic advocate of "concealment." There it signified the use of mechanical gimmicks ("Never let your husband see you without your make-up on"); here it is something that springs from within. For that matter, "wit" and "love" have very different meanings here from what they have in other places in Swift— "Some call it witty to reflect/On ev'ry natural Defect"; Cassinus and Peter are "special Wits, and Lovers both." It is not such "wit" and such "love" that Swift recommends that marriage be founded on. "The peculiar Swiftian twist to the theme that Cælia ————," says Brown, "is the notion that there is some absolute contradiction between the state of being in love and an awareness of the excremental function of the beloved." Undoubtedly there is such a contradiction in the "state of being in love" as Cassinus and Strephon conceive it. But Swift holds no brief for this "state," which is something very different from the serious and mature love he is speaking of in the concluding part of the poem. The romantic or the Freudian may smile at the naïveté of Swift's view of love (which is also the view of the Gospels) as something that transcends the merely material, the physical, the self-regarding. But that is not our concern. Our concern, as literary students, is to point out that, on the basis of a reading of the plain sense of these three poems, Swift's concept of the relationship between men and women is that neither of a romantic nor of a Freudian, nor, above all, of a neurotic, but simply the view of an orthodox Christian moralist.

Yet it may seem to some readers, committed to neither the romantic nor the Freudian position, a remarkably sane, healthy, and profound view. Far from being, as Brown says, "variations on the theme 'Oh, Cælia, Cælia, Cælia ————'," the three poems are rather variations on the theme "Who, except neurotic egotists like Strephon and Cassinus, *cares* whether Cælia————?" To mature and genuine love between adults, such matters seem quite irrelevant; and that Swift was fully aware of what genuine love is (and was no misogynist) is clear when one reads his last birthday poem to Stella (he sixty, she forty-six), one of the most tender and genuinely convincing love poems ever written:

> This Day, whate'er the Fates decree,
> Shall still be kept with Joy by me:
> This Day then, let us not be told,
> That you are sick, and I grown old. . . .

Take Pity on your pitying Friends;
Nor let your Ills affect your Mind,
To fancy they can be unkind.
Me, surely me, you ought to spare
Who gladly would your Suff'rings share
Or give my Scrap of Life to you,
And think it far beneath your Due. . . .

To Swift, Freud's and Brown's agonies because "Love has
pitched his mansion in/The place of excrement" would have
seemed as pointless as they came to seem to Yeats: Crazy Jane's
retort to the Bishop, "Fair and foul are near of kin," is closer to
Swift, and to the Christian view of the matter, than the Freud-
Huxley-Brown approach. "Should I the Queen of Love refuse,/
Because she rose from stinking Ooze?" Rather, we should bless
our ravished sight to see "such Order from Confusion sprung."
Swift would have smiled sardonically at the scene in *Lady Chat-
terley's Lover* where Mellors declares passionately to Constance,
"I'm *glad* you piss and shit," and would have felt that Lawrence's
emphasis in the other direction was equally irrelevant to the basic
question; but he would perhaps not have been wholly unsympathetic to it as a corrective to Huxley's view. If Swift makes
much frank mention of the human excremental function, it is in
order to discount its importance and satirize those who think it
is important, in the hope that those obsessed by its importance
may come to revise their values; if, in *Gulliver's Travels*, he points
out that the most admired female breast, when examined closely,
displays repulsive blemishes, it is to try to persuade us that human love ought to rest on something deeper and more permanent than temporarily fashionable Hollywoodish "opinion" about
the "desirability" of the female mammary glands.

We are animals, we are Yahoos, and have been ever since
the Fall; the wonderful thing is that through God's grace and
the use of our God-given reason we can nevertheless become
capable of love. Almost without exception, modern critics ignore
the *real* ending of *Gulliver's Travels*. This does not take place when
Gulliver, arriving home, realizes that he is irretrievably a Yahoo,
and falls into hysterical despair. Although this "breakthrough of
truth," as Brown puts it, is traumatic, yet if one has been living

in a fantasy world of ego-bolstering self-deception, it must be experienced and lived through: "Ye shall know the truth," painful as it may at first be to those who have lived in illusion, but in the end "the truth shall make you free." Five years after Gulliver's homecoming, his concern, he tells us, is "to apply those excellent lessons of virtue which I learned among the Houyhnhnms, to instruct the Yahoos of my own family as far as I shall find them docible animals, to behold my figure often in a glass"—to remind himself that he is a Yahoo. This is the old Christian program: soberly to recognize and accept the fact of one's sinful and imperfect nature, yet at the same time to strive to transcend it (for, by love and rationality, it is possible to do so), and to teach others to do the same. Perhaps Cassinus in time will learn to behold his "tawny Hyde" and legs "well Embrown'd with Dirt and Hair" in a glass, and come to tolerate a Cælia who sh——; perhaps even, in the end, to bless his ravished sight to see such order from confusion sprung. "You shall love your crooked neighbor/With your crooked heart": a great deal of the writing of the Very Reverend Jonathan Swift boils down to this paraphrase by a modern poet of the Great Commandment; and perhaps Swift's advice in these poems to the Strephons and Cassinuses of the world is adequately summed up in some other lines by the same poet:

> Thou shalt not be on friendly terms
> With guys in advertising firms . . .
> Nor, above all, make love to those
>   Who wash too much.

CHRISTINE REES

Gay, Swift, and the
Nymphs of Drury-Lane

'True Poets' wrote Swift in one of his admirable, casually analytic
poems to Stella, 'can depress and raise;/Are Lords of Infamy
and Praise'.[1] For Augustan poets like himself and Gay, it is not
an inflated claim: nor indeed would it have seemed so to earlier
generations of poets apropos the subject of woman, which Swift
has just been considering. But after implying that poetry begins
with an act of judgment, he outlines the manner of its execution,
by which the poet himself is judged:

> They are not scurrilous in Satire,
> Nor will in Panygyrick flatter.
> Unjustly Poets we asperse;
> Truth shines the brighter, clad in Verse;
> And all the Fictions they pursue
> Do but insinuate what is true.
>
> (55–60)

Coming from Swift in particular, that final couplet arrests our
attention. In practice, surely Swift's use of lyric conventions—his
'fictions'—diverges sharply from what he suggests here? If his
fictions insinuate truth, it is not through expressing the truth of
the imagination, but because he destroys their credibility and

---

This essay first appeared in *Essays in Criticism* 23 (1973): 1–21. Reprinted with
permission.

concedes nothing to suspended disbelief—at least according to the critical view of his verse as in some sense anti-poetic.[2] So these lines defining 'True Poets' are either ironic, or present a deliberate serious contrast. If we extend the definition to John Gay, we may feel that he eludes it for another reason: his charm of manner insinuates the fiction rather than the truth. But however unlike Swift in this respect, Gay often chooses similar subjects and bases his treatment on broadly similar assumptions. Instead of setting up tensions within an image, both poets concentrate on the tension existing between literary image and literal fact, which results in an interesting and complex relation of truth and fiction in their work. I want to examine one particular fiction used by Gay and Swift, since it allows us to appreciate their distinctive characteristics on common ground, and to measure their verse against Swift's theoretic standard. The fiction in question is that of the 'nymph' whose beauty is satirically defined by the conflicting principles of art and nature. Traditionally, this conflict links the fiction to moral judgment; it commonly occurs in poems where infamy is disguised as praise.

The literary antecedents for the nymphs of early eighteenth-century poetry are extensive, and more than one tradition is involved. It would be superfluous to trace in detail one prominent line of descent, that of conventionally grotesque satire directed against female use of cosmetic arts, since several scholars have already fully established this line.[3] But one general point is worth noting: although, in its narrowest form, this type of satire throws up remarkably similar versions in different periods (for instance, Turberville's sixteenth-century lyric 'To An Olde Gentlewoman, That Painted Hir Face' meets an eighteenth-century reflection in Thomas Parnell's 'Elegy, to an Old Beauty'), yet when writers interpret it in depth they almost inevitably combine the simple motif with the larger literary themes which dominate a given period. And so the woman who paints to allure men and defy age becomes an imaginative focal point for contemporary attitudes to sexuality and death. To prove the point, we have only to remember the anti-cosmetic satire in Jacobean drama, where it manifests the all-pervading theme of human mortality (Tourneur, for example, in *The Revenger's Tragedy* imagines 'false forms' as bone-deep so that not only paint but flesh itself is an obscene and delusive mask). Normally, however, paint is the emblem of art, flesh the emblem of natural beauty; and this kind of distinction crosses over from satire to pastoral.

As her name suggests, the nymph is also entitled to a pastoral pedigree, a literary line of descent even more important than the one derived from pure satire. For whereas the cosmetic motif represents one specific variation on the nature/art antithesis, the fundamental relation between nature and art is one of the most serious moral and philosophical issues that pastoral is designed to express. Indeed E. W. Tayler describes the pastoral genre as the analogue in literature of the debate in philosophy.[4] Also, although the most obvious relation between nature and art in pastoral is the antithetical one, several of the poets writing in this essentially sophisticated genre are drawn further to explore the range and complications, the possible harmonies as well as conflicts, which the dual concept involves. In spite of this, it remains true that where woman is concerned the theme is too easily and too often coarsened into cliché. When the nymph migrates to the town, uniting, so to speak, with her satiric image, she then creates a new image with paint and mannerisms instead of being content that the poet should do it for her with words. In pastoral language, she becomes seductive and evil, the profane counterpart of the innocent country nymph: they personify art and nature as morally antagonistic principles. The street ballads (an influence on both Gay's and Swift's verse) popularize this simple formula, and a ballad such as 'The Innocent Country-Maid's Delight' adds the toilette motif for good measure: the London lasses paint and powder themselves for their lovers—

> But every morning,
> Before their adorning.
> They're far unfit for Sale;
> *But 'tis not so, with we that go,*
> *Through frost and snow, when winds do blow,*
> *To carry the milking-payl.*
> (*The Common Muse*, ed. V. de S. Pinto
> and A. E. Rodway, 1965, p. 200)

Predictably, in poetry of more pretensions, the theme connects with primitivist ideals of paradise or a golden age, also deep-

rooted in pastoral and satire (the *locus classicus* in the latter case
being Juvenal's *Satire* VI). With varying skill, minor eighteenth-
century poets lament the decline from pure womanhood which
the nymph represents. Anne Finch, Countess of Winchilsea, fur-
nishes a curiosity in this line, entitled 'Adam Posed':

> Could our first father, at his toilsome plough,
> Thorns in his path and labour on his brow,
> Cloth'd only in a rude, unpolish'd skin,
> Could he a vain fantastic nymph have seen,
> In all her airs, in all her antic graces,
> Her various fashions, and more various faces,
> How had it pos'd that skill, which late assign'd
> Just appellations to each several kind,
> A right idea of the sight to frame!
> T' have guessed from what new element she came,
> To have hit the wav'ring form, or giv'n this thing a
> name![5]

If she weakens the poem's logic by an evidently post-lapsarian
Adam, she strengthens its pastoralism by the contrast between
rustic labourer and frivolous city nymph. Matthew Green's later
version of the topic lacks this slight eccentricity: he compares the
Creator's original intention with the modern female corrupted
by social arts, and declares unequivocally

> Rather than by your culture spoiled,
> Desist, and give us nature wild.
> (*The Spleen*, 248–49)

In spite of the official policy of disapproval however, it is
clear (especially from the better poetry on the subject) that it is
the sophisticated nymph and not her country sister who is by far
the more interesting. While the country maid remains a simple
figure in more senses than one, the city nymph can be meta-
morphosed into different forms depending upon her specific
environment: she may haunt the streets, the theatre, or a fashionable masquerade. As her roles overlap, her image becomes
more complicated: 'drabs of quality' and 'nymphs of Drury-Lane'
are sisters under the (painted) skin, and a writer may treat them
with a deliberately histrionic touch, highlighting costume, façade,

the sense of posturing unreality. Among seventeenth-century literary characters the whore figures as a symbol of disguised evil—
'Her body is the tilted Lees of pleasure, dasht over with a little
decking to hold colour'[6]—and the symbol survives into the eighteenth century. Certainly Defoe, who incidentally includes a form
of prose character of the whore in *Roxana,*[7] gives her a less me-
taphoric, much more earthbound social context; nevertheless,
she remains inevitably an object for fantasies, both male and
female. In effect, Gay and Swift combine two forms of presentation: in their poetry, the nymph in the shape of the whore is
not only a literal being, the professional who walks the London
or Dublin streets; she is also a creature of the imagination, mocking reality by her travesty of beauty and desire. Like a society
nymph, she dramatizes and disguises and indeed parodies nature. The literary parody expresses the living parody.

So far it appears that Gay and Swift are working within
tradition when they pursue the nymph fiction, or, at least where
pastoral is concerned, logically developing a tradition which permits its conventions to be adapted ironically while the essential
moral value, 'what is true', remains intact. But they diverge from
seventeenth-century lyric practice (whether pre- or post-Resto-
ration) in one important respect. Although the satiric and pastoral conventions associated with art, nature, and the nymph may
express attitudes to the female sex in general, it is true that in
seventeenth-century lyrics the poet is more likely to identify the
'she' of his verses with a real or supposed mistress. Rochester
flings the name 'whore' as a private gesture of abuse, a retaliation
for an abortive love affair:

> Then if, to make your ruine more,
>   You'll peevishly be coy,
> Dye with the Scandal of a Whore,
>   And never know the Joy.
>> (*Poems by John Wilmot,*
>>   *Earl of Rochester,*
>> ed. V. de S. Pinto, 1964, p. 21)

This abusiveness is of a very different kind from Swift's descriptions of nymph prostitutes: it is emotionally complicated, because
Rochester implies both degradation and lineaments of gratified

desire in his choice of term, and because it requires at least an assumed involvement. As it happens, Defoe later draws the stanza's sting by making Moll Flanders paraphrase it to describe a literal social predicament.[8] In any case, by the early eighteenth century the personal viewpoint which an imaginary relationship provides is less in evidence. The poets satirise the nymphs rather than sigh for them, although complimentary lyric still functions as social small coin. When Swift writes of his relationship to a real woman, he deliberately relegates the poetic mistress and muse to Grub Street, asserting that he and Stella belong to a different order of reality:

> Thou *Stella,* wert no longer young,
> When first for thee my Harp I strung:
> Without one Word of *Cupid's* Darts,
> Of killing Eyes, or bleeding Hearts.
> ('To Stella, Who Collected
> and Transcribed his Poems', 9–12)

Friendship and esteem take precedence of discredited romantic love. But we ought to avoid the trap of distinguishing too positively between the individual women of whom Swift and his friends write with personal feeling, and the nymphs who originate in social observation and literary convention. The poets themselves turn the distinction into a joke as well as a genuine compliment. Swift teases Stella on being unsuitable for nymphhood, and makes Venus petulantly remark of Vanessa

> 'She was at Lord knows what Expence,
> 'To form a Nymph of Wit and Sense.'
> ('Cadenus and Vanessa', 864–65)

Pope gallants it in his verse for Martha Blount without transforming her into a full-blown nymph like Belinda. For the nymph as true literary type comes into her own in poems where the poet is interested in the image or role, rather than in individuals or feelings. In other words, he gives art priority over nature: but it is his *own* art which concerns him most, and this immediately complicates the issue beyond the simple conflict of art and nature as a literary frame of reference. In fact, we return to the problematic truth-fiction-poetry triangle which is in a sense analogous to the nature-art-woman triangle.

One way of resolving the complication shifts responsibility for the fiction from the poet to the woman herself and possibly to society at large. In seventeenth-century Cavalier lyrics, a poet like Thomas Carew professes himself more than satisfied to be the creator of a woman's beauty, to make her desirable, after the manner of a court painter; after all, it gives him a bargaining position to be ironically exploited. The Restoration poets also regard themselves as 'Lords of Infamy and Praise', and, considering their flair for elegant vilification, probably in that order of priority. But as Gay and Swift move away from private pose to public satire, they become more preoccupied with confirming or destroying pre-existing images of the sex, whether created by literature, by social expectations, or by the woman concerned. This presupposes a moral distinction between the satirist's art and art used irresponsibly. However, a more subtle literary approach, also open to them, is not to resolve the complication at all but to acknowledge the poet's ambiguous position and then play upon it. If it is easy to oversimplify the moral formula of art opposed to nature, the contrary idea that art enhances nature requires more expert handling, especially when both attitudes— appreciation and disapproval—exist simultaneously. For instance, in seventeenth-century poetry Marvell's teasing and beautiful pastorals have the exact quality of ironic consciousness required, and 'The Gallery' focuses this very problem, since both mistress and poet participate in the game between nature and art played out

> In all the Forms thou can'st invent
> Either to please me, or torment

to culminate in the final shepherdess image.[9] Congreve carries overt complicity (and social allusion) further in his opalescent lyric, 'A Hue and Cry after Fair Amoret':

> Fair *Amoret* is gone astray;
> Pursue and seek her, ev'ry Lover;
> I'll tell the Signs by which you may
> The wand'ring Shepherdess discover.

> Coquet and Coy at once her Air,
>   Both study'd, tho' both seem neglected;
> Careless she is with artful Care,
>   Affecting to seem unaffected.
>   (*Complete Works of William Congreve,*
>   ed. M. Summers, 1923, iv, 74)

Set this beside Herrick's earlier treatment of precisely the same motif, the pastoral search, where he uses the pastoral convention in its prelapsarian state, so to speak, and produces an effect of 'natural' spontaneous lyricism:

> Among the *Mirtles,* as I walkt,
> Love and my sighs thus intertalkt:
> Tell me, said I, in deep distresse,
> Where I may find my Shepardesse.
> Thou foole, said Love, know'st thou not this?
> In every thing that's sweet, she is.
> In yond' *Carnation* goe and seek,
> There thou shalt find her lip and cheek . . .
>   (*Poetical Works of Robert Herrick,*
>   ed. L. C. Martin, 1956, p. 106)

Herrick has the air of discovering beauty growing wild, which reminds us of a yet older song tradition. But for Congreve, the art revealed in the errant girl's behaviour is her own creation and as much an artistic illusion as a poem written about it. The chief difference is that the one pleasure, the girl's coquetry, is precarious, the other, his poem, is permanent.

In the eighteenth century Pope develops this ambivalent nature/art theme far beyond the confines of the lyric: it is not however only the scale of *The Rape of the Lock* which accounts for increased complexity, but the awareness he displays in discriminating between different arts. Pope is investigating a world which has already evolved its own rival means of controlling or expressing nature through its etiquette, its social manœuvres, even its *objets d'art*. Within this environment, the nymph also is an artist working in her own medium to transform nature. Consequently, the scenes concerned with Belinda's adornment have a certain moral and aesthetic elusiveness perfectly mediated through the fiction of the sylphs. When criticising *The Rape of the Lock*, John Dennis perceives art and nature to be important points of reference, and so delivers himself of a familiar little homily on gilding the lily. But his evidence from pastoral ironically betrays him into the very discrepancy he condemns in Pope:

> And our Ladies who spend so much Time at their Toilettes would do well to consider, that . . . they who are most charm'd with their Persons, endeavour to retrieve their natural Beauty in Imagination at least, by divesting them of their borrow'd Ornaments, and cloathing them in the Simplicity of the rural Habit, when in their Sonnets they transform them to Shepherdesses.
>
> *(Critical Works of John Dennis,*
> ed. E. N. Hooker, 1943, ii, 334)

The fallacy contained in this argument is the age-old fallacy concerning what is 'natural': the critic fails to acknowledge that the poet's artifice embellishes nature as much as the lady's. When Pope uses pastoral convention to describe his heroine's beauty, he, and we, derive pleasure from art consciously heightening nature. Yet, as a whole, the poem's fiction insinuates a truth, as it progresses towards the final serious separation not just of art and nature but of art and art—one goes to dust, the other endures like a star.

When Gay makes use of the nymph fiction in his earlier poetry, he frames her in the conventional moral oppositions of town and country, art and nature. In *Rural Sports*, the fisherman's artificial fly images the society beauty throwing out her lures; both demonstrate art imitating nature for destructive purposes.[10] And, predictably, he pictures the country girl in terms of her opposite—

> No Midnight Masquerade her Beauty wears
> And Health, not Paint, the fading Bloom repairs.
> (259–60)[11]

Such verse does not lack charm, but it is a charm tarnished with a breath of triteness. When Gay morally separates art and nature, he is often being sentimental: allowing the two ideas to coalesce gives him the chance of a much more fascinating and variable play of irony beneath the surface. Correspondingly, the roles of the nymph coalesce in his subtlest work. In *The Beggar's Opera* it is an open question (as for their male counterparts) whether fine ladies imitate whores, or whores fine ladies. By the time he writes *The Beggar's Opera* he has perfected his ability to have a literary convention both ways, so that reminiscences of the original, whether pastoral or heroic, both satirize and enhance his material. For instance, Macheath's sweet mocking song in praise of woman, 'If the heart of a man is deprest with cares', epitomises the bruised lyricism of many of these songs in their Newgate context: a few stage-moments later, the almost Elizabethan natural imagery 'Roses and lillies her cheeks disclose' gives place to Macheath's banter with the whores on the subject of 'the repairs of quality', cosmetic paint (*The Beggar's Opera,* II, iii and iv). Somewhere between the directness of *Rural Sports* and the indirectness of *The Beggar's Opera,* the description of the nymph-prostitute in *Trivia* appears to mark an intermediate stage in Gay's development of the fiction. On the one hand, with regard to its placing in the general scheme of the poem, Gay might have made more of possible cross-references, as he does in *The Beggar's Opera* where fine filaments of style are constantly thrown out to connect different worlds, and different sets of social and artistic conventions. On the other hand, *within* the actual description of the nymph he captures a shuddering allurement as well as a moral judgment. He succeeds in suggesting the fantasy element surrounding such a figure: the whore's masquerade hints at a sinister imitation of the society masquerade, and also bears a kind of left-handed relation to the theatre. In addition to her line of patter, this nymph masks herself with what might almost be the remnants of stage costume, including, like Roxana, a Quaker guise:

> In riding-hood near tavern-doors she plies,
> Or muffled pinners hide her livid eyes.
> With empty bandbox she delights to range,
> And feigns a distant errand from the *'Change*;
> Nay, she will oft' the Quaker's hood prophane.
> And trudge demure the rounds of *Drury-Lane.*
>
> (iii, 275–80)

In every detail, highlighted like her hectic cheeks, Gay does not merely contrast art with nature but displays its active perversion. He pulls the entire fiction together through the corresponding town/country theme: corrupt town pastoral blights country pastoral in the person of the 'hapless swain' whom the 'fraudful nymph' entices and infects. It is vividly done; and yet, paradoxically, Gay is creating a fantasy image at the same time as he ostensibly destroys it. There is some hiatus between moral intention and this vital travesty, which is less apparent in works where Gay pretends not to have a moral stance towards his fiction, or where his art can support a genuinely ambivalent attitude.

Such ambiguities are more available to him when he treats the subject of the society nymph and her masquerades, instead of the nymph-prostitute. Gay's shepherdesses inherit the mantle of Congreve's Amoret, in that they, too, consciously create an image to be admired: indeed the masquerade itself licences these disguises. The fine lady no longer depends on the poet to turn her into a nymph, but effects her own transformation with significant consequences:

> Last *Masquerade* was *Sylvia* nymphlike seen,
> Her hand a crook sustain'd, her dress was green;
> An am'rous shepherd led her through the croud,
> The nymph was innocent, the shepherd vow'd;
> But nymphs their innocence with shepherds trust;
> So both withdrew, as nymph and shepherd must.
>   ('The Tea-Table', 21–26)

Gay duplicates this pastoral logic in another poem, the 'Epistle to Pulteney', in an exquisite mannered piece describing *la dolce vita*:

> When the sweet-breathing spring unfolds the buds,
> Love flies the dusty town for shady woods.
> Then *Totenham* fields with roving beauty swarm,
> And *Hampstead* Balls the city virgin warm;
> Then *Chelsea*'s meads o'erhear perfidious vows,
> And the prest grass defrauds the grazing cows.
> 'Tis here the same; but in a higher sphere,
> For ev'n Court Ladies sin in open air.

What Cit with a gallant would trust his spouse
Beneath the tempting shade of *Greenwich* boughs?
What Peer of *France* would let his Dutchess rove,
Where *Boulogne*'s closest woods invite to love?
But here no wife can blast her husband's fame,
Cuckold is grown an honourable name.
Stretch'd on the grass the shepherd sighs his pain,
And on the grass what shepherd sighs in vain?

(101–16)

In an emphatically moral reading, S. M. Armens defines this pastoral as a 'social perversion', equating the defrauded cows with the defrauded husbands (*John Gay, Social Critic*, 1954, pp. 172–73). But decadence of this kind is beautiful and amusing as well as morally deplorable, and Gay is caught up in his fiction for its own sake as he experiments here with literary convention. Certainly we are meant to see that this sexual behavior could be more harshly termed prostitution and adultery, and this appears as 'truth' on one level. Yet the fiction allows for a more complex truth, because Gay persuades us, if only momentarily, that the springtime does indeed metamorphose courtiers into shepherds, that Arcadia does border on the environs of London. Instead of town and country as moral opposites, nature herself bewilderingly turns temptress. Gay so phrases the love invitation as to go beyond the simple nostalgic appeal of spring pastoral to a jaded city: in fact, he alludes to another form of pastoral, not the one which Armens claims is perverted. When Armens writes about 'the debasement of country love, simplicity, and innocence by . . . hypercivilized shepherdesses' he idealizes and limits the genre almost as much as the neoclassical theorists. Here (as elsewhere) Gay seems if anything closer to the Caroline tradition than to the neoclassical. He alludes ironically and specifically to the conventions of *libertin* pastoral, casting the passage into the mould of a Golden Age set-piece extolling free love, but giving it a post-Dryden satiric overtone by locating his Golden Age historically and geographically. Compared with the past, the present age is crass in its regulation of such affairs, and Gay mimics this lapse of taste in a couplet bridging Caroline irony and Augustan satire:

> But since at Court the rural taste is lost,
> What mighty summs have velvet couches cost!
>
> (131–32)

He makes an interesting parallel use of the Golden Age convention, demonstrating clearly the art/nature link, in his 'Prologue Design'd for the Pastoral Tragedy of *Dione*':

> There was a time (Oh were those days renew'd!)
> Ere tyrant laws had woman's will subdu'd;
> Then nature rul'd, and love, devoid of art,
> Spoke the consenting language of the heart.
>
> (1–4)

Again, morality is not the whole truth: he undercuts this opening sentiment, which could have affinities with Tasso or with Guarini,[12] by mischievously suggesting that he prefers 'tyrant laws' because they add spice to love affairs:

> I envy not, ye nymphs, your am'rous bowers:
> Such harmless swains!—I'm ev'n content with ours.
> But yet there's something in these sylvan scenes
> That tells our fancy what the lover means . . .
>
> (13–6)

Indeed there is, and it goes far towards explaining our response to the Pulteney passage. Even granting the evident irony, it is hard to accept the single-minded view of Gay as Augustan moralist. A further indication of the extent to which the almost Caroline quality of his verse modifies its Augustanism is the gap between Gay's pastoral irony and Swift's. The couplet

> Stretch'd on the grass the shepherd sighs his pain,
> And on the grass what shepherd sighs in vain?

compares with Swift's

> *Corinna*, Pride of *Drury-Lane*,
> For whom no Shepherd sighs in vain.
> ('A Beautiful Young Nymph
> Going to Bed', 1–2)

But where Gay conveys his innuendo with finesse, leaving the pastoral art intact, Swift lays bare his meaning in a manner which defiles pastoral convention itself by association.

When Swift demolishes art, he does not spare—indeed he singles out—the fictions of poetry. In his descriptions of nymph-prostitutes, he literally strips down the image and forces us to watch it fall apart. But nature can provide no moral alternative to art, since pastoral nature is tainted by literary illusion, and what is natural to human beings, mentally and physically, is yet more deeply corrupt. Starting from these premises, however, Swift can still develop the conjunction of art, nature, and the nymph in a number of poems in order to make statements about what is true and what is delusion. One especially interesting example occurs at the end of 'The Lady's Dressing Room', where the poet offers an apparent compromise solution to the problem of how Strephon should sort out the confusion of art and nature, appearance and reality, sharply impressed upon him by Celia's squalor:

> When *Celia* in her Glory shows,
> If *Strephon* would but stop his Nose;
> (Who now so impiously blasphemes
> Her Ointments, Daubs, and Paints and Creams,
> Her Washes, Slops, and every Clout,
> With which he makes so foul a Rout;)
> He soon would learn to think like me,
> And bless his ravisht Eyes to see
> Such Order from Confusion sprung,
> Such gaudy Tulips rais'd from Dung.
>
> (133–42)

The speaker implicitly condemns both Strephon's original illusion and his violent disillusion as ferments of a diseased imagination, but his own insinuating answer is no less ironic, and no more tenable. He invites Strephon to learn to think like him, yet at a price, for in order to do so Strephon cannot afford to admit reality through all his senses: he must look and stop his nose, smell no evil so to speak. In place of suppressed imagination, the speaker voices a disillusioned intelligence, prepared to accept Celia's image for the artefact it is. Without the irony, the argument that art produces order from confusion would be a perfectly respectable philosophical and poetic proposition. But Swift has forced 'Confusion' upon the reader too intimately and menacingly in the whole poem for 'Order' to be anything other than an abstract and highly satiric compensation (he does not create Celia's 'Glory' for us as Pope does Belinda's: the difference in strategy corresponds to a different conception of the theme). His actual rejection of the nature/art compromise is confirmed by the final image 'Such gaudy Tulips rais'd from Dung' and its fascinating, if minor, literary history. Since the 1630s, when tulips were the rage of Europe, poets commonly associated references to these flowers with a certain type of beauty flaunting itself in the eye of the beholder. In the context of art and nature, the cultivation of tulips (especially the flamboyant streaked varieties) signifies a triumph of art. Consequently, an aura of moral ambivalence clings to the lyric image of the tulip (as to Perdita's gilly-flowers in *The Winter's Tale,* IV, iii) ironically like a fragrance that the flower itself does not possess. James Shirley exiles both tulips and women from his melancholy lovelorn garden:

> Those Tulips that such wealth display,
> To court my eye, shall lose their name,
> Though now they listen, as if they
> Expected I should praise their flame.
> (*The Cavalier Poets,*
> ed. R. Skelton, 1970, p. 233)

Marvell represents nature corrupted by art (with a side-glance at female cosmetics) in his more celebrated tulip image from 'The Mower against Gardens':

> The Tulip, white, did for complexion seek;
> And learn'd to interline its cheek.
> (*Poems & Letters,* ed. Margoliouth, i, 40)

And Cowley provides a conclusive seventeenth-century example, highly detrimental to female beauty and tulips:

Beauty, Thou *active, passive* Ill!
Which *dy'st* thy self as fast as thou dost *kill!*
Thou *Tulip,* who thy stock in paint dost waste,
Neither for *Physick* good, nor *Smell,* nor *Tast.*
(*Poems of Abraham Cowley,*
ed. A. R. Waller, 1905, p. 116)

Nor are the nuances lost upon an eighteenth-century poet and garden enthusiast: Pope shows that the image survives transplantation to a different kind of poetry—[13]

Ladies, like variegated Tulips, show,
'Tis to their Changes that their charms they owe;
Their happy Spots the nice admirer take,
Fine by defect, and delicately weak.
(*Epistles to Several Persons,*
ed. F. W. Bateson, 1961, p. 53)

It is not necessary to suppose that Swift must have known and modelled his allusion on specific earlier examples; those quoted simply prove how strong the combined associations are, how easily poets might come to see the tulip as the harlot of the garden. The image of 'gaudy Tulips' to represent woman's art and beauty is unlikely to have been chosen at random.

Swift is perhaps most dazzlingly subversive in exploiting the pastoral fiction of the nymph when he writes 'The Progress of Beauty' and 'A Beautiful Young Nymph Going to Bed'. The descriptions spark and flare into their own wildfire poetic logic, again forming a dialectic of art and nature. In effect, the earlier poem 'The Progress of Beauty' has a regressive structure: the poet's art fails when simple rearrangement makes a mockery of all his metaphors; the nymph's cosmetic repairs prove futile against natural deficiency—

But, Art no longer can prevayl
When the Materialls all are gone—

art, the poor mortar of crumbling nature, has nothing left to hold together. Paradoxically, however, Swift's art does 'prevayl' because it has the makings of myth. The symbolic identification of whore and moon is more than a neat ironic antithesis of poetic praises addressed to the virgin goddess.[14] Perhaps unexpectedly, the image probes a nerve, touches upon much older and deeper human fantasies expressed in nature myth. The link between the moon and female sexuality is the dark reverse of the bright chastity image, a source of fear and possible repulsion. When Swift works out the parallel between a syphilitic moon, gradually eaten away night by night, and rotting Celia strolling the street, he follows his customary stylistic practice which compounds what is comic and what is intolerable. As in *A Modest Proposal*, he releases the imagination's own sources of power, but, for once, it is a power also generated in traditional poetry and myth. Through the chosen fiction, 'The Progress of Beauty' insinuates what is imaginatively as well as morally 'true' about its subject.

The later poem 'A Beautiful Young Nymph Going to Bed' also cuts deep, since it starts from a familiar erotic situation which is both literary topic and personal fantasy. Again, however, Swift goes beyond simple parody. Geoffrey Hill expresses a commonly felt uneasiness about this poem when he remarks that 'it may seem that the superior intelligence can assert itself only by extravagant gestures of revulsion' (*The World of Jonathan Swift*, p. 207). Surely, however, (as his own penetrating analysis of the final lines would bear out) the chief gesture made by the superior intelligence is precisely the art of the poem. Swift organizes it meticulously through a controlling metaphor made literal, one of his most impressive techniques. Just as he developed the whore-moon parallel in 'The Progress of Beauty', so here he develops a dominant image of physical dissolution on this side of the grave, the nightmare of a human creature falling apart into the components of a hideous art form:

> Then, seated on a three-legg'd Chair,
> Takes off her artificial Hair:
> Now, picking out a Crystal Eye,
> She wipes it clean, and lays it by.
> Her Eye-Brows from a Mouse's Hyde,
> Stuck on with Art on either Side,
> Pulls off with Care, and first displays 'em,
> Then in a Play-Book smoothly lays 'em.
>
> (9–16)

Nature takes her revenge on the nymph both in the physical
ravages she suffers, and in the grotesque mauling of her property by the creatures. In the morning, Corinna must recreate
her image—

> But how shall I describe her Arts
> To recollect the scatter'd Parts?
>
> (67–68)

So the poet says, intimating that he and his 'bashful Muse' must
withdraw; and by this point, the reader is only too ready to wel-
come the withdrawal as a heavily ironic concession to sensibility.
But in fact, this attitude dovetails into the logic of the poem, and
indeed of Swift's general treatment of art and the nymph. If the
satiric poet's function is to strip the nymph-prostitute of the image which she creates for herself or which society and literature
pervertedly apply to her, then the controlling metaphor in 'A
Beautiful Young Nymph' exactly corresponds to this intention
and theme. Swift ruthlessly takes apart Corinna's image in the
going to bed sequence: he cannot participate as poet in the process of rebuilding this image. The poem as it stands is his creation set against hers; and for the poem—if not for its nymph
heroine—the whole is more than the sum of the parts.

To return then to the initial question of how Gay and Swift
differ in manipulating fiction and truth, and whether or not they
are 'True Poets' according to Swift's definition: neither is as simple a case as the definition implies. For Gay, theatrical and pastoral illusions are—to adapt a phrase from Marianne Moore—
like imaginary gardens inhabited by real toads. At his best, he
solves the problem of truth and fiction, not by discrediting fiction
but by exaggerating it to a point where we are forced to make
comparisons with reality, as when he holds the deliberately
framed fairytale ending of *The Beggar's Opera* against a known
and real Tyburn. Swift, on the other hand, does not hesitate to
debase fiction in the name of truth. Yet 'truth' in his poems is
not therefore independent of fiction, a straight synonym for reality. If it were, we might argue, he would not be writing verse at
all. However wary he may be of the power of poetry as an equivalent of private fantasy, reinforcing certain sexual images, for
example, and repressing others, it is this same power that he

harnesses as a destructive counter-force in his nymph poems. Where truth and nature *are* to be found, in the Stella poems, he uses fiction as a context, a test of their mutual integrity: the worth of human personality is weighed by plain statement, and truth shines the better in verse which does not shine. And so in one of the birthday poems (1721) he tosses away 'Art or Time or Nature' as sops to the women who attempt to bribe this tyrannous triumvirate. For Stella such propitiation is needless, just as for her poet 'all the Common-Places/Worn out by Wits who rhyme on Faces' are eminently dispensable.

Both Gay and Swift make original poetry out of the nymph fiction because they have the wit to see how, in conjunction with the concepts of art and nature, this convention can relate to ultimately serious themes. But it must be said that satire against the nymphs, like the antecedent pastoral convention, is all too easily trivialized by lesser talents. When this happens, the poets level meaningless infamy with meaningless praise, and are lords no longer. Nevertheless the theme, in one or other of its forms, continues to attract major artists. Yeats's version in *A Woman Young and Old* which might stand as a splendid lyrical riposte to Swift's satire, despite its totally different philosophical basis, further proves the intellectual and imaginative vitality of the subject:

> If I make the lashes dark
> And the eyes more bright
> And the lips more scarlet,
> Or ask if all be right
> From mirror after mirror,
> No vanity's displayed:
> I'm looking for the face I had
> Before the world was made.

Notes

1. 'To Stella, Who Collected and Transcribed his Poems', 53–54. All quotations from Swift's poetry are from *Poetical Works*, ed. Herbert Davis, 1967.

2. v. H. Davis, 'Swift's View of Poetry' (*Jonathan Swift: Essays on his Satire, and Other Studies*, 1964).

3. For a convenient summary, v. *The World of Jonathan Swift*, ed. B. Vickers, 1968, pp. 23–24, footnote 10.

4. *Nature and Art in Renaissance Literature*, 1964, pp. 4–6.

5. *Minor Poets of the Eighteenth Century*, ed. H. I'a. Fausset, 1930, p. 71. The germ of this poem was presumably Donne's line describing a courtier, 'A thing, which would have pos'd Adam to name' (*Satyre* iv, 20).

6. 'A Whoore' (*The 'Conceited Newes' of Sir Thomas Overbury etc.*, ed. J. E. Savage, 1968, p. 112). Cf. John Webster, *The White Devil*, III, ii, 78–101.

7. *Roxana*, ed. Jane Jack, 1964, pp. 132–3.

8. *Moll Flanders* (first edition), ed. Bonamy Dobrée and Herbert Davis, 1961, pp. 74–5.

9. *The Poems and Letters of Andrew Marvell*, ed. H. M. Margoliouth, 2nd ed. 1952, i, pp. 29–30. For a relevant discussion of this poem v. Winifred Nowottny, *The Language Poets Use*, 1962, pp. 94–6.

10. *Rural Sports*, first version (1713), 135—38.

11. Gay's alterations in his revised version (1720) do not substantially change his presentation in these particular instances, although he omits one couplet from the earlier description of the rural maid which is perhaps redundant through over-emphasizing the point:

> Upon her Cheek a pure Vermilion glows,
> And all her Beauty she to Nature owes.
>
> (247–48)

All quotations from Gay's works are from *Poetical Works*, ed. G. C. Faber, 1926.

12. Cf. Tasso's *Aminta* (1573), Guarini's *Il Pastor Fido* (1589), and the conflicting *libertin* and moral versions of the Golden Age convention in seventeenth-century English poetry (for instance, Carew and Randolph provide examples of the former, and the earlier poet, William Browne, of the latter).

13. Claude Rawson draws attention to Pope and Swift's tulip images in 'Order and Cruelty: a Reading of Swift (with some comments on Pope and Johnson)', *Essays in Criticism*, Jan. 1970.

14. Cf. Kathleen Williams's assessment of this poem (*Jonathan Swift and the Age of Compromise*, 1958, p. 149).

RICHARD H. RODINO

Blasphemy or Blessing?
Swift's "Scatological" Poems

The disproportionate critical attention given to Swift's poems about women (probably more than has been given to the rest of his poetry put together) until recently seemed to have resulted from intuitive and rather myopic fascination with the materials of coprophilia and misogyny which litter these poems. The late eighteenth- and nineteenth-century reactions to Swift's "scatology," from Johnson through Thackeray ("horrible, shameful, unmanly, blasphemous") and Taine ("toutes ces ordures"), are too well known to need much rehearsing. And more recently, in the hands of Huxley and Middleton Murry, this traditonal revulsion crystallized into quasi-psychoanalytical pronouncements about Swift's aberrations, obsessions, and lunatic compulsions.[1] If the early judgments seem at least unfair, however, most modern defenses of Swift's motives are also apt to make us uneasy. Norman O. Brown's classic (and pivotal) essay, "The Excremental Vision," subsumed the vague defenses offered by Swift's scholarly readers into enthusiastic appreciation and vindication. Brown ranged beyond Swift's poetical works to make a case for the affinities between Swift's "scatology" and modern psychological theory: "We no longer try to explain away Swift's literary achievements as mere epiphenomena on his individual neurosis.

This essay first appeared in *Papers on Language and Literature* 14 (1978): 152–70. Reprinted with permission.

Rather we seek to appreciate his insight into the universal neurosis of mankind."[2] Still, Brown's essay obviously raised more questions than it solved. Even modern scholars are apt to be rather uncomfortable with the notion that Swift fits so easily into the mainstream of modern theories of the subconscious. And we still did not understand the intended purpose of such delineated insight. For all the provocative connections it made, Brown's theory really only established a basic theme running through Swift's writings: "the conflict between our animal body, appropriately epitomized in the anal function, and our pretentious sublimations."[3] Even such a convincing statement of theme raises many crucial questions about literary motive and effect. Additional problems are raised by another modern tendency to find sober Anglican teaching in these poems, despite the well-documented historical evidence that few readers have experienced them as such. In order to answer these questions it is necessary to begin with the matters of form and structure.

We may begin to solve a number of critical quandaries about Swift's verse if we remember that Swift's formal strategies underwent a series of significant changes over the course of his career. From 1730 to 1733, when most of the "unprintables" were written, Swift's major accomplishments in verse were written in the "vexatious" mode of Gulliver's last voyage or *A Tale of a Tub*. The reader is forced into an urgent, but seemingly impossible, choice between fraudulent alternatives—between fools and knaves, Yahoos and Houyhnhnms, or blasphemy and delusive "blessing." Yahoos, knaves, and misanthropic blasphemy are sufficiently horrible to permit us no ambivalence, but the alternatives are equally repulsive, the more we think of them. It is no coincidence that Swift so energetically repudiated the Horatian apologia of *The Life and Genuine Character of Dr. Swift* during the early 1730s, for his literary motives were changing, and by 1731 he had completed the "vexatious" *Verses on the Death of Dr. Swift*. The latter poem is intended to shock the reader into a more intense realization of his own base motives than would be possible through any "poetry of statement." The exaggerated but not ridiculous encomium in the second half of the poem is meant to evoke, and thereby "prove," the universal jealousy and self-interest Swift predicted in the first half of the poem. "The Day of Judgement" strips away the comforting props of religious formulas from all men through Jove's biting indifference to human expectations of orderly reward and punishment. "The Beasts Confession to the Priest" builds up an elaborate analogy between vicious human imposture and bestiality, and then decides with chilling unconcern that human nature is actually too base for a didactic fable. The "scatological" poems vexatiously treat the physical relations of men and women by offering plausible but deceptive speakers who court the reader's comradely agreement, and then trap him into a moral position he cannot wish to hold.

If we accept Swift's profession that his poetry was always written "with a moral view," then it is clear that his strategies of moral purpose changed significantly over the course of his career. In any age that values rational thought, "moral" writing proceeds from a contemplative definition of normative human dignity and virtue. Each literary application has the effect of insulating and codifying these standards, a process which continually creates new problems for the really sceptical moralist who distrusts the tendency to think of moral definitions as the product of reasoned agreement.[4] Swift was keenly aware that "moral" literature, in its extreme and popular forms, tends to create a comforting dualism which appeals to human pride, to man's complacent sense of his own perfectability. This is the source of his early disdain for L'Estrange's emphasis upon the "Morals and Reflections" attached to his fables, evidence of a general tendency to "fix" moral definitions and the dualism they nourish. From 1730 to 1733, Swift's intention in his poetry is to shatter conventional moral definitions without replacing them. The reader may feel uneasy with the notion of a "moral view" in these poems, so tenuous or at times mocking are any implications of normal, virtuous human behavior. The "moral" quality of Swift's "vexatious" poetry differs in kind, not merely in degree, from his more conventionally "moral" poems, especially those written from 1715 to 1730. The later poems proceed from a drastic reduction of human potential, so that the ideal of a normal, virtuous man seems nearly impossible or even irrelevant. Since man is by nature perverse and vain, at best "A Mingled Mass of Good and Bad," the satirist professes indifference as to the beneficial moral effect of his satire. That is, satire of man's pride in the sufficiency of his reason is not particularly hopeful about the possibility of man's redeeming himself by means of this same corrupt faculty. Thus the "vexatious" satirist courts the impression of being "misanthropic"; he detaches himself from sympathy with the human predicament, refuses to be identified with a definable moral solution. Rejecting the comforting distinctions of a moral dualism, "vexatious" satire offers the human race only the slight chance that the resentment it arouses will be turned to thoughtful humility rather than offended pomposity.

"Vexatious" writing is "moral" only by the extent to which it allows the reader some motive, however tenuous, to resist its own extreme indifference to moral reform and to seek a way out of the impasse. William Empson remarked of this sort of satire that

> the fundamental impulse of irony is to score off both the arguments that have been puzzling you, both sets of sympathies in your mind. . . . It is because of the strength given by this antagonism that it seems to get so safely outside the situation it assumes, to decide so easily about the doubt which it in fact accepts. This may seem a disagreeable pleasure in the ironist but he gives the same pleasure more or less secretly to his audience, and the process brings to mind the whole body of their difficulty with so much sharpness and freshness that it may give the strength to escape from it.[5]

However, this kind of satire may be less potent and purposive than Empson suggested. Such structures always threaten to collapse into burlesque or to deny moral values so thoroughly that to take the fiction seriously requires toughening rather than increased sensitivity. The historical evidence shows that the poems of 1730–33 have been found to imply "incurability" (to use Claude Rawson's term) at least as often as they have been found to imply the possibility of escape and solution.[6] From Swift's time to our own, there have always been readers to refuse Swift the title of "moral poet" on the basis of the "vexatious" verses.

Swift's poems about women before 1730 were generally organized around rational, discriminating relationships between poet and reader. The poems from 1698 to 1712, notably "Verses wrote on a Lady's *Ivory Table-Book*," "To *Mrs*. Biddy Floyd," and "*Apollo* Outwitted," depended upon the "normative" Augustan formal properties of balance and poise, structural relationships which appeal to the moral and social "good sense" of the reader, and which imply, at least, some sense of transcendent ideals. From 1719 to 1730, after the "private" resolution of *Cadenus and Vanessa*, Swift's muse took a public turn, and he wrote a short series of "moral tales" about women and marriage. In these poems, extreme and unnatural situations are narrated to their unhappy conclusions in such a way that no explicit moralizing is necessary. The typical manner of "Phillis, Or, the Progress of Love" (1719) and "The Progress of Marriage" (1722) is to make early and complete moral distinctions, with unambiguous invitations for the reader to share Swift's comic and morally wholesome overview. "An *Elegy* on *Dicky* and *Dolly*" (1728) is rather more interesting. The tercet stanzas, with ten or eleven syllables but only four beats to a line, develop a ghastly lightheartedness about the deaths of a husband and wife. If this is a more difficult attitude to share, Swift nevertheless forces acceptance upon us by his bald and unequivocal discriminations:

> *Dick* Sigh'd for his *Doll* and his mournfull Arms Cross'd,
> Thought much of his *Doll,* and the Jointure he lost,
> The first vex'd him much, but the other vex'd most.[7]

Another series of poems, aimed more or less directly at Swift's sometime friend, Lady Acheson, must be read in the spirit of this special, intimate motive. If Thomas B. Gilmore is correct that, in "A Panegyrick on the Dean in the Person of a Lady in the *North*" (1730), Swift suggests that scatological filth "should be regarded in the spirit of comedy, with tolerance or indulgence," it is one of the few times we are allowed to laugh and to tolerate so easily.[8] For this poem, which begins with some clever mockery of Swift himself and ends with some equable comedy about Lady Acheson and the goddess Cloacine, is unique among the "scatological" verses written in 1730. As with all the other poems about Lady Acheson, the tonality of "A Panegyrick" "suggests that Swift is writing, not out of fascinated disgust or angry contempt, but under the obligation to amuse."[9]

The exception to the typical manner of the "Progress"

poems and "moral tales" during the period before 1730 is "The Progress of Beauty" (1719). Here Swift ultimately declines to take the reader into his confidence, as in the later "scatological" poems, and the result is a vexing confrontation with urgent but seemingly impossible moral choices. The beginning of "The Progress of Beauty" relies not upon parody of "poetical" language, but upon patent evocation of what a certain type of poetry was expected to be like. Rather than ironically making clear the vast discrepancies between the satiric object and the conventional ideal with which it is nominally identified, here Swift insists that the identification between Celia and the Moon is all too true; he debunks our usual poetical standards at the same time that he indicates a universal "natural" problem of female beauty (ll. 1–16).

The "exact Parallel" with the Moon seems to accept the possibility of redemption by reference to eternally recurring cycles of renewal and hope. The detached unconcern of the speaker about Strephon's "blasphemy" also emphasizes the hopeful aspects of the analogy. The judicious reader will be suspicious from the start, however; the language of ideal renewal is cursory and vague, and it is massively outweighed by the gleeful detail which records the ugly discomposure of both Moon and nymph. The imbalance continues through the stanzas which describe Celia's cosmetic applications: proper makeup is "gracefull," but its eternally opposing *bête noir* is "frightfull hideous" and leaves one with a "Purple" nose (ll. 17–24). Though the speaker keeps insisting that the ideal recovery subsumes "blasphemy," is a "blessing" and a "wonder," the language of praise suggests "reduction" (l. 33) and ephemeral retrenchment, self-admiration, and a curious ironic ambiguity, as in "Celia's the Wonder of her Sex" (l. 42). When the speaker essays a mythological conceit for all this praise, he gravely allows it to collapse into bathetic reduction (ll. 49–52).

The first fifteen stanzas form a complete and almost separate unit.[10] The speaker concludes them with an ecstatic appreciation of applied beauty, which by now we wholly distrust, and we are left to choose between the debilitating "blasphemy" of obsessive outrage and the delusory "blessing" of fair appearances: "Delude at once and Bless our Sight" (l. 58). At this point Swift requires of us a problematical "fool or knave" decision.

"Blasphemy" denies all acceptance of the human condition, but the "blessing" is a mocking deception. The possibility of other alternatives has been carefully excluded by the poem: this is how the earthly situation runs, says Swift; the traditional pattern of female beauty, the Moon, is precisely thus.

The last ten stanzas imitate a "compromise" structure of working out of the problem of specious extremes, but the "vexatious" mode is at heart only a parody of the Augustan structure of balance and reconciliation. This last section of the poem is carefully contrived to make the "transcendent middle ground" as unappetizing as the extremes. The ending insists that cosmetic beauty is inevitably connected with the bodily decay of syphilis; "delusion" leads to loss of "matter," scurrility, and death. We might protest that there is nothing inevitable about this connection, but the poem induces our horrified fascination with this "universal" fate, wrenches a kind of suspension of disbelief from us, by the inexorable "logic" of the continuing conceit that women are, indeed, exactly like the moon. The speaker's joking "scholarly" references to the absurd astrological theories of Partridge and Gadbury are so chilling and detached in the face of such a horrible predicament that we may not acknowledge for a moment that this tone of frightening rational unconcern is the "solution" to the dilemma. The terrible, tragic progress of beauty is neither a "blessing" nor a cause of "blasphemy," but a matter of little concern. The mechanical cycles of population growth will supply us with new nymphs, just as the celestial revolutions will give us new Moons. If this poem is comic, then we join in with the speaker's unconcerned laughter only at the risk of denying our own humanity.

One of the primary contributions of modern Swiftian criticism has been to make firm distinctions between the misanthropic or misogynistic personae, such as Gulliver or Strephon, and the positive ethical values implicit in Swift's controlling faculty. A residual problem exists when this view is taken too narrowly: it may suggest positive affirmations which Swift never intended to make, and it may obscure Swift's strategy of making the reader think of himself. "The Lady's Dressing Room" (1730) has been much discussed, and its major problems assumed to be solved. Strephon is a compulsive idealist, who insists upon repeatedly shocking himself by a most meticulous survey of his "goddesse's" dressing room. Although we are amused with the narrator at Strephon's exaggerated revulsion, we are ultimately the butt of a very serious joke. The narrator invites us to share his amusement and superior scorn at the expense of the poor obsessed youth; he intersperses the inventorial sequence of sordid details with exaggerated professions of mock pity, joking parodies of "English poetry from Milton to Pope," and sardonic similes which woo the reader into joining him in detaching himself from Strephon for the purposes of clinical examination.[11] For instance, the rather cruel simile of roasted "Mutton Cutlets" in lines 99–114 confides to us by sly innuendo that Celia's sexual morals were no better than they should be. "Mutton," of course, was and is slang for a prostitute, and we laugh at (perhaps a little queasily) or pity Strephon and his lamentable compulsions, his frowsy whore.[12] But the ending of the poem abruptly shatters the reader's complacent relationship with the speaker. Even Thomas B. Gilmore, making a case for the "comedy" of the poem, admits that "Swift has forced 'Confusion' upon the reader":[13]

> But Vengeance, Goddess never sleeping
> Soon punish'd *Strephon* for his Peeping;
> His foul Imagination links
> Each Dame he sees with all her Stinks:
> And, if unsav'ry Odours fly
> Conceives a Lady standing by:
> All Women his Description fits,
> And both Idea's jump like Wits:
> By vicious Fancy coupled fast,
> And still appearing in Contrast.
> I pity wretched *Strephon* blind
> To all the Charms of Woman Kind;
> Should I the Queen of Love refuse,
> Because she rose from stinking Ooze?
> To him that looks behind the Scene,
> *Satira's* but some pocky Quean.
>
> When *Celia* in her Glory shows,
> If *Strephon* would but stop his Nose;

(Who now so impiously blasphemes
Her Ointments, Daubs, and Paints and Creams,
Her Washes, Slops, and every Clout,
With which he makes so foul a Rout;)
He soon would learn to think like me,
And bless his ravisht Eyes to see
Such Order from Confusion sprung
Such gaudy Tulips rais'd from Dung.[14]

Norman O. Brown proposed that Swift was urging upon Strephon the notion that sublimation was still possible and necessary. Donald Greene countered that Swift's argument was that all beauty is born of chaos and imperfection; Swift was not urging sublimation, but Christian acceptance of reality. John M. Aden seconded Greene's view (with modifications): "if Strephon would but discount the argument from his senses . . . he could, like the poet, find the spectacle of beauty out of such noisome origins a source of wonder, and not, as he has, of despair."[15] If these critics have distinguished Swift from Strephon, they are still confusing him with the speaker of the poem. The speaker is not addressing Strephon at all, but rather his Olympian companion, the "judicious reader," whose company he has been at pains to solicit. Strephon's quandary is solved: stop blaspheming and appreciate the "blessing." Our dilemma has just begun.

The reassuring idea that everyone is disgusting "behind the scenes," but a "blessing" up front, collapses into ironic vexation. What is up front stinks as badly as what is behind, and as our speaker records with equanimity his relish for "Woman Kind," the stinking ooze, the "pocky Quean," the "gaudy Tulips rais'd from Dung"—all one has to do is hold one's nose!—the horrible insouciance and immoderation make it more than difficult to take this attitude as Swift's genuine pronouncement on the matter. Swift has lured his reader into a position he cannot want to hold. The action is almost the reverse of *A Modest Proposal,* where our initial horror collapses in relief as the speaker "gives himself away." Here the speaker is painstakingly ingratiating and plausible as a satirist in order to startle us with the sudden revelation that his moral scorn of Strephon has concealed an equally repugnant grossness. Reality is vastly imperfect, and certainly must be accommodated, but one shrinks from calling a "pocky Quean" a goddess, or smiling luridly while holding one's nose. Such "order" is "ravishment," illusory and degrading. We have been tricked into nearly accepting "gaudy Tulips rais'd from Dung" as a "blessing."[16]

This is "vexatious" poetry; the wonderful compressions of octosyllabic couplets allow Swift ironically to associate "Glory" with nose-holding, "Blessing" with "Dung," with a minimum of obtrusive disturbance. There may be a morally sound and attractive "mean" somewhere between Strephon's compulsive idealism and the speaker's offensively eager pragmatism, but Swift has engineered the poem so that the "mean" is notably hard to find. Swift's main attack is on complacency and moral obtuseness. "The Lady's Dressing Room" does not simply delineate the ambiguities and dilemmas of the "fair and foul" female paradox, it forces the reader to redeem himself from complacency, to participate in the saving act of creating some kind of tenable moral position from a universal situation fraught with obstacles. Swift does not "teach" us anything at all, really; he forces us to teach ourselves or be damned. Unlike Belinda, whom Pope reveals to us with confident and affectionate amusement, Celia is a phenomenon demonstrably hard to face.

"A Beautiful Young Nymph Going to Bed" (1731) presents a different order of difficulty, but one which is equally "vexatious." The poem is no less tough-minded than "The Progress of Beauty," but the narrator openly declares the terms of the problem and insists upon them to the end. The opening lines seem to establish a particular, traditional mode of satire: call a repulsive, dissolute whore a "bright goddess," and see how the terms of praise develop sarcastic puns and double entendres:

> CORINNA, Pride of Drury-Lane,
> For whom no Shepherd sighs in vain;
> Never did Covent Garden boast
> So bright a batter'd, strolling Toast.
>
> [517]

The initial rhyme sound induces the sardonic undercutting of "in vain," while the "poetical" alliteration in line 4 mockingly disguises a satiric incongruity as it did in "The Progress of

Beauty," lines 51–52. The incongruity leads to further amusement: try another conventional rhyme for a famous beauty, and
the sarcastic context turns "Toast" into a particularly insulting
pun. Having established Corinna as a horrible joke, Swift suspends the sarcasm somewhat for a matter-of-fact chronicle of the
nymph's dismantling (boosted just once by "lovely Goddess" in
line 23), and this allows a different response to develop. The
chilling account of the mechanical operation merges into the
very human pathos of cruel dreams:

> With Pains of Love tormented lies;
> Or if she chance to close her Eyes,
> Of *Bridewell* and the *Compter* dreams,
> And feels the Lash, and faintly screams;
> Or, by a faithless Bully drawn,
> At some Hedge-Tavern lies in Pawn;
> Or to *Jamaica* seems transported,
> Alone, and by no Planter courted;
> Or, near *Fleet-Ditch*'s oozy Brinks,
> Surrounded with a Hundred Stinks,
> Belated, seems on watch to lye,
> And snap some Cully passing by;
> Or, struck with Fear, her Fancy runs
> On Watchmen, Constables and Duns,
> From whom she meets with frequent Rubs;
> But, never from Religious Clubs;
> Whose Favour she is sure to find,
> Because she pays them all in Kind.
>
> [518]

The tone of this passage is peculiarly difficult to describe. There
is little discernible sympathy in the narrator's account, and no
one is going to find it sentimental. But Swift shows us something
we have not been allowed to see in earlier poems; for all her
absurd and disgusting artifices, Corinna shares (too much) the
basic human tragedies of loneliness and victimization. The
reader cannot help but feel a measure of sympathy as Corinna's
tortured dreams refuse to go away, as the passive verbs build up
into a massive state of helplessness and terror. But Swift does not
permit our sympathy to dissolve the moral toughness with which

we began; the dream passage closes (almost disconcertingly) with the same cavalier scorn of the opening lines:

> But, never from Religious Clubs;
> Whose Favour she is sure to find,
> Because she pays them all in Kind.
>
> [518]

The narration continues with a tone of elaborate ironic portent (ll. 57–64) which may remind us of *The Dunciad*; but as in *The Dunciad*, this tonality has acquired a curious complexity. For Corinna's personal tragedies (like the public tragedies of *The Dunciad*) cannot be dismissed by comedy. Corinna's pitiful daily retrenchment is sadly deplorable as well as amusingly outrageous. The final section of the poem (ll. 65–73) does have some of the essential qualities of comedy, "the persistence of the usual," but in the structure of the entire poem, the human comedy of renewal is a delusive perspective.[18] Swift brings us up short with a final line which insists upon an attitude different from any other in the poem: "Who sees, will spew; who smells, be poison'd" (519). There is no sympathy at all in this last line, but also there is none of the sardonic and superior amusement which balanced sympathy through the poem. Eight inexorable words, abruptly and brutally chopped into four syntactical units, record the last attitude of the poem as spare, factual acknowledgement of cause and effect. Unlike the earlier poems, the "extremes" of attitude in "A Beautiful Young Nymph" are not fraudulent or mutually exclusive, but they are inadequate alone in the face of such persistent fact. Sympathy will not make the fact go away, nor will rational detachment. The final line will not let us deny what it reports, and admitting the hard fact may be, rather than callous insensitivity, the first step to real human engagement.

The adventures of Strephon are resumed in the longest and least successful of the "scatological" poems, "Strephon and Chloe" (1731). Despite the insistence of Huxley and others that the second part of the poem is an instance of Swift's neurotic analism, "Strephon and Chloe" was one of the first of Swift's "scatological" poems to be seriously defended for its moral import. The defense is usually based upon the ostensible clarity of the poem's structure: the equally nauseating extremes of poetic

idealization and "great Society in Stinking" are scorned and tran-
scended by the moral sermon which concludes the poem. More
recently, critics of Swift's verse have noticed that so much of what
goes on in the poem has little relevance to this clear moral pattern. John M. Aden decided that the poem fails "not because of
any moral fault, but because it fails of poetical economy and
thematic consistency"; there are so many passages that seem "excessive of [their] contribution to the point and movement of the
poem."[19] The problem with Aden's criticism is that it requires us
to dismiss a considerable portion of the poem as bungling, especially passages in the last section where the sententious ser-
monizing deliberately falls flat. For the speaker of this poem is
conspicuously unreliable. He establishes his relation to the
reader more as satirical clown than as rational companion. He
begins with a winning burlesque of Grubstreet's clichéd ideali-
zations, which begins to turn our stomachs a bit as his paraphrase
develops into a series of foul details mockingly presented as su-
perlative compliments by the repeated interposition of "no"
(ll. 3–24). Although the speaker invites us to share his delight in
burlesquing the worn-out platitudes of female beauty, he re-
serves the right to turn the same mocking attention upon his
audience. He offers up the mythological paraphernalia of the
wedding with tongue-in-cheek solemnity for our enjoyment; but
after urging us to smile with him at poor Strephon's comical
delusions about his "goddess," the speaker flouts us with an insolent address which momentarily denies us such Olympian overview and includes us in the satire:

> Now, *Ponder well ye Parents dear*;
> Forbid your Daughters guzzling Beer;
> And make them ev'ry Afternoon
> Forbear their Tea, or drink it soon;
> That, e'er to bed they venture up,
> They may discharge it ev'ry Sup; . . .
> Keep them to wholsome Food confin'd,
> Nor let them taste what causes Wind; . . .
> O, think what Evils must ensue;
> Miss *Moll* the Jade will burn it blue:
> And when she once has got the Art,
> She cannot help it for her Heart;

But, out it flies, even when she meets
Her Bridegroom in the Wedding-Sheets.
[522–23]

The clown historically enjoys a unique freedom as a satirist.
He makes no special commitment to his audience. By special
dispensation, he turns to mock them along with the victims of
his tale. Like the court jester, the speaker has made us laugh (a
little grudgingly, perhaps) by the end of this whimsical address
(ll. 115–36) with his sly flatulent causeries. Having regained our
(reluctant) intimacy, he feeds us a bit of specious morality:

BUT, after Marriage, practise more
Decorum than she did before;
To keep her Spouse deluded still,
And make him fancy what she will.
[523]

"Delusion" is suspicious as the intended solution to the problem
of marital cleanliness, and the insouciant "make him fancy what
she will" should warn us that the speaker is describing a "fool
among knaves" situation, though he is careful to offer it up with
the solemn magic word, "Decorum."

During the account of the grotesque wedding night, the
reader becomes again the speaker's companion in mirth, though
the latter seizes convenient opportunities to slyly tease his comrades: "SAY, fair ones, must I make a Pause?/Or freely tell the
secret Cause" (ll. 161–62). The jester performs his tricks to the
great enjoyment of all present. If the bawdy humor of "Let fly
a Rouzer in her Face" (l. 191) is a little rough for the ladies (who,
as the speaker knowingly anticipated, could hardly wait to be
shocked by it), the dismissal of absurd romantic conventions in
lines 193–202 is a purely wholesome and rational pleasure for
all. The climactic scene of degradation between husband and
wife (ll. 203–18) is slyly funny, but, we agree with the speaker,
disgraceful nevertheless.

We are ready for the moral of the story, but, characteristically, the playful speaker gives us both more and less than we
expect. Donald Greene pointed out that the next 73 lines (219–
93) are not meant to be taken seriously—"the philosophy of the

advertising man."[20] In fact, the speaker offers us several high-sounding but ultimately empty sermonettes and analogies. First he pompously equates "Decency" with "Opinion." Then he sententiously warns us not to laugh too quickly at romantic nonsense (though he has obviously been guilty of urging us to do just that throughout). Next he lectures Strephon for his compulsive idealism, managing his argument so that Strephon's choice is either to "lick her leavings" or "find a filthy Mate" (ll. 235–44), then grandly concluding with the (often overlooked) pronouncement that he himself finds nothing attractive about women anyway:

> Your Fancy then had always dwelt
> On what you saw, and what you smelt;
> Would still the same Ideas give ye,
> As when you spy'd her on the Privy.
> And, spight of *Chloe*'s Charms divine,
> Your Heart had been as whole as mine.
>
> [526]

The clown traditionally stands apart from his audience; he has little stake in the moral solution of his story, little serious commitment to the moral education of his audience. After the usual appeal to "AUTHORITIES both old and recent," the speaker delivers a little "judicious" criticism of females: they get lazy and sloppy and disgusting after the battle for the marriage crown is won. Unlike good soldiers, they "throw all their Weapons down" (l. 262). If we have failed to notice that this language echoes the silly "battle" between Strephon and Chloe on their wedding night (ll. 145–60), the speaker makes his irony more distinct by reinforcing this sententious point with a political analogy:

> Though by the Politicians Scheme
> Whoe'er arrives at Pow'r supreme,
> Those Arts by which at first they gain it,
> They still must practise to maintain it.
>
> [526]

It need not be said that solemn analogies to "political arts" hardly indicate a straightforward intention on Swift's part. After some abuse for women who imposture by trying to be "wits," the speaker gravely advises all females to learn from the "Puppet-

Man" the arts of deception and illusion. One is almost tempted
to say of the final eight-line sermon: we have had the "ladder"
and the "stage-itinerant," now for the "pulpit." But the tone of
these lines seems to exclude any ironic intention. As the analogy
to the "PRUDENT Builder" indicates, true "Decency" in marriage
is hard to come by: it needs a "Foundation sound," not the delusive arts and wiles which make instead for a partnership of
fool and knave. The closing lines are bare of analogies and pomposity:

> ON Sense and Wit your Passion found,
> By Decency cemented round;
> Let Prudence with Good Nature strive,
> To keep Esteem and Love alive.
> Then come old Age whene'er it will,
> Your Friendship shall continue still:
> And thus a mutual gentle Fire,
> Shall never but with Life expire.
>
> [527]

Had the poem ended before these lines, its relation to the
other "vexatious" poems about women would be clear: it would
demonstrate the dangers of easy and inadequate analogies and
preaching as solutions to the problem of illusion and disgust,
blasphemy and blessing. As it stands, "Strephon and Chloe" does
supply the "positives"; we might say that it leaves us, not with
the experience of moral difficulties, as do the earlier "scatological" poems, but with propositional truth and value. And yet, the
(now) reasonable and congenial narrator leaves us really with
merely a catalogue of abstract terms—perhaps as a "reward" for
having weathered the difficulties of being his audience or as an
emblem of a truth which may not be propositional at all.

In the 1734 quarto pamphlet which Matthew Pilkington arranged to be published, "Cassinus and Peter" was preceded in
order by "A Beautiful Young Nymph" and "Strephon and
Chloe." As the "lead" poem, "A Beautiful Young Nymph" was
naturally also the advertised title of the pamphlet, and it is reasonable to assume that Swift wanted his readers to experience
the tough-minded, vexing problems of that poem before they
went on to the "solutions" in the two poems which were "added."

"Strephon and Chloe," though flawed in its overall design as I read it, provides a kind of climax for the "scatological" poems: the "middle ground" of the problem of blasphemy or blessing is at last positively, though abstractly, affirmed. Furthermore, as its title suggests, "Strephon and Chloe" gives something like equal weight to the contributing failures of both men and women, where "The Progress of Beauty" emphasized female delusions, "The Lady's Dressing Room" stressed the degrading attitudes of men, and "A Beautiful Young Nymph" revealed the tawdry fate of women. "Cassinus and Peter" rights the balance, as it were, for "Celia" is no more than an emblematic touchstone for the absurd degradations of Cassinus. And, following the "earned" resolution of "Strephon and Chloe," this final poem exploits the release of "vexation" in pure comedy.

As Gilmore noted, "Cassinus and Peter" is an "elaborately sustained joke"; the heretofore problematical choice between blasphemy and blessing gives way to a different and temporary ironic quandary, for Cassy's sensibility seems to include both extremes. Our first sight of the "College Soph" (ll. 11–24) convinces us that Cassinus certainly has no idealistic compulsion for cleanliness or "Nicety." An ostensible paradox is soon constructed, however. For this "special Wit" also indulges himself in "Rapture sweet," and Peter's periphrastic salute allows us to savor Cassy's silly romantic posturings better than anything Swift could have put into the latter's own mouth:

> WHY, *Cassy,* thou wilt doze thy Pate:
> What makes thee lie a'bed so late?
> The Finch, the Linnet and the Thrush,
> Their Mattins chant in ev'ry Bush:
> And, I have heard thee oft salute
> *Aurora* with thy early Flute.
>
> [528–29]

Peter, like Strephon in the earlier poems, is possessed of pitiable idealist delusions. But Cassinus, like the speaker of "The Progress of Beauty," is coldly indifferent to the imagined tragedies of his lover's death or disease; and, like the speaker of "The Lady's Dressing Room," he is altogether too equable about the charms of a "pocky Quean":

271

> Come, tell us, has she play'd the Whore?
> Oh, *Peter*, wou'd it were no more!
> Why, Plague confound her sandy Locks:
> Say, has the small or greater Pox
> Sunk down her Nose, or seam'd her Face?
> Be easy, 'tis a common Case.
>   Oh *Peter!* Beauty's but a Varnish,
> Which Time and Accidents will tarnish:
>   [529]

By this time, we are beginning to be aware that Swift is ironically rehearsing the various fraudulent voices and attitudes of the other "scatological" poems, and we may not be totally unprepared to hear Cassinus spout a little specious nonsense which reminds us of the language employed by the narrator of "Strephon and Chloe":

> Oh *Peter!* Beauty's but a Varnish,
> Which Time and Accidents will tarnish:
> But, *Caelia* has contriv'd to blast
> Those Beauties that might ever last.
> Nor can Imagination guess,
> Nor Eloquence Divine express,
> How that ungrateful charming Maid,
> My purest Passion has betray'd.
>   [529]

Not only does Cassy's fatuous talk of "lasting Beauties" unknowingly parody the ending of "Strephon and Chloe" (indicating again how readily such comforting abstractions can be perverted), but the reader has the added delight of recognizing the comical accuracy of Cassinus's inadvertent bawdy allusion:

> And, Love such Nicety requires,
> One *Blast* will put out all his Fires.
>   ["Strephon and Chloe," ll. 135–36]

> But, *Caelia* has contriv'd to blast
> Those Beauties that might ever last.
>   ["Cassinus and Peter," ll. 53–54]

Cassinus is presented to us as a mock paradox: a romantic

dreamer who is nevertheless quite willing to relish pocky whores. Of course, Swift has an answer to the pseudoproblem in store for us, but his comic intentions require the suspense to build up before the secret of Cassy's monomania is revealed. Therefore, after the tragical youth delivers himself of some dark hints about "A Crime that shocks all human Kind," he indulges in a bit of inflating self-pity, imagining his martyr's journey to Hades. The comic technique of self-indulgent overstatement is quite obvious, but essential to the genuine comedy of the poem. Cassinus's extreme affectation of sensibility is Swift's means of allowing his reader the healing grace of detachment and humorous condemnation. After Cassy's absurd projection of self-heroism, he produces a reprise of his earlier portentous hints before allowing the secret to escape in a final line that was probably even more amusing when the last word had to be indicated by the decent obscurity of a dash. The revelation does indeed explain Cassy's tortured state of mind, though obviously not in the way he intended.

The last of the "scatological" poems is one version of the "perfect" ending to the series. Swift bestows upon Cassinus and Peter all the extreme, debilitating attitudes which "vexed" the reader in the earlier poems. By allowing the reader to detach himself so completely from the absurd duo, Swift fulfills the "promise" of a shared positive commitment in "Strephon and Chloe." That is, "Cassinus and Peter" is not a "vexatious" poem, but is rather a genially transparent imitation of one, which finally dissolves the mock paradox in favor of relying upon the reader's human engagement and moral good sense. The comedy of the poem is a kind of reward for the reader who has undergone the "vexation" of the earlier poems. There, comedy is either a specious alternative, or is at the expense of the reader himself; here, it is the gift of a shared experience of comic discrimination which subsumes blasphemy and blessing.

Notes

1. Aldous Huxley, *Do What You Will* (London, 1929), pp. 93–106;

RODINO

John Middleton Murry, *Jonathan Swift: A Critical Biography* (London, 1954), pp. 432–48.

2. *Life Against Death* (Middletown, Conn., 1959), pp. 179–201; rpt. in *Swift: A Collection of Critical Essays*, ed. Ernest Tuveson (Englewood Cliffs, N.J., 1964), p. 37.

3. Ibid., p. 38.

4. Irvin Ehrenpreis, "The Meaning of Gulliver's Last Voyage," *Review of English Literature* 3, no. 3 (July 1962): 18–38, has an important discussion of Swift's relation to eighteenth-century "definitions of man." A. O. Lovejoy, "The Parallel of Deism and Classicism," *Modern Philology* 29 (1932): 281–99, remains one of the best discussions of the pervasiveness of morality as "reasoned agreement" in the eighteenth century.

5. *Some Versions of Pastoral* (1935; rpt. London, 1950), p. 62.

6. "Order and Cruelty: A Reading of Swift with some comments on Pope and Johnson," *Essays in Criticism* 20 (1970): 24–56.

7. *Swift: Poetical Works*, ed. Herbert Davis (London, 1967), p. 338. Subsequent references to the poem are from this edition and are cited parenthetically in the text by page.

8. "The Comedy of Swift's Scatological Poems," *PMLA* 91 (January 1976): 41. See also the exchange among Gilmore, Donald Greene (Swift is recommending "good sense" to the "Cassinuses and Strephons of this world"), and Peter J. Schakel ("the scatological poems show us a more human Swift, fallible, uncertain, struggling—trying to work through his feelings, but not succeeding entirely") in the "Forum" section of *PMLA* 91 (May 1976): 464–67.

9. Geoffrey Hill, "Jonathan Swift: The Poetry of 'Reaction,'" *The World of Jonathan Swift,* ed. Brian Vickers (Cambridge, Mass., 1968), p. 209.

10. There are several stanzas in the manuscript which were omitted in the printed version. These are largely composed of sordid details which Swift's friends apparently thought tipped the balance of the first part of the poem toward "Blasphemy." See *The Poems of Jonathan Swift,* ed. Harold Williams, 2nd ed., 3 vols. (Oxford, 1958), 1:225–29.

11. Herbert Davis, "A Modest Defense of 'The Lady's Dressing Room,'" *Restoration and Eighteenth-Century Literature: Essays in Honor of Alan Dugald McKillop*, ed. Carroll Camden (Chicago, 1963), p. 42. See Louise K. Barnett's discussion of the unreliability of the narrator in "The Mysterious Narrator: Another Look at 'The Lady's Dressing Room,'" *Concerning Poetry* 9, no. 2 (Fall 1976): 29–32. I am encouraged to find general agreement between our accounts of how the poem works, though at least part of Barnett's explanation of Swift's motives ("the poet pleads for cleanliness and order . . .") is obviously different from my own.

12. *O.E.D.*, 6:802, notes the usage of "mutton" to refer to "loose women and prostitutes" as early as 1518. For a contemporary example,

see Rochester's *A Ramble in St. James Park*, ll. 45–62, in *The Complete Poems of John Wilmot, Earl of Rochester*, ed. David. M. Vieth (New Haven, 1968), where the joke about the first "knight" centers on his ignorance of the lascivious second meaning of "mutton." For modern usage see Yeat's anecdote about Ernest Dowson and Oscar Wilde in *The Trembling of the Veil*, 4:14.

13. P. 40.

14. *Swift: Poetical Works*, pp. 479–80. David Vieth, *Notes and Queries* 220 (1975): 562–63, corrects "Satira" in the Davis and Williams texts to "Statira," probably a reference to Nathaniel Lee's tragedy *The Rival Queens*. The correction sharpens the contrast between make-believe (the stage) and real (the "pocky" actress who plays the role).

15. Brown, p. 40; Greene, "On Swift's 'Scatological' Poems," *The Sewanee Review* 75 (1967): 672–89 [reprinted in this volume]; Aden, "Those Gaudy Tulips: Swift's 'Unprintables,'" *Quick Springs of Sense: Studies in the Eighteenth Century*, ed. Larry S. Champion (Athens, Ga., 1974), p. 21.

16. See A. B. England, "World Without Order: Some Thoughts on the Poetry of Swift," *Essays in Criticism* 16 (1966): 32–43 [reprinted in this volume]; and Christine Rees, "Gay, Swift, and the Nymphs of Drury Lane," *Essays in Criticism* 23 (1973): 1–21 [reprinted in this volume], for views which agree with mine on the ending of the poem. Rees points out the little history of "tulip imagery," noting that tulips were associated with "flaunting beauty," so that "a certain moral ambivalence" clung to the image.

17. Despite Rees's interesting argument that the poem was intended to "defile" the traditional Caroline pastoral, it is the grotesque tradition itself which Swift calls into question.

18. The phrase is from Thomas R. Edwards, Jr., *This Dark Estate: A Reading of Pope* (Berkeley, Calif., 1963), p. 1. Gilmore, p. 35, suggests that "Corinna's daily resurrections link her with Falstaff."

19. Pp. 23, 25.

20. P. 683.

IX. *On Poetry: A Rapsody*

C. J. RAWSON

"'Tis Only Infinite Below"
Speculations on Swift,
Wallace Stevens, R. D. Laing
and Others

Wallace Stevens has a poem entitled 'Frogs Eat Butterflies. Snakes Eat Frogs. Hogs Eat Snakes. Men Eat Hogs'.[1] The poem, like many of Stevens's, is about poetry and its relation to the great processes of life and death. The cycle of rapacity which the title describes is an ineluctable fact of nature. From this, squarely recognising death, the poet starts. . . .

Swift also has a poem about poetry, *On Poetry: A Rapsody* (1733), in which various images of self-nourishing, reciprocal feeding, and a chain of rapacity occur. Chickens take a month to fatten, but are quickly eaten; similarly, poems long toiled over 'Are swallow'd o'er a Dish of Tea' and go 'where the *Chickens* went before'.[2] Again, if you have published a poem anonymously and the town is running it down, keep the secret, 'Sit still, and swallow down your Spittle' (*Poems*, II. 644). Most famously, there is a picture of universal devouring in the animal kingdom:

This essay, here condensed to approximately two-thirds its original length, first appeared in *Essays in Criticism* 22 (1972): 161–81. It also appears, in slightly different form, as Chapter 3 in Rawson's *Gulliver and the Gentle Reader: Studies in Swift and Our Time* (London and Boston: Routledge and Kegan Paul, 1973), pp. 60–83. Reprinted with permission.

> *Hobbes* clearly proves that ev'ry Creature
> Lives in a State of War by Nature.
> The Greater for the Smallest watch,
> But meddle seldom with their Match.
> A Whale of moderate Size will draw
> A Shole of Herrings down his Maw.
> A Fox with Geese his Belly crams;
> A Wolf destroys a thousand Lambs.
>
> *(Poems, II. 651)*

Poets, and fleas, are like this too, differing only in three special emphases or implications. They reverse the order of nature, so that it is the smallest who bite the greatest; they do this in an unending chain; and the chain is cannibalistic:

> The Vermin only teaze and pinch
> Their Foes superior by an Inch.
> So, Nat'ralists observe, a Flea
> Hath smaller Fleas that on him prey,
> And these have smaller Fleas to bite 'em,
> And so proceed *ad infinitum*:
>
> *(Poems, II. 651)*

There is no need to insist that Swift's emphases, unlike Stevens's, are satirical. He is dealing with bad critics and bad poets. The self-feeding, and the cannibal activity, are unproductive, barren, but not with the paradoxical 'aridity', the true 'poverty' of Stevens's poet, which 'becomes his heart's strong core' (*C.P.*, 427). Characteristic Swiftian effects quickly develop. *Unnaturalness* is massively emphasised, not only the simple reversal of 'due Subordination' (*Poems*, II. 650), but perversions of natural feeding patterns which compound, and cut across, the cannibal chain. Thus, the poetasters have left their native Grub Street, are now not only tolerated outside (and above) their proper station, but actually fed by the Court:

> Degenerate from their ancient Brood,
> Since first the Court allow'd them Food.
>
> *(Poems, II. 652)*

The whole fantasy is elaborated with a sour loftiness of which Swift was a unique and perfect master.

My special emphasis, however, is on the *infinity* of the flea-biting chain. This infinity is not one which completes itself in a circle, like the constant renewals of the life-cycle. It is a teeming but negative endlessness, applicable especially to poetry, which (unlike other things in nature) has an upper but no lower limits:

> From bad to worse, and worse they fall,
> But, who can reach the Worst of all?
> For, tho' in Nature Depth and Height
> Are equally held infinite,
> In Poetry the Height we know;
> 'Tis only infinite below.
>   (*Poems*, II. 653–4)

The ever-receding limits of badness ('who can reach the Worst of all?') recall an important satiric pattern in *Gulliver's Travels*. But against this denial of a closing circle, where end and beginning, top and bottom, meet, runs another configuration. In the damaging sense, there *is* a circle, and top and bottom *do* meet in the '*low Sublime*' (*Poems*, II. 652, 657):

> With Heads to Points the Gulph they enter,
> Linkt perpendicular to the Centre:
> And as their Heels elated rise,
> Their Heads attempt the nether Skies.
>   (*Poems*, II. 654)

Such polarisations and circularities are an old preoccupation of Swift's, going back at least as far as the *Tale of a Tub* and the *Mechanical Operation of the Spirit*:

> . . . whereas the mind of Man, when he gives the Spur and Bridle to his Thoughts, doth never stop, but naturally sallies out into both extreams of High and Low, of Good and Evil; His first Flight of Fancy, commonly transports Him to Idea's of what is most Perfect, finished, and exalted; till having soared out of his own Reach and Sight, not well perceiving how near the Frontiers of Height and Depth, border upon each other; With the same Course and Wing, he falls down plum into the lowest Bottom of Things; like one who travels

281

the *East* into the *West*; or like a strait Line drawn by its own Length into a Circle.[3]

The unending series, and the closed circle, can, by a happy chance, coexist mathematically, and Swift is quick to seize on the joke (though its use in satire was not new: Marvell used it in the *Rehearsal Transpros'd*).[4] What really interests Swift is not the mathematical viability of this joke, but the opportunity it gives the satirist for having it both ways. Endless chains, closed circles, crossing poles and the like would be thrust into unsettling proximities even if scientific explanations had not been available for some of them.

Of course Swift is at the same time laughing at scientific propositions about the ultimate circularity of the straight line, or whatever; and at the paradox-mongering which 'makes us fond of furnishing every bright Idea with its Reverse':

> Whether a Tincture of Malice in our Natures, makes us fond of furnishing every bright Idea with its Reverse; Or, whether Reason reflecting upon the Sum of Things, can, like the Sun, serve only to enlighten one half of the Globe, leaving the other half, by Necessity, under Shade and Darkness: Or, whether Fancy, flying up to the imagination of what is Highest and Best, becomes over-shot, and spent, and weary, and suddenly falls like a dead Bird of Paradise, to the Ground. Or, whether ... I have not entirely missed the true Reason....
>
> (*P.W.*, I. 99)

The *Tale* is concerned with the human mind, not merely bad poets, and the example helps us to see the Grub Street hacks of the poem, like their ancestor in the *Tale*, resolving themselves into instances of a radical perversity of man, endlessly refining or 'modernising' itself into fresh heights or depths of folly. The Bird of Paradise was popularly supposed to lack feet, and to be doomed to fly in the air until death. Bacon has a mocking remark about this bird, which Swift may be recalling.[5] But in Coleridge's *Eolian Harp* there was to be a lovely celebration, where 'Footless and wild' and 'hovering on untam'd wing', neither pausing nor perching, the bird of Paradise becomes an emblem of high imaginative enchantments, associated with 'Melodies round honey-dropping flowers'—sweetness and light! As so often, Swift's mockeries of mad moderns prefigure the imaginative explorations of later men, as though the modernism had finally come into its own, outfacing Swift. We may well also feel a kind of tragic beauty erupting lawlessly from Swift's own jeer about the bird, Swift himself becoming a modern *malgré lui,* unruly in his restless intensities. . . .

Such short-circuits of violence find their stylistic reflection in certain 'gratuitous' shocks in what we have become accustomed to call the literature of 'cruelty'. I have argued elsewhere[6] that certain sudden violences in Swift's prose style, notably at moments of rambling tortuosity or in other mimicries of protracted or limitless folly, may be taken as an intuitive (though doubtless not in those terms conscious or avowed) rendering of this.

Violent interruption is not the same as polarised vision, but it has here a similar purpose, of breaking the spinning formlessness of 'all complexities of mire or blood'. In Swift, and in Yeats and Mailer, there is a powerful tendency, at their most vivid moments or in their most crucial writings, to think in terms of strongly paired opposites. The whole range of Yeats's doctrines of the mask and antiself, Mailer's dichotomising of Hip and Square (and his related interest in the concept of the 'White Negro') or Cannibals and Christians,[7] have a real relation with Swift's pairing of Ancients and Moderns, Fools and Knaves, big men and little men, Houyhnhnms and Yahoos.

Politically, such polarising outlooks tend to be 'radical' (whether of the left or of the right) rather than 'liberal', fostering a Hobbesian domination of unruly human nature, or an opposite project of 'perpetual revolution'.[8] Swift knew the old truths about the closeness of anarchy to tyranny, of the extreme left to the extreme right, and he professed himself a 'moderate'. But we should not be misled by that. His professed 'moderation' and his conservative attachment to the 'common forms', and to established accommodations and 'middle ways', were accompanied by an often strongly manifested element of dislike for these self-same things. Swift saw man's condition as being by its psychological nature inclined to 'perpetual revolution' (an eternal 'modernism'), and he did not exempt himself from this. His moderation is itself an extreme position, committed to the *status quo* and slow piece-meal improvement as a desperate protection from the disruptive forces that are, in himself as in all of us, ready to erupt at the least failure of vigilance.

His political outlook is thus profoundly pessimistic. Where the Marxists regard the 'dialectic spiral' as tending upwards, towards 'higher reformulation' at each dialectical 'leap' or synthesis,[9] Swift saw the spiral as most characteristically tending downwards. Indeed, as he said, "Tis only infinite below'. This is so because of that restless perversity of our psychological constitution, of which the 'moderns', Grub Street hacks and flea-like poetasters, are a particularly disreputable manifestation. That perversity, as we know especially from the *Tale*'s 'author', involves an unchecked submission to instantaneous impulse, and an undisguised cherishing of mere undisciplined experience. . . .

The Unnamable's broodings [in Beckett's play] go on to explore alternative patterns. For the moment, however, his configuration is like Swift's, but even bleaker. Both posit that the spiral has a limit in one direction, and none in the other.

> For, tho' in Nature Depth and Height
> Are equally held infinite,
> In Poetry the Height we know;
> 'Tis only infinite below.
> *(Poems,* II. 653–4)

But for Swift the limit is a fixed and positive height, while for Beckett's hero it is just a dead end. Of course, that Swiftian 'positive' is flattened and back-handed, since, unlike its opposite, the goodness has its limits, and since, by a queer kind of irony I have already noted, it is made to appear *unnatural*: for in *nature*, height or depth *are* infinite. The passage should be taken seriously. That its main business is to jeer at 'bad poets' does not reduce it to a mere specialised joke, for 'bad poets' are (as in the *Tale*) human nature in its unregulated state and also (as in both the *Tale* and Pope's *Dunciad*) a desperate symptom of cultural sickness. Still, Swift can laugh at them in the name of established standards, and his treatment of them or of the hack in the *Tale* is, despite some self-implication, at least sufficiently externalised to prevent compassionate sympathy. Beckett's Unnamable, like the *Tale*'s 'author', is quizzically conscious of himself as a writer, and of his predicament as a mad one. 'How, in such conditions, can I write, to consider only the manual aspect of that bitter folly?' he asks.[10] The Unnamable's *physical* difficulties are more absolute than those of Swift's occasionally bed-ridden and hungry garretteer, since his very shape and physical identity are in question. But the mental anguish of his consciousness is very stark. 'And yet I am afraid, afraid of what my words will do to me, to my refuge, yet again':[11]

> Labyrinthine torment that can't be grasped, or limited, or felt, or suffered, no, not even suffered, I suffer all wrong too, even that I do all wrong too . . .[12]

Here, the Unnamable joins Camus's Sisyphus, sufferer of ever-renewed, 'absurd' and meaningless torment. Swift would not have denied meaning to the suffering, but would have hung on to a belief in its 'decorum', as well as its justice. For this reason, it might almost be said, he held back from attributing serious suffering to his hacks. That would not only have dignified them unduly, but perhaps removed their difference from himself.

These torments Swift, like Beckett or Camus, regarded as given, as well as self-inflicted. But the quality of self-infliction was, for him, a peculiarly culpable thing, and he shows what Beckett and certainly Camus do not: the special exasperations of guilt, and of a rigid commitment to values which are perpetually under subversion from that condition of restlessness which is given. The bottomless chain of self-complicating perversity in *Gulliver* is seen in relation to very uncompromising and very plain standards of Nature and Reason. The plainness gives an added hopelessness to the sense of the folly of sin, but also an inevitability, since only the most irrepressible energies could be supposed strong enough to break such strong and simple rules. Hence the peculiarly personal testiness which enters into Swift's uses of the satiric commonplace of the world's unmendability: the 'I told you so' spikiness with which he renders Gulliver's annoyance that the world is still uncured six months after the publication of his book (*P.W.*, XI. 6), or the Modest Proposer's belief that a cannibal-project will seem more acceptable than the sensible 'other Expedients' which he (and Swift) had once been 'visionary' enough to advocate (*P.W.*, XII. 116–17). The rhetorical posture of a noble, protesting madness is allowed to curdle into a pathological absurdity, in which the distinction between the vicious and the virtuous folly becomes horribly and insultingly blurred, and in which rhetorical madness (of both kinds) becomes medical—and perhaps incurable.

The configurations of limitlessness and incurability in *On Poetry: A Rapsody* are, of course, in a lighter vein. The cannibalism *ad infinitum* of the poetic fleas should not be approximated too closely to the outrageous nastiness of the *Modest Proposal*. That Swift was capable, in moods ranging from an unsettling playfulness to the most chilling sarcastic astringency, of himself expressing certain destructive velleities not unlike that of the *Proposal*, I have argued elsewhere.[13] My concern here is with his own paradoxical involvement in the bottomlessness of the fleas' cannibal activity, and with the simultaneous very rigid sense that the bottomlessness (as well as the habit of eating people) is wrong. The playfulness does not remove a powerful element both of self-involvement and of distaste.

Another highly stylised, and perhaps more externalised, variant of the *ad infinitum* configuration occurs earlier in the poem, when Swift advises critics who want to quote Longinus, but do not know Greek, to buy Welsted's translation,

> Translated from *Boileau's* Translation,
> And quote *Quotation* on *Quotation*.
> *(Poems*, II. 649)

The quip takes its place among the whole network of jokes about circularities or infinities of consumption in the poem, and calls to mind the *Tale's* joke about nesting boxes: 'But not to Digress farther in the midst of a Digression, as I have known some Authors inclose Digressions in one another, like a Nest of Boxes . . .'(*P.W.*, I. 77). The example shows the set of boxes not, as in the poem, externalised into a fairly specific (and actually finite) perversion of plagiarism, but instead internalised into wanderings of mental self-elaboration. Moreover, the 'author' not only actually says he will no longer do what he has just done, but will shortly give us a formally labelled 'Digression in Praise of

Digressions'. These playful notions of circularity or of infinite regression are, of course, a highly patterned, self-completing joke, and have some effect of taming or enclosing infinity itself. In both poem and *Tale*, however, they coexist with another kind of open-endedness. Both works contain the old mock-learned joke that what we are reading is a scholarly edition of itself, with a scholarly apparatus or other indications that draw attention to the fact that there are gaps in the MS., and in particular that it is unfinished at the end. Thus the poem ends with asterisks and *Caetera desiderantur* (*Poems*, II. 657),[14] and the *Tale* with the 'author' planning to resume his pen, after a pause for feeling the world's pulse and his own (*P.W.*, I. 135).

If the poem and *Tale* become, in these ways, the thing which they mock, that is partly the mere nature of the parody, although many critics have felt (with the *Tale* at least) that Swift's self-implication runs deeper than that. The infinities evoked by these open endings are part closed-system, and part gaping void. The *Tale*'s 'author', in particular, is considering a modern experiment to '*write upon Nothing*', letting 'the Pen still move on' beyond the exhaustion of his subject and the exhaustion of his book (*P.W.*, I. 133).[15] Compare his fellow-dunce, Cibber, 'Sinking from thought to thought, a vast profound!', whose mental abyss is of Miltonic dimensions:

> Plung'd for his sense, but found no bottom there,
> Yet wrote and flounder'd on, in mere despair.
> (*Dunciad*, I. 118–20)[16]

Swift's 'author' has not made the 'mere despair' conscious to himself, and it would be unlike Swift to claim Miltonic splendours and miseries for his creatures, or for himself (though a 'despair' of the modern 'vast profound' he did, in another and very anguished sense, share with Pope). But the aptness of Milton's Chaos and Milton's Hell to our subject is real, for his Satan saw Hell as both mental prison and bottomless drop:

> Which way I flie is Hell; my self am Hell;
> And in the lowest deep a lower deep
> Still threatning to devour me op'ns wide.
> (*Paradise Lost*, IV. 75–7)

This kind of 'vast vacuitie' (II.932) is the reward, and the domain, of guilty folly: it is infinite space, yet totally imprisoning, and, in one important sense, *situated in the mind* (the spiralling mental hell of Dostoyevsky's *Notes from Underground* is a still more completely psychologised version).[17]

The freedoms of these spaces of the mind, and their entrapments, are Swift's subject, in anguish and in wit. In his parody of Anthony Collins, *Mr. C——ns's Discourse of Free-Thinking, Put into plain English, . . . for the Use of the Poor,* Swift shows his foolish Freethinker asserting the right of all men to 'think freely', even those who are incapable of 'thinking freely':

> Whoever cannot *think freely,* may let it alone if he pleases, by virtue of his Right to *think freely*; that is to say, if such a Man *freely thinks* that he cannot *think freely,* of which every Man is a sufficient Judge, why then he need not *think freely,* unless he *thinks* fit.
>
> (*P.W.,* IV. 38)

The parody is gross. But the notion it conveys of spiralling vacuities which are both unlimited and self-imprisoning is vividly and characteristically Swiftian, even if it distorts what Collins really said. Swift's Freethinker was answering the objection that most men are not qualified to think at all, 'and if every Man thought it his Duty to *think freely,* and trouble his Neighbour with his Thoughts (which is an essential Part of *Free-thinking,*) it would make wild work in the World'.

Troubling one's neighbour with one's thoughts, that 'essential Part of *Free-thinking*', takes up the point made a little earlier, that 'free-thinking', like all forms of schism or anarchy, quickly turns tyrannical: 'It is the indispensable Duty of a *Free Thinker,* to endeavor *forcing* all the World to think as he does, and by that means make them *Free Thinkers* too' (*P.W.,* IV. 36). Swift's belief that dissenting attitudes in religion or politics should be tolerated so long as they are not expressed or displayed in public is well-known. But since dissent and doubt are radical to man, his point extends beyond the political forms of dissent to that potential private subversiveness which is in himself also. Hence his insistence on a peculiarly reductive moral discipline, and on massive self-restraint and self-suppression, rather than on any hopeless project of eradicating the vicious impulses themselves. In one of his 'Thoughts on Religion' he said 'I am not answerable to God for the doubts that arise in my own breast' provided he conceals them from others, tries to subdue them, and prevents their 'influence on the conduct of my life' (*P.W.,* IX. 262). His extension, in *Mr. C——ns's Discourse,* of the more technical and restricted sense of 'free-thinking' to the most literally anarchic implications of the term, is no mere debating-point, but rooted in a profound sense of real relation. The 'wild work in the World' which he foresees from any spread of free-thinking must be understood in the light of a short undated piece, 'Some Thoughts on Free-thinking', in which he approvingly quotes a remark made to him by an Irish prelate, 'that if the wisest man would at any time utter his thoughts, in the crude indigested manner, as they come into his head, he would be looked upon as raving mad'. This made it clear how essential it was to keep our thoughts, 'as they are the seeds of words and actions', under 'strictest regulation': 'So that I cannot imagine what is meant by the mighty zeal in some people, for asserting the freedom of thinking . . .' (*P.W.,* IV. 49).

That way madness lies. And when in 1738 Swift wrote, with a tart jokeyness, of his 'Age, Giddyness, Deafness, loss of Memory, Rage and Rancour against Persons and Proceedings', he chose to convey this self-mocking portait of senile decay in an image of endless spiralling regression from his former healthy self: 'I have been many months the Shadow of the Shadow of the Shadow, of &c &c &c of Dr. Sw——.'[18] We should not take this too solemnly (and certainly not as evidence of actual insanity!) But this infinite chain of self-attenuation may reasonably be put side by side with the equally playful and equally tart image of the cannibal chain of fleas and poets in *On Poetry: A Rapsody.* Grub Street poets and sectarian freethinkers are but images of the unregenerate self, and their mad cravings and hungers can, at a certain level, be translated and internalised into 'that hunger of imagination which preys incessantly upon life' which was Johnson's more compassionate formulation of man's radical restlessness (*Rasselas,* Ch. XXXI[I]). Modern psychology has taught us to think of the internalised self-reference of cannibal fantasies, and of related fantasies of eating and devouring.[19] We need not suppose that Swift or Johnson would be conscious of this in any cold technical sense, any more than Wallace Stevens was when he spoke in 'Frogs Eat Butterflies. Snakes Eat Frogs. Hogs Eat Snakes. Men Eat Hogs', not only of the life-cycle, but of the imagination's rootedness in, as well as analogy with, this cycle. Where, he asked in another poem,

> . . . shall we find more than derisive words?
> When shall lush chorals spiral through our fire
> And daunt that old assassin, heart's desire?[20]

'That old assassin' is Johnson's 'hunger of imagination', turned into affirmation. It is perhaps not too fanciful to say that he is also the Swiftian flea, not mocked but celebrated in 'more than derisive words'. In yet another poem, Stevens spoke of 'the never-resting mind', but saw (unlike Swift, or Johnson) 'in this bitterness, delight'—the source of poems, 'flawed words and stubborn sounds': 'The imperfect is our paradise' (*C.P.*, 194).

Notes

1. *Collected Poems of Wallace Stevens*, London, 1955 (hereafter *C.P.*), p. 78.

2. *The Poems of Jonathan Swift*, ed. Harold Williams, 2d ed., Oxford, 1958 (hereafter *Poems*), II. 642.

3. *Tale of a Tub*, Section VIII: *Prose Writings of Jonathan Swift*, ed. Herbert Davis and others, 14 vols., Oxford (Blackwell), 1939–68 (hereafter *P.W.*), I. 99.

4. See *Tale of a Tub*, ed. A. C. Guthkelch and D. Nichol Smith, 2d ed., Oxford, 1958, p. 158n., citing *Rehearsal Transpros'd*, 1672, p. 206.

5. Bacon, *Works*, ed. J. Spedding *et al.*, London, 1857–74, XII. 43. Cited Brian Vickers, ed., *The World of Jonathan Swift*, Oxford (Blackwell), 1968, p. 121.

6. 'Order and Cruelty: A Reading of Swift (with some comments on Pope and Johnson)', *Essays in Criticism*, XX (1970), 24–56.

7. On Mailer's tendency 'to think in "couples"', see Tony Tanner, 'On the Parapet. A Study of the Novels of Norman Mailer', *C.Q.*, XII (1970), 160–61. See also the amusing conversation between Nicolas and the Detective in Ionesco's *Victims of Duty*, about the need in the theatre to replace the old psychology, based on 'the principle of identity and unity of character', by a new 'dynamic psychology' capable of rendering not static being, but the complex 'formlessness of becoming', and which

is at the same time 'a psychology based on antagonism' and on polarised 'contradiction' (*Plays*, Volume II, London, 1962, p. 308).

8. For another conception of political process as a 'polarised circuit', with renewals envisaged as following upon death by self-devouring ('The serpent shall swallow itself . . . Then we can have a new snake'), see D. H. Lawrence, *Kangaroo*, ch. XVI, Harmondsworth, 1968, pp. 333–34. Lawrence's hero desires liberation from some specific contemporary manifestations of this circuit, in 'a new recognition of the life-mystery'.

9. R. N. Carew Hunt, *The Theory and Practice of Communism*, Harmondsworth, 1966, p. 46.

10. Samuel Beckett, *Molloy, Malone Dies, The Unnamable*, London, 1959, p. 303.

11. Ibid., p. 305.

12. Ibid., p. 316.

13. 'Order and Cruelty', p. 27; 'Nature's Dance of Death. Part I: Urbanity and Strain in Fielding, Swift, and Pope', *E.C.S.*, III (1970), 316–20.

14. By an ironic coincidence, some cancelled fragments of the actual poem have survived, and are sometimes printed by editors immediately after the final words, *Caetera desiderantur* (*Poems*, II. 639, 658–59).

15. Cf. Beckett's Unnamable: '. . . I had nothing to say and had to say something . . .' (*Molloy*, etc., p. 400). For some suggestive insights into the relation of madness to configurations of limitless nothingness, see Michel Foucault, *Madness and Civilization. A History of Insanity in the Age of Reason*, trs. Richard Howard, New York and Toronto, 1967, pp. 224 ff., esp. 227–28; and p. 100.

16. On the Miltonic elements of this see, in addition to the Twickenham note, Arthur Sherbo in *M.L.R.*, LXV (1970), 505.

17. *Notes from Underground*, I. iii, v; trs. A. R. McAndrew, New York, Toronto and London, 1961, pp. 97, 103.

18. *Correspondence*, ed. Harold Williams, Oxford, 1963–65, V. 89.

19. E.g., *The Divided Self*, p. 49; and see the chapter on 'Food' in Norman O. Brown, *Love's Body*, New York, 1966, which also cites related passages from more ancient (especially religious) symbolisms.

20. Wallace Stevens, *Opus Posthumous*, London, 1959, p. 66.

X. *Verses on the Death of Dr. Swift*

BARRY SLEPIAN

The Ironic Intention of
Swift's Verses on His Own Death

Swift's intention in his 'Verses on the Death of Dr. Swift' has puzzled many people. In 1738, having kept the finished poem in manuscript for six years, Swift sent a copy to Dr. William King, Principal of St. Mary Hall, Oxford, with directions that the poem should be printed in London.[1] By way of the Earl of Orrery this copy, or a transcript of it, reached Pope, who wrote to Orrery on 25 September: 'I return the Verses you favor me with, the latter part of which is inferior to the beginning, the Character too dry, as well as too Vain in some respects, & in one or two particulars, not true.'[2]

In January 1739 the London printer Charles Bathurst published a version of the poem vastly different from Swift's manuscript. Besides numerous changes of individual words, all Swift's footnotes and 171 of the original 484 lines had been omitted, and more than 60 lines from another poem by Swift, 'The Life and Genuine Character of Dr. Swift', had been added.[3] Almost all these changes occur in the latter part of the poem.

Dr. King, who made the publication arrangements, was understandably nervous about the liberties that had been taken with the Dean's poem. During the winter of 1738–39 he sent four letters to Dublin—two to Swift and two to Martha Whiteway,

This essay first appeared in *The Review of English Studies* n.s. 14 (1963): 249–56. Reprinted with permission.

Swift's cousin—explaining why the alterations had been made and denying, in the case of most of them, personal responsibility. He wrote to Swift on 5 January, about ten days before the London edition appeared: 'I have done nothing without the advice and approbation of those among your friends in this country, who love and esteem you most.... As they are much better judges of mankind than I am, I very readily submit to their opinion.'[4] On 23 January he wrote to Swift: 'All the rest of your friends on this side of the water must share the blame with me; for I have absolutely conformed myself to their advice and opinion as to the manner of publication.'[5] He himself, he told Swift in this letter, would accept responsibility for the omission of two passages which he 'durst not' print: one (lines 183–8) that would have offended Queen Caroline, and another (presumably lines 379–430) that the government might have thought treasonous. He said nothing to Swift about certain parts seeming vain.

Writing to Mrs. Whiteway, Dr. King was more circumstantial and more frank. In a letter dated 30 January he said: 'I ... doubt much whether [Swift] will be satisfied with the manner in which he finds it published; to which I consented in deference to Mr. Pope's judgement, and the opinion of others of the Dean's friends in this country.'[6] And in another, dated 6 March, he said:

> The Doctor's friends, whom I consulted on this occasion, were of opinion, that the latter part of the poem might be thought by the public a little vain, if so much were said by himself of himself. They were unwilling that any imputation of this kind should lie against this poem, considering there is not the least tincture of vanity appearing in any of his former writings, and that it is well known, there is no man living more free from that fault than he is. They were of opinion that these lines,
>
> > He lash'd the vice, but spared the name,
> > No individual could resent
> > Where thousands equally were meant,
>
> might be liable to some objection, and were not, strictly speaking, a just part of his character; because several persons have been lashed by name, a Bettesworth, and

in this poem, Charteris and Whitshed, and for my part,
I do not think, or ever shall think, that it is an imputation on a satirist to lash an infamous fellow by name.[7]

In this same letter to Mrs. Whiteway, Dr. King also wrote:

I was not a little mortified yesterday, when the bookseller brought me the Dublin edition, and at the same
time put into my hands a letter he had received from
Faulkner, by which I perceive the Dean is much dissatisfied with our manner of publication, and that so many
lines have been omitted, if Faulkner speaks truth, and
knows as much of the Dean's mind as he pretends to
know. Faulkner has sent over several other copies to
other booksellers, so that I take it for granted this poem
will soon be reprinted here from the Dublin edition,
and then it may be perceived how much the Dean's
friends have been mistaken in their judgement, however
good their intentions have been.

The Dublin edition referred to, printed by George Faulkner,
Swift's Irish printer, is held by the principal modern editors of
Swift, Mr. Herbert Davis and Sir Harold Williams, to be 'practically identical' with the manuscript Swift sent King.[8] Dr. King
must indeed have been 'not a little mortified'.

That Dr. King omitted parts of the poem for political reasons is not strange, but that Pope omitted parts on the ground
that they were too vain and that Swift restored them certainly is.
The publication history of 'Verses on the Death of Dr. Swift'
leads to one or the other of the following conclusions: that Swift,
who so often directed his satire against the sin of pride, was
himself vain on at least two occasions, when he wrote the poem
and when he restored the cuts; or that Pope seriously misunderstood Swift's poetic intention.[9]

Each of these possibilities has been suggested within the last
few years. John Middleton Murry, in *Jonathan Swift: a Critical
Biography*, wrote: 'In truth the latter part of this famous poem is
unworthy in every way. It lacks the vitality and vividness, and
above all the humour, of the former; and it is morally incongruous with it. The sardonic objectivity gives place to an extrav-

agance of self-laudation. So striking a lapse from decorum must be ascribed to a radical weakening of Swift's vigour of mind.'[10] Mr. Maurice Johnson, the author of the only book-length critical study of Swift's verse, wrote, in a brief note in *Notes and Queries*: 'Exaggerated praise for the "dead" Dean, in [the poem's] latter part, has the structural function of balancing the exaggerated weakness of character Swift imputes to himself in early lines, especially 13–72, and the account of indifference to news of his death, lines 73–298. The satiric pattern for "Verses on the Death of Dr. Swift" is that of opposed exaggerations from which the middle ground of truth is to be inferred.'[11] I think that a close look at 'Verses on the Death of Dr. Swift' will disclose that Jonathan Swift had a better understanding of the poem than Alexander Pope and John Middleton Murry.

First, though, we may dispose of Murry's biographical explanations: that Swift's 'vigour of mind' was 'weakening', and, as he says earlier,[12] that Swift's mind was 'wandering'. Both are untenable. Swift's senility dates from the early 1740's. Though 'Verses on the Death of Dr. Swift' was published as late as 1739, it was composed in 1731 and 1732.[13] 'During this period', writes Thomas Sheridan in his life of Swift, 'his faculties do not seem to have been at all impaired by the near approaches of old age, and his poetical fountain, though not so exuberant as formerly, still flowed in as clear and pure a stream. One of his last pieces, "Verses on his own Death," is perhaps one of the most excellent of his compositions in that way. Nor are two of his other productions, written about the same time, intitled "An Epistle to a Lady;" and "A Rhapsody on Poetry" inferior to any of his former pieces.'[14] Such well-sustained poems as 'The Lady's Dressing Room', 'The Day of Judgement', 'A Beautiful Young Nymph Going to Bed', 'The Beast's Confession to the Priest', and 'The Legion Club'—to name but a few—were also written in the 1730's. In 1732 Swift's mind was not 'weakening'.

Nor was it 'wandering'. On 1 December 1731 Swift wrote to Gay: 'I have been several months writing near fine hundred lines on a pleasant subject, only to tell what my friends and enemies will say on me after I am dead. I shall finish it soon, for I add two lines every week, and blot out four and alter eight.'[15] If Swift was vain in 'Verses on the Death of Dr. Swift', he cannot be excused on the grounds of carelessness or senility.

The clues to Swift's intention in 'Verses on the Death of Dr. Swift' can be found in the poem's subject, structure, and technique. In subject, it is a series of illustrations of a maxim by La Rochefoucauld: *Dans l'adversité de nos meilleurs amis nous trouvons quelque chose, qui ne nous deplaist pas.* The maxim is quoted and translated on the title-page and paraphrased by Swift at the beginning of the poem proper:

> In all Distresses of our Friends
> We first consult our private Ends,
> While Nature kindly bent to ease us,
> Points out some Circumstance to please us.
>
> (7–10)

Later in the introductory section of the poem, the subject is restated:

> VAIN human kind! Fantastick Race!
> Thy various Follies, who can trace?
> Self-love, Ambition, Envy, Pride,
> Their Empire in our Hearts divide.
>
> (39–42)

The accusation of Pope and Murry, then, is that in a poem whose announced theme is self-love, pride, and vanity, Swift himself was too vain! One might suspect that Swift was up to his usual ironical tricks.

The structure of 'Verses on the Death of Dr. Swift' supplies another clue to Swift's intention, for, on close examination, the controversial 'latter part' turns out to be not, as Murry calls it, an 'incongruous addendum'[16] but the necessary completion of a complex pattern. The poem can easily be divided into three parts. The first part, lines 1–72, is set off from what follows by the concluding couplet:

> THUS much may serve by way of Proem,
> Proceed we therefore to our Poem.

The second part, lines 73–298, begins:

> THE Time is not remote, when I
> Must by the Course of Nature dye:
> When I foresee my special Friends,
> Will try to find their private Ends.

In this part, which includes the famous game of quadrille passage, Swift tells what his friends will say and do when they learn of his impending death, how they will act after his death, and how, within a year, he and his writings will be forgotten. This second part deals not with Swift, but with other people. The third part, lines 299–484, begins:

> SUPPOSE me dead; and then suppose
> A Club assembled at the *Rose*;
> Where from Discourse of this and that,
> I grow the Subject of their Chat:
> And, while they toss my Name about,
> With Favour some, and some without;
> One quite indiff'rent in the Cause,
> My Character impartial draws.

This part, which is approximately the same length as the second part, deals not with other people, but with Swift.

Significantly, the pattern of the whole poem is the same as the pattern of the first part of the poem, the seventy-two-line 'proem'. Mr. Maurice Johnson, as we have seen, holds that lines 13–72 deal with Swift, but that is an over-simplification. The first part of the proem, lines 1–12, introduces and paraphrases the maxim from La Rochefoucauld and then, in the final couplet, introduces the illustrations of the maxim that follow:

> IF this perhaps your Patience move
> Let Reason and Experience prove.

The second part of the proem, lines 13–42, gives illustrations of the maxim drawn from common experience, as:

> WE all behold with envious Eyes,
> Our *Equal* rais'd above our *Size*;

Who wou'd not at a crowded Show,
Stand high himself, keep others low?
(13–16)

The third part, lines 43–70, gives illustrations drawn supposedly
from Swift's own experience, as:

ARBUTHNOT is no more my Friend,
Who dares to Irony pretend;
Which I was born to introduce,
Refin'd it first, and shew'd its Use.
(55–58)

Like the poem as a whole, the proem consists of three parts: a
brief introduction followed by two longer sections of approximately the same number of lines. The first of these longer sections deals with other people; the second deals with Swift. Thus,
the structure of 'Verses on the Death of Dr. Swift' is, as
Mr. Johnson says, balanced (though in a far trickier way than he
suspected). The neatness of the pattern suggests that this balance
is not the result of chance but of conscious planning. One might
suspect that Swift thought the last part of the poem to be related
in some meaningful way to the rest of the poem.

Both this suspicion and the suspicion that Swift's self-praise
in the last part of the poem may be ironical are confirmed by
an examination of Swift's technique. Throughout the poem, both
in the verses proper and in Swift's own footnotes, the sources of
the comedy are irony and exaggeration. The amazing total of
122 words are superlatives or absolutes. *Ever, universal, universally,*
without the least, numberless, greatest, utmost, alone, still, mere, absolute,
and *any* occur once; *not one, not a, utterly,* and *nothing* occur twice;
the most, always, and *only* occur four times. *Every* occurs six times;
never, twenty times; *no,* twenty-three times; and *all*—perhaps the
key word in the poem—forty-one times.

In commenting on the first two parts of the poem, no critic
has mistaken Swift's ironies and exaggerations for statements
intended literally. No one, for example, has used the passage last
quoted to prove that Swift broke off with Dr. Arbuthnot when
the latter began to write ironically, or that the proud Dean really
believed that he alone was 'born to introduce' irony into the

language. Nor has anyone used the game of quadrille passage as evidence that Swift thought his female friends were all stony-hearted ingrates. Pope and Murry raised no objections to anything in the first two parts of the poem. But Swift's technique in the last part is just the same. A close look at a few of the passages that Pope cut out and Murry objected to will show, I think, that both critics missed the point and joke of the last part of the poem.

Consider, for instance, this couplet, which Dr. King said Swift's friends thought 'might be liable to some objection, and . . . not, strictly speaking, a just part of [Swift's] character':

> Yet, Malice never was his Aim;
> He lash'd the Vice but spar'd the Name.
> (459–60)

Pope cut it out, because, as Dr. King wrote, in Swift's other writings 'several persons have been lashed by name, a Bettesworth, and in this poem, Charteris and Whitshed'. Actually, in addition to Francis Charteris and William Whitshed, the following persons are lashed by name or title in this poem: King George, Queen Caroline, Sir Robert Walpole, Edmund Curll, James Moore Smyth, Colley Cibber, Lewis Theobald, John Henley, Thomas Woolston, William Wood, and Sir William Scroggs. Middleton Murry quotes the line and writes: 'Shades of the Duchess of Somerset! Presumably Swift now believed it; but it is almost incredible that he did.'[17] Shades of 'The Shortest Way with the Dissenters'! Murry misses the point. Swift was hardly so absent-minded as to forget that he had just finished attacking thirteen people by name: the line must be meant as a joke.[18]

Swift wrote:

> To steal a Hint was never known,
> But what he writ was all his own.
> (317–18)

Pope solemnly removed the couplet from the poem. But George Birkbeck Hill noticed that the second of these lines is itself stolen from Denham's elegy on Cowley:

> To him no author was unknown
> Yet what he wrote was all his own.[19]

None of Swift's over-solicitous English friends caught the allusion or the irony.

Using these two examples as a key to the poem, we can now go through Murry's Popean interpretation of the last section, systematically substituting the word *ironic* wherever Murry writes *not true.* Murry quotes this couplet which was cut out by Pope;

> His satyr points at no Defect,
> But what all Mortals may correct;
> (463–64)

and comments: 'Again, it is not true. Half the satire of the Yahoos is directed against the inescapable physical conditions of human existence.'[20] Of course. That is the point. Murry quotes:

> HAD he but spar'd his Tongue and Pen,
> He might have rose like other Men:
> But, Power was never in his Thought;
> And, Wealth he valu'd not a Groat:
> (355–58)

and comments: 'The first two lines are true enough; the second two are not.'[21] Once again, of course.

Swift wrote:

> Fair LIBERTY was all his Cry;
> For her he stood prepar'd to die;
> For her he boldly stood alone;
> For her he oft expos'd his own.
> (347–50)

Who, familiar with Swift's characteristic biting verse, could suppose this flight of sublimity was seriously intended?

Throughout his life, Swift directed his satire against the sin of pride or vanity. 'Verses on the Death of Dr. Swift' is on that same familiar subject. The first part of the introduction or 'proem' says that people are vain; the second part that other men are vain; the third part that Swift is vain. The second part of the poem shows that other men are vain. The third part shows that Swift is vain. When Swift, in the final section's eighty-nine octosyllabic couplets, while snarling at the Whigs and the Irish, informs us that he himself is humble, fearless, altruistic, diligent, innocent, and resolute, he is not presenting an apologia, but making an assertion of his own vanity necessary to complete his thesis that all mankind is egotistical, selfish, and proud.

In the course of this display of his vanity, Swift has left clues in the way of self-contradictions and stylistic flights to show that he was not really taking himself seriously. Had he not left such clues, the last section would indeed seem an incongruous departure from the comic tone of the rest of the poem. But had he omitted the last section, or cut it as drastically as Pope did, the poem would have been incomplete in both design and statement.

Notes

1. *The Poems of Jonathan Swift,* ed. H. Williams (Oxford, 1937), ii. 551. All quotations from the poem are taken from this edition; line numbers are indicated in the text. Sir Harold reprints the first Irish edition, with blanks completed from early copies.
2. *The Correspondence of Alexander Pope,* ed. G. Sherburn (Oxford, 1956), iv. 130.
3. The omitted lines are 15–16, 183–88, 281–98, 303–06, 309–14, 317–18, 325–38, 345–434, 443–54, 459–60, 463–78. Williams, ii. 552, is the authority for the number of lines introduced from the earlier poem.
4. *The Correspondence of Jonathan Swift,* ed. F. Elrington Ball, vi (London, 1914), 107–08.
5. Ibid., pp. 109–10.
6. *Correspondence of Swift,* ed. Ball, vi. 111.
7. Ibid., pp. 114–15.
8. Williams, ii. 552; H. Davis, 'Verses on the Death of Dr. Swift', *The Book-Collector's Quarterly,* March–May 1931, pp. 56–73. Sir Harold repeats Mr. Davis's arguments; both use the phrase 'practically identical'.
9. It is not known who actually did the revision, but I suspect Pope, since I cannot imagine who else among the Dean's English friends would have been so bold. Even if somebody else was responsible, my argument that follows remains the same.
10. (London, 1954), p. 459.
11. 'Verses on the Death of Dr. Swift', *N. &Q.,* cxcix (1954), 474.
12. P. 457.

13. Williams, ii. 551–53.

14. *The Works of the Rev. Jonathan Swift*, ed. T. Sheridan and J. Nichols (London, 1808), i. 278–79.

15. Ball, iv. 273.

16. P. 457.

17. P. 459.

18. Faulkner prints blanks for the King, Walpole, and Whitshed, but the context leaves no doubt as to whom Swift was talking about. In the omitted couplet, the Dean's implied argument that the ideal satirist will attack vices rather than individuals is moral: the satirist thus himself avoids the vice of malice. Perhaps Swift believed in this conventional ideal or perhaps not, but in any case he must have realized that sometimes he could not or would not live up to it. It is of interest that, when writing privately in the so-called 'Holyhead Journal' of 1727, he chides Pope and Gay for naming their victims, solely for the reason that by so doing they help to preserve names that would otherwise be forgotten (*The Prose Works of Jonathan Swift, D.D.*, ed. T. Scott, xi [London, 1907], 395–96.) Here, morality is of no concern, but simply what is practicable. 'Heaven forgive Mr. Pope . . . [for] transmitting so many names . . . full at length.' In reality, it would seem that Swift had no objection to initials and dashes, which maliciously make the victim known to his contemporaries, but leave him unknown to posterity.

19. Samuel Johnson, *Lives of the English Poets* (Oxford, 1905), iii.56, n. 3.

20. P. 459.

21. P. 458. These lines, too, were cut out by Pope. Hill comments on them (iii. 22, n. 1): 'On April 5, 1711, [Swift] wrote of the assurances given him by the ministers: "They may come to nothing, but the first opportunity that offers and is neglected, I shall depend no more, but come away." On May 23 he wrote:—"To return without some mark of distinction would look extremely little; and I would likewise gladly be somewhat richer than I am."'

MARSHALL WAINGROW

Verses on the Death of Dr. Swift

In a recent interpretation of *Verses on the Death of Dr. Swift* Barry
Slepian (*Review of English Studies*, N.S., XIV [1963], 249–256)
attempts to save Swift from the imputation of a poetically destructive personal vanity (notably by Middleton Murry, in *Jonathan Swift*, New York, 1955, pp. 457–459) by reading the alleged
incriminating passages as intentional exhibitions of self-irony, the
purpose of which is "to complete his thesis that all mankind is
egotistical, selfish, and proud." The choice between reading the
last part of the poem as "an unqualified eulogy" set down "in
flat contradiction to the first part" (Murry) and as a piece of
inverted irony perfectly consistent with the first part (Slepian) is
a poor choice for the critics to offer or for us to accept. The
eulogy is neither unqualified, nor is it qualified by a totally negating irony. But I should say that Mr. Slepian's praise is in effect
more damning than Mr. Murry's blame, for it lays Swift open to
a charge more serious than vanity, and that is a pointless humility. However great a leveler Swift may be in his satire in general, or however elusive his positive exemplars, in this work he
seems perfectly willing to offer himself as a model of moral perception and behavior, though—when the time comes for explic-
itness—in the decorous third person. I shall maintain that the
poem is written in both serious and thoughtful praise of the
satirist. Even the attribution of self-irony confers a distinction;

This essay first appeared in *Studies in English Literature* 5 (1965): 513–18. Reprinted with permission.

as Dr. Johnson remarked, "all censure of a man's self is oblique praise. It is in order to shew how much he can spare." Mr. Slepian's thesis needs to be reconstructed: "All is vanity. My life is no exception. But I know it. Therefore. . . ." Such a distinction is crucial for satire, where it is the very absence of self-knowledge in the subjects (knaves no less than fools) that gives the satirist his licence to "teach." So Swift is vain; but the poem shows that *his* vanity is knowledgeable, that it doesn't disguise his kinship with other men, and that upon such knowledge virtue may be built.

The *Verses* begin, however, in quite a different key, with the satirist's traditional low view of human nature, this time "occasioned" by a maxim of La Rochefoucauld which Swift translates thus:

> In all Distresses of our Friends
> We first consult our private Ends,
> While Nature kindly bent to ease us,
> Points out some Circumstance to please us.
>
> (7–10)

(Quotations are from *The Poems of Jonathan Swift*, ed. Sir Harold Williams [Oxford, 1937], II, 553ff.) In a letter to Gay, Swift described his subject as "pleasant"—meaning, of course, merry or jocular. He is writing, he says, "near five hundred lines . . . only to tell what my friends and enemies will say on me after I am dead" (quoted Williams, p. 551). Death is a jest and all things show it? In the poem it is a jest that turns earnest, for the maxim that informs the subject, though "pleasant," is disagreeable. La Rochefoucauld himself suppressed it in later editions, and Swift admits: "This Maxim more than all the rest/Is thought too base for human Breast" (5–6). All the more reason, then, for Swift to demonstrate the truth of it, a task he goes about performing in his favorite way of presenting the extreme case. If it shocks our sense of the dignity of human nature to conceive of taking comfort in the distresses of others (especially friends), can we bear the thought of deriving any satisfaction whatsoever from their last distress, death? The *Verses* do not broach the question directly or at once. Rather, Swift "by way of Proem" offers assorted exempla of "Self-love, Ambition, Envy, Pride" (41), including his own envy of his friends' talents. Envy, the discomfort we experience in the success of others (especially friends), is simply the other side of the infamous maxim; turn this success into failure and the envious are comforted. Ironically, what appear to be the most self-regarding of emotions are shown in fact to be utterly dependent upon the condition of others. As Swift puts it, putting a proper word in its proper place: ". . . when you sink, I seem the higher" (46).

The reader should now be prepared for the worst:

> The time is not remote, when I
> Must by the Course of Nature dye:
> When I foresee my special Friends,
> Will try to find their private Ends:
> Tho' it is hardly understood,
> Which way my Death can do them good;
>
> (73–78)

The only apparent "good" done his friends by his dying is explained in the lines: "Then hug themselves, and reason thus;/'It is not yet so bad with us'" (115–116). Such comfort can be destroyed by the outbreak of sympathetic pain, which prompts the sufferer to a more attentive solicitude towards the dying Swift and a greater lament over his death than is shown by the unfeeling friends. But Swift is not deceived. The imaginary identification which is hypochondria only sharpens the separation of selves; it is by no means the same as that imaginative identification which is true sympathy. Swift illustrates the perversity of equating one's good with another's ill in the case of the friend who, having prophesied his end, would "rather chuse that I should dye,/Than his Prediction prove a Lye" (131–132), and the absurdity of the same process of thought in the case of the false security derived by the (no matter how slightly) younger from the older:

> The Fools, my Juniors by a Year,
> Are tortur'd with Suspence and Fear.
> Who wisely thought my Age a Screen,
> When Death approach'd, to stand between:

> The Screen remov'd, their Hearts are trembling,
> They mourn for me without dissembling.
> (219–224)

"Without dissembling," only in the sense of not pretending a concern; but the concern remains unmistakably for the self.

The *Verses,* taking their cue from the maxim of La Rochefoucauld, convey a subtle critique of friendship: just as one envies friends more than foes, so friends demonstrate better than foes self-seeking, a preoccupation with private ends. Friendship comes to be seen as a state of alienation, even at times a state of open hostility and aggression:

> When, *ev'n his own familiar Friends*
> Intent upon their private Ends;
> Like Renegadoes now he feels,
> Against him lifting up their Heels.
> (403–406)

In contrast, Swift, according to his spokesman, was ever concerned to preserve and protect friendship:

> Without regarding private Ends,
> Spent all his Credit for his Friends.
> (331–332)

> Nor made a Sacrifice of those
> Who still were true, to please his Foes.
> (363–364)

Yet for Swift friendship is an ideal relationship capable of, indeed demanding, enlargement, so as to include strangers, if not enemies, and in the last analysis the general public. The news of his legacy scandalizes his friends:

> What has he left? And who's his Heir?
> I know no more than what the News is,
> 'Tis all bequeath'd to publick Uses.
> To publick Use! A perfect Whim!
> What had the Publick done for him!
> Meer Envy, Avarice, and Pride!
> He gave it all:—But first he dy'd.
> And had the Dean, in all the Nation,

> No worthy Friend, no poor Relation?
> So ready to do Strangers good,
> Forgetting his own Flesh and Blood?
> (154–164)

Swift hardly needed to invent his sympathetic interlocutor—
"One quite indiff'rent in the Cause" (305)—when he could exact
such tribute from his imagined critics.

The rationalization of private ends into a narrowly-con-
ceived benevolence is just the attitude that is being satirized in
the poem. The concluding lines both state a biographical fact
and suggest a metaphor:

> He gave the little Wealth he had,
> To build a House for Fools and Mad:
> And shew'd by one satyric Touch,
> No Nation wanted it so much:
> That Kingdom he hath left his Debtor,
> I wish it soon may have a Better.
> (479–484)

Swift's last will and testament is the symbolic capstone of his
career as a satirist. Public uses, not private ends—this is the code
(Mandeville aside) of the moralist, and in this light the claim
made in the last section of the poem for the unimpeachability
of Swift's ethics as a satirist cannot be drawn into a pattern of
self-irony without blunting the main point. The two (related)
questions at issue are (1) the spirit in which the satire is under-
taken:

> Yet, Malice never was his Aim;
> He lash'd the Vice but spar'd the Name.
> (459–460)

and (2) the end which satire hopes to accomplish:

> His Satyr points at no Defect,
> But what all Mortals may correct;
> (463–464)

These are familiar answers to familiar charges from Roman
times onward, but for our present purpose they are better con-

sidered in the context of the poem than in the tradition of the apology for satire. Granting that Swift doesn't spare the name (not even in this poem that asserts he does), the disavowal of malicious intent is to be taken seriously as Swift's means of distinguishing himself, not merely from other, culpable satirists, but from the run of people in general. In other words, the claim is a direct rebuttal of La Rochefoucauld's maxim: Swift—or the satirist (the man and the rôle have become one by this point in the poem)—is just that person who does *not* take comfort in the distresses of others. In support of this claim and correlative with it, the second couplet, and the lines following, assert that Swift abided by the well-established (if often breached) rule of satire prohibiting the ridicule of natural infirmities, and limited his warfare to human affectations. Malice surely is better pleased by the former than by the latter objects, but the question is, is the claim just? Mr. Slepian notes that the couplet was omitted in the shortened version of the poem printed by Charles Bathurst (apparently on the authority of Pope); that Murry rejected the assertion as false ("Half the satire of the Yahoo is directed against the inescapable physical conditions of human existence."); and concurs, with the understanding that Swift knew it to be false. But the point of the claim—and the point of Swift's satires in general—is that the *worst* defects of human nature are defects of attitude (including our attitudes towards our physical defects), and are therefore at least potentially correctable.

The foundation of the *Verses* is that one absolutely inescapable physical condition of human existence, the necessity of dying. It is not this defect (which no mortal may correct) which inspires the satirist, but the corruption of mind which results from it. The middle section of the poem surveys the various imagined responses to the death of Swift on the part of friends and foes, and discovers attitudes of glee, scorn, self-serving, easy resignation, banal piety, and (a year later) obliviousness. The presence of Pope, Gay, and Arbuthnot among the respondents (for their poor capacity for mourning) only strengthens the general indictment: what all mortals may correct is how they ignore their own mortality, and in ignoring it, how they live ignobly, or, at best, trivially. The lesson of the Struldbruggs, we may remember, is how people live who (think they) are going to live forever.

Swift's fiction in making himself a witness to the drama of his own death is a form of exemplary behavior, which distinguishes him as a human being whose natural vanity has not suffered the corruption of mind. He remains "preserved" in death; the autopsy shows no cause within why the man dies:

> For when we open'd him we found,
> That all his vital Parts were sound.
>
> (175–176)

In remaining superior to his fate the satirist is justified, first as an individual, but last as an example. The ironic understatement of the early couplet:

> Tho' it is hardly understood,
> Which way my Death can do them good;
>
> (77–78)

vanishes before the force of the poem's expanding moral. That private end which is death can indeed have its public uses.

313

ARTHUR H. SCOUTEN AND ROBERT D. HUME

Pope and Swift
Text and Interpretation of
Swift's Verses on His Death

Critics are at present in radical disagreement about how to read
the *Verses on the Death of Dr. Swift.* In the last few years the poem
has been damned for exaggerated self-praise, defended for the
"ironic intention" of that praise, taken as a serious *apologia pro
vita sua,* and read as a seventeenth-century style religious meditation on death. No agreement at all has been reached about the
basic nature of the poem. Such variance seems odd, since most
of the critics agree that the *Verses* are one of Swift's greatest
works, and indubitably some of its passages are among his finest
efforts. One must ask, though, whether the poem does possess
a basic structural coherence. We believe so, and will try to demonstrate it.

One reason for the confusion about the poem is probably
its checkered textual history—a history which has never yet been
fully expounded, although most of the truth has become apparent in the course of the last forty years. Since the *Verses* seem to
have given readers trouble from the 1730's on, and since this
trouble helped complicate the textual tangle, text and interpretation seem logically to go together: the one sheds light on the

This essay first appeared in *Philological Quarterly* 52 (1973): 205–31. Reprinted
with permission.

other. Swift's poem exists in four distinct but entangled versions: we hope that by tracing and comparing them we can perhaps arrive at a better sense of the nature of the poem as Swift wanted it and so make some sense out of the current critical muddle.

I

The reason critics have only recently paid the *Verses* much serious attention is that until Sir Harold Williams printed Swift's text in 1937, the poem was generally available in a corrupt text of 545 lines, an amalgam of three different versions of two separate poems. How this monstrosity came into being is a fascinating story, and we are now in a position to add something to the pioneering studies of Herbert Davis and Harold Williams.[1]

The earliest printings state on the title page that the poem was "Written by Himself: Nov. 1731," and this date is supported by Swift's letter to Gay of 1 Dec. 1731.[2] Swift's note to line 379 of the Dublin printing (1739) is dated "this present third Day of May, 1732": he could have added notes or made revisions at any time before the 1739 printings. Probably he made no substantial additions, since he describes the piece in 1731 as "near five hundred lines," and the Dublin edition is 484. At any rate, in 1738 Swift entrusted the MS of the *Verses* to Dr. William King, Principal of St. Mary Hall, Oxford, who was to supervise the printing of the poem in London, and C. Bathurst brought out the first edition in 1739—on 19 January, the *Daily Advertiser* tells us.[3] Unfortunately, a good deal was done to the manuscript before it was printed. From King's letters to Swift and Mrs. Whiteway we can reconstruct the sequence of events: advised by Pope and others, King gave Bathurst a radically altered version; Swift was furious and promptly had Faulkner print the original version in Dublin, with an advertisement protesting the London alterations and omissions.

> King to Swift, 5 Jan. 1738–39: "At length I have put *Rochefaucault* to the press. . . . But I am in great fear lest you should dislike the liberties I have taken. Although I have done nothing without the advice and approba-

tion of . . . your friends in this country . . . if . . . you shall still resolve to have the poem published as intire as you put it into my hands, I will certainly obey your commands."

(Correspondence, v, 133)

King to Mrs. Whiteway, 30 Jan. "I am in some pain about *Rochefoucauld,* and doubt much whether he will be satisfied with the manner in which he finds it published; to which I consented in deference to Mr. *Pope's* judgment, and the opinion of others of the Dean's friends in this country."

(v, 136–37)

King to Mrs. Whiteway, 6 March. "I was not a little mortified yesterday when the bookseller brought me the *Dublin* edition, and at the same time put into my hands a letter he had received from *Faulkner,* by which I perceive the Dean is much dissatisfied with our manner of publication. . . . It may be perceived how much the Dean's friends have been mistaken in their judgment, however good their intentions have been."

(v, 139)

The nature of these changes and the reasons for them we will take up in due course. The immediate point of note is simply that, as of the first printings in 1739, two drastically different versions of the poem had appeared, both seeming outwardly to possess authority.[4]

An examination of Bathurst's text bears out King's admission that numerous changes had been made. Collation shows that "Swift's friends" in London received a MS of 484 lines; they excised 165 and added 62 new lines—the additions being extracted from "The Life and Genuine Character of Doctor Swift. Written by Himself," a poem published in 1733, evidently by Swift, although he denied authorship. This second "Rochefoucauld" poem—which will be discussed in the next section—is generally considered an experimental version of the *Verses.* In any case, Bathurst printed a composite text of 381 lines. Since King makes no mention of additions to Swift's version (though he discusses the reasons for *his* making several deletions),

Dr. Teerink was probably right in his conjecture that Pope was responsible for the additions, the major deletions, and the restructuring; as Barry Slepian adds, who else would have been so bold?[5]

Pope's revisions (he supplied no lines of his own) are instructive to students of both Pope and Swift. After the deletion of the Wolston episode (ll. 281–98),[6] he cut out the long panegyric, the "Character" presented by the "impartial" spokesman at the Rose. As a substitute for this extended eulogy, Pope inserted ten different extracts from the "Life and Genuine Character," concocting from them a heated debate among the gossips at the Rose. In Pope's version, when one speaker praises Swift, another retorts,

> Sir, I have heard another Story;
> He was a most confounded Tory;
> (ll. 82–83 of "Life")

> And grew, or he is much bely'd,
> Extremely dull, before he dy'd.
> (ll. 88–89 of "Life," amended)

When another defender endorses Swift, "'Twas he that writ the *Drapier's Letters*," a denigrator replies, "He shou'd have left them for his *Betters*" (l. 98 of "Life"). Other sneers appear: "You never can *defend* his *Breeding*" (l. 102 of "Life"); and "What *Scenes* of Evil he unravels,/In *Satyrs, Libels, Lying Travels*" (ll. 111–12 of "Life").

As we look at the Pope version, we can see what Joseph Horrell rightly points out, that Pope was replacing the long eulogy (whether serious or ironic) with an interspersion of "rapid-fire dialogue," a characteristic feature of Horace's apologia.[7] Furthermore, we see Pope revising in precisely the fashion explained by George Sherburn in his well-known essay "Pope at Work."[8] Sherburn prints passages from MSS to show that Pope liked to work with verse paragraphs (not merely couplets), and gives us one passage of 53 lines from which Pope later pulled 7 lines to use in his "First Satire of the Second Book of Horace Imitated" (1733) and 22 lines to put into the *Epistle to Dr. Arbuthnot* (1735). This is precisely what Pope does in altering Swift's poem on the present occasion: he goes to the "Life and Genuine Character" and extracts couplets and passages of 4, 8, 14, and 20 lines to insert at appropriate places in the latter half of Swift's text in order to sustain the newly-conceived controversial dialogue on Swift's place in history. Since Swift had actually constructed "The Life and Genuine Character" on the Horatian model, one can fairly say that Pope was only trying to enforce the same organization on Swift's new poem. Swift at work displays a different set of habits. When he completed a poem, he was through with it. When he was not satisfied with a plan, he discarded it and substituted another, as we can see in comparing "The Life and Genuine Character" with the *Verses* or the drafts of his intended reply to Tindal with the finished product of *An Argument Against Abolishing Christianity*. Unlike Pope, he was not in the habit of composing simultaneously on several different poems or borrowing passages from earlier work.

The Bathurst version of the *Verses* contains 319 lines corresponding to Faulkner's first edition (and presumably to Swift's MS), plus 62 lines from "The Life and Genuine Character of Doctor Swift."[9] As a matter of fact, the use of these lines is our best piece of evidence for the authorship of the "Life." Swift had actually written to Pope (1 May 1733) and Oxford (31 May), explicitly denouncing the poem as "spurious" and a "sham."[10] But Pope cannot have been convinced (the poem's dedication to Pope is dated April Fool's Day), or he would scarcely have borrowed from the poem when preparing Swift's *Verses* for publication.

Thus far, the textual history is relatively clear and straightforward. Had nothing worse happened to Swift's poem, little harm would have been done. The Pope-Bathurst version could have been examined as a useful curiosity and no bad poem in its own right. Certainly it gives us an interesting example of Pope at work. Unfortunately, the two texts became badly entangled: the result was a monstrosity of a 545-line poem, a maze without a plan.

Even the history of this coalescing of texts has remained a matter of confusion. The usually reliable Harold Williams and Herbert Davis both assume that Sir Walter Scott started the process by inserting into his second edition of his *Swift* (1824) the 62 borrowed lines of the Bathurst printing—putting them in the footnotes as lines "rejected by Swift, when he revised the piece."

Scott did indeed place these lines in the notes, but an examination of successive editions of Swift's works shows that the Bathurst text and the authentic Dublin text of Faulkner had been joined as early as 1756.

We have been unable to identify the culprit, but he was an editor who was very much aware of what he was doing. In the eight-volume *Works* published by A. Kincaid (and others) in Edinburgh, and R. Urie (and others) in Glasgow (1756; Teerink-Scouten No. 95) the composite text makes its appearance. After some snide remarks about Hawkesworth's editorial work, the Scots editor provides an analytic table showing the eleven different places in the poem where he has added lines (170 in all) from the Dublin printing to the 375 lines of the text in the 1742 *Miscellanies* (derived from the 1739 Bathurst), and he provides the line numbers. The net result is to place Pope's additions after the passage where the gossips assemble at the Rose, thus presenting the "impartial" spokesman's harangue after the argumentative dialogue. The editor concludes by accurately stating that the resulting poem is composed of 484 lines corresponding to the Dublin text and 61 to the London text: one line (Bathurst 372) has been dropped.

This 545 line composite text appears in subsequent Edinburgh editions of 1757, 1759, 1766, 1768, 1774, 1778, (etc.), and in Dublin editions of 1758 (G. Ewing) and 1767. The first apparent London printing of the composite text is an undated edition (Teerink-Scouten No. 59) for which Harold Williams conjectures a 1750 date (*Poems*, I, lvii), but David Foxon very kindly examined it and found bibliographical evidence to indicate that it was a piracy of the 1760's, possibly printed in Edinburgh. But when the booksellers' project, the *Works of the English Poets* (for which Samuel Johnson wrote his *Lives of the English Poets*) appeared in 1779, it carried the 545-line text, as did subsequent editions of this series and such other collections as Robert Anderson's *Works of the British Poets* (1795). In 1824 Scott did insert the extra lines in the notes, a practice followed by Mitford in 1833. But in 1843 when Dr. Aikin brought out *The Select Works of the British Poets* in London for Longmans, he followed Scott's text but raised the extra lines from the notes.

Fate had one more unkind twist in store for Swift's poem.

In 1910 W. E. Browning brought out a two-volume edition of Swift's verse. He states that his source for the text of this poem was "a copy of the original edition, with corrections in Swift's hand, which I found in the Forster collection."[11] Whatever "original" means, no one else has ever been able to find such a copy in the Forster collection. Harold Williams charitably surmises that Browning "mistook the hand in the copy completed by Forster"—but that copy was, of course, a *Faulkner* printing. The composite text had been in print for 154 years when Browning made his claim: what he prints is 484 lines from the Dublin edition, plus 61 lines from Bathurst. Where he got the amalgam is no puzzle.[12] Worse yet, Browning's text was standard in modern times until the appearance of Williams' definitive edition in 1937—and as a result the composite 545-line text appeared in almost all the popular school editions: for example, Bredvold, McKillop, and Whitney (*Eighteenth Century Poetry and Prose,* 1939), Odell Shepard and Paul Spencer Wood (*English Prose and Poetry, 1660–1800,* 1934), and especially William Alfred Eddy's Oxford Standard Authors edition of *The Satires and Personal Writings of Jonathan Swift* (1932, and reprinted regularly through the 1950's). Only in the last few years has the genuine text supplanted the amalgam for student use, and in the meantime whole generations of scholars have grown up thinking of the poem as a structural disaster, a display of brilliant patches. No doubt this helps explain lack of critical interest in the *Verses* until the last decade. But even with the Williams edition available for the last thirty years, no agreement has been reached on the impact of the structure as Swift himself wanted it, and so the import of the whole poem has remained a disputed puzzle. Consequently we think it worthwhile to go back to the genesis of the tangle to try to see why Pope and others wanted to make the changes they did, what sort of poem resulted, and whether a comparison with the "Life and Genuine Character" and the Bathurst version are any help.

II

Of the four versions of Swift's "Rochefoucauld" enterprise which we possess, one—the 545-line amalgam—is worse than worthless, and another—"The Life and Genuine Character of Doctor Swift"—is distinctly enigmatic. Its genuineness now seems beyond dispute, but Swift does seem to have been burlesquing his own style, and the paraphernalia of the put-on with which the poem is prefaced have discouraged serious interpretive attention. If we agree with Williams that the piece is genuine, two possibilities present themselves. Joseph Horrell conjectures "that the poem is preliminary work superseded by the *Verses*."[13] Or it could simply be, as Herbert Davis believes, a satirical joke, largely on Pope.

The tone of the "Life and Genuine Character" is altogether lighter than that of the *Verses,* especially near the outset: "Whenever *Fortune* sends/*Disasters,* to our *Dearest Friends,*/Although, we *outwardly* may Grieve,/We oft, are *Laughing in our Sleeve.*" Or again, the little anecdote which begins, "*Tom* for a *wealthy Wife* looks round,/A *Nymph,* that brings *ten thousand* Pound," is far more flippant in spirit than the material in the *Verses.* Nonetheless, the parallels are considerable: the beginning with La Rochefoucauld, reference to poetic rivalry, a gout episode, the supposition of the Dean's death and imagined responses to the news, the *Medals* episode, the Drapier, and a discussion of satire appear in both poems. The bulk of the "Life and Genuine Character" (which totals only 202 lines) is devoted to a Horatian debate on Swift's merits. The anti-Swift speaker finds him "too *airy* for a *Dean*"; "a most *confounded Tory*"; "*a Misanthrope*"; the author of "*Satyrs* running riot" and "*Libels, lying Travels*"; and "Not sparing his own *Clergy-Cloth,*/But, eats into it, like a *Moth*—!"

Swift obviously takes a sardonic pleasure in mocking himself and insinuating double-edged "libels":

> had We made him *timely* Offers,
> To *raise* his Post, or *fill* his *Coffers,*
> Perhaps he might have truckled down,
> Like other *Brethren* of his *Gown.*
> (138–41)

The gay tone of the bulk of the poem seems to reduce the emotional impact of the final apologia, as in the reference to a clerical *Moth,* or in the couplet, "*Poor Man!* he went, all on a sudden—!/ H'as drop'd, and *giv'n the Crow a Pudden!*" The anti-Swift speaker in the debate is allowed some effective sneers, but is made to occupy foolish positions, as in his jibe at Swift's *Breeding*, his assertion that "We had a Hundred *abler Men*" when the Drapier's accomplishments are raised, and especially his reference to Swift on Walpole:

> But, why wou'd he, except he *slobber'd*,
> Offend our *Patriot*, Great Sir R———,
> Whose *Councils* aid the Sov'reign Pow'r,
> To *save* the *Nation* ev'ry hour?
>
> (107–10)[14]

Obviously a key point in the interpretation of this poem is to determine the proper response to the pro-Swift speaker. One of the few critics to pay the matter any attention, Ronald Paulson, suggests that he is "detached and reasonable" while his opponent's views are dictated by prejudice—which seems to us essentially accurate. But Paulson goes on to say that "Swift leaves the reader, as in many of his works, to make out for himself the real Swift who is somewhere between. Taking this as an early version of the *Verses,* we might suppose that Swift lost patience with the vague and unsatisfactory approximation of the median and in the later poem while still suggesting a median ("They toss my Name about,/with Favour some, and some without") he substituted the ideal instead."[15] This last suggestion we will consider later. But is the reader really left to puzzle out a median in the earlier poem? Essentially everything the pro-Swift speaker says is indeed "detached and reasonable," though sometimes couched in a style Swift disliked. Two particularly obvious deflations of high-flown rhetoric in the defense involve triplets, which Swift despised. First, replying to a complaint about Swift's presumption in applying "the *Whip,*" his defender launches into a grandiloquently moral tirade which is more than a little let down by its concluding triplet.

> If you *resent* it, who's to blame?
> He neither knew *you,* nor your *Name;*
> Shou'd *Vice* expect to 'scape rebuke,
> Because its *Owner* is a *Duke?*
> *Vice* is a *Vermin;* Sportsman say

No *Vermin* can demand *fair* Play,
But, ev'ry Hand may justly slay.
(121–27)

Even more disconcertingly, just before the final couplet, Swift's writings are defended in a fashion in which content and style ill accord:

'Tis plain, his Writings were design'd
To *please,* and to *reform* Mankind;
And, if he often miss'd his Aim,
The *World* must own it, to their *Shame;*
The *Praise* is *His,* and Theirs the *Blame.*
(196–200)

Thus although much of the defense of Swift's position on religion (148–79) seems essentially "straight," the reader's trust in the seriousness of the whole enterprise is undercut by the mostly flippant tone, the style, and the manner of the dedication to Pope. So much protestation about the *genuineness* of the poem and the accuracy of the copy breeds instant suspicion in a reader versed in the tricks of the Scriblerians—as Swift apparently intended it should. The following paragraph of "L. M.'s" note to the reader is a real teaser:

I have shewn it to very *good Judges,* and *Friends* of the *Dean,* . . . who are well acquainted with the *Author's* Stile, and Manner, and they all allow it to be *Genuine,* as well as perfectly *finished* and *correct;* his particular *Genius* appearing in every Line; together with his *peculiar* way of *thinking* and *writing.*

To an experienced reader of Swift, this claim appears half true and half outrageous. The handling of the octosyllabic couplets, the wry humor, such examples as Tom in search of a nymph, are all highly characteristic. The serious praise is not, nor is the extensive employment of "Breaks, Dashes, and Triplets (which the Author never made Use of)." This last comment is Faulkner's in a preface to the 1746 edition: he adds that the object was "to disguise his Manner of Writing."

Consider the impact of the piece. The prefatory material

and title trumpet the poem as Swift's genuine work, yet some very obvious stylistic devices seem to belie the claim. Anyone familiar with such works as "A Panegyric on the Reverend D— n S—t" (1730) would be exceedingly suspicious about what was going on. At the outset, the poem might seem to be only a *jeu d'esprit*. Given the ostentatious attribution to Swift, it might turn out to be a travesty on him, an expectation fed for a while by the outspoken criticism of him. One would not anticipate the poem's move toward a fairly serious defense of Swift:

> Whole *Swarms* of *Sects,* with grief, he saw
> More favour'd, than the *Church by Law:*
> Thought *Protestant* too Good a Name
> For *canting Hypocrites* to claim.
>
> (168–71)

Under these circumstances, we are told, "the *Dean's* disgust" is justified.

Assessed strictly on its own terms, "The Life and Genuine Character" is a good poem and a fine personal defense by Swift. Obfuscating his authorship, starting with a very light tone, and continuing to play stylistic tricks, he successfully avoids any sense of heavy special pleading or personal advocacy. The long passage on the church is slipped in late in the poem, prefaced and followed by light-hearted jokes about Swift as a clergyman. "What *Writings* had he left behind—? . . . *not one Sermon,* you may *swear.*" Certain criticisms could be levelled, especially in comparison with the *Verses.* "The Life and Genuine Character" lacks the intriguing personal references to Pope, Gay, and Arbuthnot, the apparent display of self, and such dazzling passages as the card game. But as a personal defense, it is really very effective. La Rochefoucauld does not seem especially relevant, but one comes away with a good sense of Swift's detractors and his justifications. At least one distinguished critic has felt that the "Life and Genuine Character" is the better apologia[16]—and indeed, that is what the poem, disguised by flippancy and deception, seems to be.

Whatever Swift intended when he went on to write the *Verses,* his friends seem not to have liked the result. The longer poem, "save for general idea and parallelisms," is "transparently different"[17] from the "Life and Genuine Character." True enough, but how far does the similarity in "general idea" extend? According to Paulson (quoted above), Swift decided to be even blunter in his self-recommendation. We propose to dispute this point, but indubitably there is evidence to show that Swift's friends saw the matter this way.

George Sherburn prints a letter from Pope to Lord Orrery (25 Sept. 1738) which includes this statement: "I return the Verses you favor me with, the latter part of which is inferior to the beginning, the Character too dry, as well as too Vain in some respects, & in one or two particulars, not true"[18] From this Sherburn argues that the allusion is to *Verses*, and that Pope, King, and possibly Orrery made revisions in it. One wonders, if the MS was circulating in London in mid-1738, why Swift then sent a copy by way of King. But Pope's phrases sound so much like what King reports, and suggest so well what he was to do, that Sherburn's conjecture seems highly plausible.

Certain of the changes King seems to take responsibility for.

> There are some lines, indeed, which I omitted with a very ill will, and for no other reason but because I durst not insert them, I mean the story of the medals: however, that incident is pretty well known, and care has been taken that almost every reader may be able to supply the blanks. That part of the poem which mentions the death of queen *Anne,* and so well describes the designs of the ministry, . . . I would likewise willingly have published, if I could have done it with safety: but I don't know whether the present worthy set of ministers would not have construed this passage into high treason, . . . at least a lawyer . . . gave me some reason to imagine this might be the case.
>
> (*Correspondence,* v, 135)

In a later letter, King says that the Wolston lines "are plainly a mistake, and were omitted for that reason only; for *Wolston* never had a pension, on the contrary, he was prosecuted for his blasphemous writings. . . . *Wollaston* . . . was indeed much admired at *Court*" (*Correspondence,* v, 140). In the same letter King says that he omitted the last two lines "because I did not well understand them; a *better* what?"—and goes on into grammatical quibbles.

These changes range from the perhaps overly cautious (the Medals, etc.), to the dense ("a *better* what?"), to the stupid (the Wolston passage). This last deserves notice, since King's blunder has been endorsed by Horrell and Murry.[19] Swift *does* mean Wolston, the blasphemous clergyman who claimed to show "That *Jesus* was a Grand Impostor" (294). That Wolston received no pension (and was actually prosecuted before he died in 1733) proves nothing at all. Swift is *imagining* a scene with Lintot a year after his death; the title page is dated Nov. 1731; and as the note on "Chartres" says, the poem "preserves the Scene and Time it was writ in." Swift is excoriating Lintot, courtiers, and "Court Ladies" by suggesting that they all dote on Wolston, and Lintot's rejoicing that "The Rev'rend Author's good Intention,/Hath been rewarded with a Pension" is no mistake, but rather a piece of savage sarcasm from an *un*pensioned Irish Dean.

The major part of the changes, however, seem not to be King's.

> The Doctor's friends, whom I consulted on this occasion, were of opinion, that the latter part of the poem might be thought by the public a little vain, if so much were said by himself of himself. They were unwilling that any imputation of this kind should lie against this poem. . . . They were of opinion that these lines,
>
>> He lash'd the vice but spared the name,
>> No individual could resent
>> Where thousands equally were meant—
>
> might be liable to some objections and were not, strictly speaking, a just part of his character; because several persons have been lashed by name, a *Bettesworth,* and in this poem, *Charteris* and *Whiteshed.*
>
> (*Correspondence*, v, 139–40)

In light of these awkward faults, some repairs were clearly in order.

Plainly Pope, King, & Co. took the long eulogy dead seriously. We propose to disagree, yet to claim that we can read Swift better than Alexander Pope could is presumptuous indeed. If the eulogy is at least partly ironic, why should Pope (who knew

Swift extremely well) fail to see the irony? The answer, we believe, is very probably that Pope expected something quite different from what is actually there. Already familiar with one "Rochefoucauld" poem, "The Life and Genuine Character," which did contain, however disguised, a serious apologia, Pope expected another, and the two poems do follow much the same pattern of development. Pope, we suspect, made much the same assumption as Ronald Paulson—that Swift "substituted the ideal" for a pro-con debate. Anticipating a serious presentation of self, one might well find the panegyric a "little vain" and "not true" in all particulars.

Conjectures aside, we do know precisely what Pope saw fit to do with the *Verses*—which was to rebuild them on the model of "The Life and Genuine Character." The result is a fine poem. Herbert Davis, anxious to preserve the purity of Swift's texts, dismissed Pope's version with some severity, and subsequent critics have mostly been content to ignore it. Actually, it is a substantial poem in its own right, and well deserves study. As we have seen, the poem remains pretty well intact up to the scene at the Rose. Like the "Life and Genuine Character," both the Bathurst and Faulkner versions open with roughly seventy lines giving examples of Rochefoucauld's maxim in practice. The introduction of Swift's friends is a highly effective device; the tone is more sardonic, less flippant than in the earlier poem. Swift's later version is altogether more gripping, and the verse seems less choppy; Pope cuts only two lines and takes full advantage of the material. The second section too Pope leaves alone (only the Wolston part is dropped); it has no real precedent in the 1733 poem, which went straight on to the debate on Swift's character. Swift takes a sardonic pleasure in dwelling on imaginary chat about his decrepitude and the casual response to news of his death. All this illustrates La Rochefoucauld perfectly. Swift had devoted some two hundred lines to this section, then giving roughly equal length to the "impartial" spokesman. Pope cuts this last section by half, and takes more than half of the remaining material out of the "Life and Genuine Character," turning the one long speech into a rapid-fire debate. Only a few innocuous lines are retained from Swift's version.

The result is certainly a well-constructed poem, as we might expect from so expert a writer of Horatian satires. One can well believe King's claim that the Bathurst version was a great success, widely acknowledged "to be a just and a beautiful satire."[20] Far better than the 1733 poem, it moves smoothly from some general (though personalized) illustrations of the maxim, to a very telling illustration of it with reference to Swift's supposed death, to a pendant debate on what Swift's worth really was. Pope does rather gut the 1733 defense by failing to bring in the long speech on religion, but the result is polished and relatively non-controversial, a perfect amalgam of the first two sections of the *Verses*—indubitably an improvement—with the discreet argumentative method of the "Life and Genuine Character."

We may wonder, with Herbert Davis, why the man who had just written the *Epistle to Dr. Arbuthnot* was so chary of vanity. The answer probably lies in method. Pope was perfectly capable of a passionate personal defense, but he arranges it with vast rhetorical care, replying to serious attacks and abuse, and not presuming to present an extended and allegedly "impartial" eulogy on himself. The next question is obvious: was Swift trying to do so? We have already agreed that the "Life and Genuine Character" seems to be an attempt at something of the sort, but we are by no means convinced that *Verses on the Death of Dr. Swift* works in the same fashion.

III

J. M. Murry takes the panegyric dead seriously. He calls it "an unqualified eulogy," "an incongruous addendum," "garrulous and inconsequent," and says that the poem's publication was "probably due to the clouding of Swift's faculties." "Sardonic objectivity gives place to an extravagance of self-laudation." Murry proceeds through the poem, objecting to "fantasy" and statements which are "not true"—and he finds plenty of them. He quotes "He lash'd the Vice but spar'd the Name," and comments: "Presumably Swift now believed it; but it is almost incredible he did. Even Dr. William King" knew better. Murry can account for this only by supposing that Swift's "actual memory of the past had become quite unreliable," and that "the incoherence of *The*

Death of Dr. Swift was due to the weakening of his faculties which
he describes in the earlier and better part of the poem."[21]

Murry marks one extreme. Mr. Barry Slepian, in a reply to
Murry which remains the most helpful treatment of the poem
and to which we are indebted, moves toward another extreme by
seeing the whole poem as ironic. "The accusation of Pope and
Murry, then, is that in a poem whose announced theme is self-
love, pride, and vanity, Swift himself was too vain! One might
suspect that Swift was up to his usual ironical tricks." Quite right,
and Slepian is able to make some very telling points. He quotes
the line "He lash'd the Vice but spar'd the Name," lists *thirteen*
people lashed by name or title in this poem alone, and comments: "Swift was hardly so absent-minded as to forget that he
had just finished attacking thirteen people by name: the line
must be meant as a joke." Or again, he takes the couplet: "To
steal a Hint was never known,/But what he writ was all his own,"
and points out that Pope suppressed it, failing to see the joke in
an obvious falsehood—the joke being that Swift has stolen the
second line from Denham.[22] Such false statements as "His Satyr
points at no Defect,/But what all Mortals may correct" (463–64)
Slepian finds—rightly we believe—part of a systematic self-der-
ogation by exaggeration. All that Murry cites as evidence of mental deterioration, Slepian can convincingly explain as conscious
and deliberate irony. But when Slepian concludes that Swift is
"not presenting an apologia, but making an assertion of his own
vanity necessary to complete his thesis that all mankind is egotistical, selfish, and proud"—we find him only half-right. Com-
pleting a thesis, yes. To assert that Swift really believed what he
said in the eulogy can only make him out to be a senile fool. But
Slepian's reading does ignore a great deal in those two hundred
lines of which Swift was genuinely proud—the Drapier's letters,
for instance—and which we have no reason to suppose he was
ironically repudiating. In short, the issue is not so simple: we
have here neither pure apologia nor pure irony.

In a reply to Slepian, Professor Marshall Waingrow finds his
praise for the *Verses* "more damning that Mr. Murry's blame, for
it lays Swift open to a charge more serious than vanity, and that
is a pointless humility."[23] He has a point: the poem seems rather
long and complicated to be merely an ironic assertion of Swift's

own selfishness and pride. Brilliant but pointless might then be the verdict. What Waingrow tries to do, however, is to whitewash Swift on the charges Murry had brought against him. He claims that Swift is "perfectly willing to offer himself as a model of moral perception . . . in the decorous third person." Such a reading seems a blatant contradiction of the announced point of this "Rochefoucauld" poem, and our confidence in it is not improved when Waingrow airily dismisses Swift's refusal to spare the name and cooly asserts that he "limited his warfare to human affectations." Waingrow concludes that Swift's moral superiority is proved by his bodily preservation, evidenced in the lines "For when we open'd him we found,/That all his vital Parts were sound" (175–76). But the logic and the reading here seem to us entirely wrong. Waingrow is quoting from a collection of fatuous doctors, "tender of their Fame," who are disclaiming responsibility for Swift's demise. How this can be construed as a boast about Swift's "preserved" state, we do not see at all.

An even more extreme reading has recently been offered by Mr. John Irwin Fischer,[24] who ignores all studies but Waingrow's while arguing that this "meditative exercise" is an "instructive satire and a model for us." Fischer starts with a good point: the "problem is to discover the relationship between the panegyric with which Swift's poem ends and the maxim of La Rochefoucauld which, Swift tells us in his headnote, occasioned the entire poem."[25] Waingrow proposes that Swift is *rebutting* La Rochefoucauld, using himself as the example of perfection. (Vanity indeed!) Fischer sees the connection as part of a complex argument: Swift too is guilty (Fischer's proof is the *beginning* of the poem), but in recognizing his "sin," he teaches us a lesson— "trust in God."

There is just enough that is plausible in this interpretation to make it confusing. Fischer says that the *Verses* are "controlled, *though unobtrusively and with great delicacy,* by the three traditional topics of the meditation on death: a recognition and repentance of sin, a true contempt for that which is purely worldly and, finally, that reliance on God which makes possible charity towards man."[26] The lines on Pope, Gay, and Arbuthnot he reads as "a confession of Swift's envy." But look at the passage. Are we to gather that "Arbuthnot is no more my Friend," and that Swift seriously believed that he was "born to introduce" irony, "Refin'd it first, and shew'd its Use"? Nonsense: the whole passage is a graceful compliment to Swift's friends and an ironically self-deprecating joke. Swift thoroughly enjoyed maligning himself, a habit exhibited in this poem and others.[27] To read this high-spirited passage as a serious confession of sin seems to us entirely to miss its essential and obvious character. Indeed, this objection applies to Fischer's whole essay. He seizes on and magnifies minor, peripheral, and speculative points, while ignoring the tone and most of the text. He argues that the work is "highly allusive," that the "allusions are mostly to Scripture," that this "process of allusion . . . sutures his good works to his faith," and hence that the poem is basically a statement of religious faith.[28]

To find scriptural allusions in Swift's poems is no great trick; he was, after all, a clergyman. But only great insensitivity to the pervasive humor, the complex ironies, and the biographic distortions and jokes could lead one to consider this poem a serious religious meditation. If that was what Swift was trying to produce, he failed miserably, for a Jesuitical subtlety is required to catch his point. We do not doubt that Swift was familiar with the "formal meditation" tradition, though Fischer's evidence is weak—vague reference to "Swift's friend" Nicholas Rowe back at the beginning of the century. Fischer's argument that "it would be strange" if Swift "were unaware that in so reflecting on his death he was participating in that great meditative tradition,"[29] seems unpersuasive, a case of special pleading which necessarily ignores most of the content of the poem. Like Waingrow, Fischer assumes that the panegyric is meant utterly seriously; he does not even try, however, to meet Murry's strenuous objections to its inaccuracies. *If* we are to take the panegyric "straight," we have only two choices: to agree with Murry that Swift was senile, or to show that his charges of distortion are unfounded. The former appears biographically nonsensical to us; the latter impossible.

IV

Verses on the Death of Dr. Swift is organized to juxtapose and contrast the clashing views of a variety of speakers. Few authors have managed a more brilliant use of point of view, but since many readers seem to have had trouble following Swift's sustained but changing ironies, some explication is needed.

Swift begins with a general exposition of La Rochefoucauld's maxim, developed through four hypothetical examples: "my Friend," the heroic winner of "Lawrels," poor *Ned* with the gout, and the poet jealous of his rivals (13–34). Swift then makes a generalized observation which turns out to be the theme of the poem.

> Vain human Kind! Fantastick Race!
> Thy various Follies, who can trace?
> Self-love, Ambition, Envy, Pride,
> Their Empire in our Hearts divide.
>
> (39–42)

Following a common eighteenth-century practice, he then proceeds thoughout the poem to the particulars which illustrate the general truth. Various points of view will be presented, but all illustrate the maxim's point. Swift begins by using the first person, with himself as the speaker, and he chooses to use real people, with their names given: Pope, Gay, Arbuthnot, Bolingbroke, and Pulteney. With humorous self-deprecation Swift uses himself to prove his point, though each episode turns out to be a compliment to the person named. With the end of the "proem" at line 72, however, Swift drops the first person and launches into the buzz of anonymous voices, offering unflattering commentary on the decrepit Dean. These speakers are not identified, and their acerbic comments are placed in indirect discourse. A good deal of wry humor runs through these comments: "he must make his Stories shorter,/Or change his Comrades once a Quarter"; "For Poetry he's past his Prime"; he "well remembers *Charles* the Second." This is a brilliant passage, with its dry levity well-maintained, despite Swift's well-known horror of physical decay, and all tends to illustrate the maxim: Swift's friends "hug themselves, and reason thus;/It is not yet so bad with us" (115–16).

Just before the announcement of the Dean's death (150), Swift moves into third person narrative, interspersed with dialogue. After the announcement, we get very rancorous comments in direct discourse. Swift's leaving his money "to publick Uses" draws the comment, "A perfect Whim!/What had the Publick done for him!/Meer Envy, Avarice, and Pride!" When the scene shifts from Dublin to London, identified speakers appear: Lady Suffolk, the Queen, Charteris, and Walpole. From the blatantly selfish comments of these enemies, attention moves to the responses of his friends; some are named, others "who never Pity felt" are not. Swift playfully insults his best friends: "Poor Pope will grieve a Month; and Gay/A Week; and Arbuthnott a Day."[30] Swift's survey of London society lights on those a year younger than Swift, who "mourn without dissembling"—another instance of selfishness—and catches the ladies at their card game, the most widely quoted passage in the poem.

The remainder of the poem takes place after a year has passed. Almost all critics (including Slepian) divide the poem: proem (1–72); responses to death (73–298); panegyric (299–484). This is not accurate. The break comes after the card game, and the third part, on the theme of Swift's reputation after his death, consists of a fifty-line speech belittling him ("Says *Lintot*, 'I have heard the Name'") balanced against the much longer "impartial" oration.

The first speech is by a real figure, the publisher Lintot, who dismisses Swift's work as *passé,* and dilates on the modern greats, Cibber, Duck, and Henley, all of whom Swift despised. Swift's own works have been despatched to Duck-lane to serve as wrappings for pastry. This passage is a brilliant imaginative flight. Fischer feels that it "verges almost on despair for this world and everything in it."[31] We would say rather that Swift is indulging in a high-spirited prank. Exaggeration is the keynote of the whole poem, and here, just before he is about to launch into a grand puff for himself, Swift playfully exalts fools and runs himself down:

> The Dean was famous in his Time;
> And had a Kind of Knack at Rhyme:
> His way of Writing now is past;
> The Town hath got a better Taste.
>
> (263–66)

Notice that Swift is maneuvering to change the direction of the poem, preparing for the scene at the Rose. Lintot's speech has a double function: to give a derogatory opinion, and to serve as a transition into an assessment of Swift as man, satirist, politician, and churchman. Hence Lintot pushes "Sir *Robert*'s Vindication," and concludes his speech with an outrageous eulogy on the egregious Wolston, who "doth an Honour to his Gown,/By bravely running *Priest-craft* down," and

> shews, as sure as God's in *Gloc'ster,*
> That *Jesus* was a Grand Impostor:
> That all his Miracles were Cheats,
> Perform'd as Juglers do their Feats:
> The Church had never such a Writer:
> A Shame, he hath not got a Mitre!
> (291–98)

This passage on Wolston, who "deserves" to be a bishop, serves as introduction for the final scene: "Suppose me dead; and then suppose/A Club assembled at the *Rose.*"[32]

In the Wolston passage, irony descends to dictionary level ("real meaning is the opposite of literal meaning"): Swift lambastes a knave with idiotic praise. Swift's irony seldom falls to so obvious a level; no reader should have the slightest problem with this pasage. Were Swift about to launch into unqualified praise of himself, we might feel that he was losing control of his poem, lurching from simple-minded, perhaps irrelevant attacks to self-praise and pity. We might well, however, heed the warnings of such critics as A. E. Dyson, C. J. Rawson, Ricardo Quintana, and John Traugott about Swift's fondness of trapping and betraying his reader. Could Swift be lulling his audience into easy stock responses immediately before a truly ironic outbursts? So it turns out. As Edward Said observes in a passing comment, "the setting of the poem's final scene is one of the most carefully engineered things Swift ever did."[33] To the club assembled at the Rose, an "impartial" speaker rebuts Lintot's cheap sarcasms with an impassioned eulogy of a perfect hero, the Dean of St. Patrick's. The statements, rhetoric, and diction of his long speech (307–484) all merit scrutiny.

The very first couplet should put us on our guard: "The Dean, if we believe Report,/Was never ill receiv'd at Court." Of course not—everyone knew that the author of *A Tale of a Tub* and *The Windsor Prophecy,* in "exile" after 1714, had always been a particular pet of each succeeding monarch. As the *Correspondence* makes clear, George II was about as pleased by Swift's Latin inscription for the Duke of Schomberg's monument (1731) as Queen Anne had been by *A Tale of a Tub.* And the first paragraph, strongly defending Swift the writer and satirist, ends with a resounding claim for his complete originality—in a line stolen from Denham.

Every speaker up to this point—including Swift in the first person—has projected an *artificial* point of view. That is, we are not meant to accept any statements as literally *true.* Does Swift "detest" St. John and Pulteney? Even when Swift is illustrating La Rochefoucauld, he exaggerates. Does the poet literally "wish his Rivals all in Hell"? or does Swift *mean* he would rather Fortune favored his enemies rather than his friends (67–70)? Structurally, there is no reason to suppose that the "impartial" speaker is not also expressing an exaggerated and artificial point of view. Just as we *half* accept the truth of Swift's illustrations of La Rochefoucauld, and grant the *partial* truth of his insistence on men's "indifference" to another's death, so we can *half* accept the panegyric.

The ironies and exaggerations in the eulogy are sufficiently prominent that no interpreter can afford to dismiss them. The mocking theft from Denham; the bland assertion that "Power was never in his Thought;/And, Wealth he valu'd not a Groat" (357–58);[34] and finally the outrageous disclaimer of personal satire are all striking grounds for suspecting a Scriblerian trick.

> Yet, Malice never was his Aim;
> He lash'd the Vice but spar'd the Name.
> No Individual could resent,
> Where Thousands equally were meant.
> (459–62)

The first couplet is ridiculous in light of this poem, and the more so in view of Swift's lifelong production of libellous poems. And he had been, as everyone knew, a savage political pamphleteer. The second couplet exaggerates the claim into the realm of the completely preposterous. Lintot, Lady Suffolk, and Charteris, we

gather, were going to feel no resentment because *thousands* of
other publishers, court ladies, and "infamous, vile scoundrels"[35]
equally were meant. This blunt description of Charteris provides
occasion to remark that Waingrow and Fischer, intent on seeing
Swift as sweet, reasonable, and above all human passion, contrive
to overlook Swift's many venomous footnotes. Pope, of course,
dropped all of them. But the notes are as much a part of the
work Swift published as the verse; they should not be ignored;
and though they are purportedly mere editorial explication, they
can be fairly described as vituperative.

Another ground for suspicion of the panegyric is its over-
blown rhetoric.

> Fair LIBERTY was all his Cry;
> For her he stood prepar'd to die;
> For her he boldly stood alone;
> For her he oft expos'd his own.
>   (347–50)

The use of "LIBERTY" is peculiar. Fischer employs it to make
Swift out as a sort of George Washington *cum* Tom Paine and
some of his activities in Ireland can be viewed in this light. Swift's
pride in his position as a champion of liberty is often apparent,
as in his epitaph for himself. But as readers of *A Tale of a Tub*
and *An Argument Against Abolishing Christianity* well know, Swift
sometimes uses the word to connote anarchy and licence, and
though he is a passionate opponent of "slavery" and tyranny, he
has quite severe views on the necessary restrictions on "liberty
of conscience."[36] Hence his flaunting the word here should make
the reader a little uncomfortable—a feeling reinforced by the
"For her... For her... For her" construction of the next three
lines. Swift attacked this sort of writing all his life: it is alien to
his style and can be found only in his juvenilia and his parodies.[37]

A good deal of the diction of the panegyric should sound
odd to anyone familiar with the rest of Swift's poetry—for example, "Our golden Dreams," "sacrifice old *England's* Glory,"
"unguarded Virtue," "Pursu'd by base envenom'd Pens." "By Innocence and Resolution,/He bore continual Persecution," taken
seriously, is as foreign to Swift's poetic diction as "Power was
never in his Thought" was to his conduct. Swift helpfully dis-

cusses the proposal that he write "serious" poetry in his "Epistle to a Lady, who desired the Author to make Verses on Her, in the Heroick Stile" (1733). There Swift has Lady Acheson beg him to drop his "*Burlesque* Stile" in order to write in "Strain sublime." He replies with a lengthy statement about persuasion and poetry, asserting that he cannot repudiate his "nat'ral Vein" to write in "Heroick Strain"; if he attempted "lofty Numbers" he would burst, and "All my *Fire* would fall in Scraps." Hence, "For your Sake, as well as mine,/*I the lofty Stile decline*" (217–18; italics added). In view of this well-established stylistic preference, we find the panegyric impossible to take absolutely straight.

Nonetheless, to call it ironic and no more (as Slepian seems to) is surely a mistake, for indubitably Swift was genuinely proud of many of the things referred to. He certainly *did* believe in the moral aim of his satire—or most of it—and his pride in his efforts on Ireland's behalf seems perfectly genuine. When he says, "not a Traytor cou'd be found,/To sell him for Six Hundred Pound" (353–54), we can scarcely be meant to find this ironically intended. Fully half of the panegyric is devoted to Swift's disgust with the English government and his struggles in Ireland. His low opinion of the Irish, rather dwelt upon, is quite genuine.

The account of the Tory ministry ("oh! how short are human Schemes!/Here ended all our golden Dreams," 371 ff.) is more complicated. Swift gives an exaggeratedly Tory view of history, and does it so well that one is very nearly convinced. He half-believed it himself, but the reader of Ehrenpreis' biography knows that his feelings were a good deal more ambivalent, then and later, than is indicated here. Emile Pons is quite right to question the "saints lives" ("cette littérature hagiographique") in this passage.[38] The high-flown diction which infests the paragraph is one hint that this romantic view of the Age of Queen Anne is just another "artifical" view. Another is the romanticized picture of Anne herself ("that precious Life"). Again Swift half believes it, but he gives a rather harsher picture of the "royal prude" in the *Journal to Stella* and "The Author upon Himself." Thus though the episode has some real rhetorical power, the very one-sided presentation sows doubts. For example, Swift mentions in a note thirty lines earlier that *Queen Anne* had put a price on his head—a part of the episode in which he takes pride that the public would not "sell him for Six Hundred Pound."

In brief, despite the presence of some serious elements, the panegyric is no more to be believed literally than is the rest of the poem. At the outset Swift maintained that "Self-love, Ambition, Envy, Pride" are common to other people, mockingly asserting that the same is true of himself—and then he slyly manipulates his material at the end of the poem to prove it. As Maurice Johnson says in a regrettably brief interpretation, Swift is over-abused in the first half of the poem and over-praised in the concluding half.[39] But why? Granting the brilliance of the trick, what is the point? Johnson suggests that out of the pattern of "opposed exaggerations . . . the middle ground of truth is to be inferred." Perhaps we can expand on this.

Any poem on the author's own character is likely to be a personal meditation, an ironic libel (like "A Panegyric on the Reverend D—n S—t"), or essentially an *apologia pro vita sua*. There is enough in the *Verses* which appears seriously felt that Slepian's interpretation (sound as far as it goes) seems to explain the technique but not the point. So Waingrow tries to take the *Verses* "straight," ignoring the many evidences of irony and satire.[40] We would have to say that the poem Waingrow wants to find is really the "Life and Genuine Character," or better yet, Pope's Bathurst version, which does provide essentially the sort of dead serious personal defense which several critics try to extract from the *Verses*. Indeed they have some justification, for the poem should strike us as more than an ironic self-libel.

Probably the key to response to the poem lies in our sense of the poet's presence in his poem. Ronald Paulson, who reads the panegyric literally, finds "an unwillingness on Swift's part to be satisfied with a persona; a tendency toward self-dramatization that connects him with the Romantic poets." Paulson finds "a shift in emphasis . . . toward the poet himself. . . . The Juvenalian satirist of the *Verses* offers a suggestive resemblance to the poets like Gray and Collins who pictured themselves withdrawn from society and as having a somehow special relationship to God."[41] No doubt Swift can be arrogant, but Gray and Collins scarcely seem good analogies. Where do they indulge in sustained irony? When so distinguished a critic as Paulson arrives at this comparison, something must be wrong.

Reading the panegyric literally has produced some bizarre explanations of the poem. For Murry, Swift must be senile to make such factual misstatements.[42] For Paulson, the poem must be a romantic self-projection in which factual accuracy is completely irrelevant. To the reader who comes to Swift by way of *Adonais*, such a reading might seem perfectly reasonable. Shelley, after all, having announced a poem in memory of Keats, proceeds to praise himself ("a pardlike Spirit beautiful and swift") to the skies. But is Swift really a proto-Romantic?[43]

If we read the eulogy as at least partly ironic, we are not forced into elaborate explanations. We can view the poem as perfectly consistent in method and outlook with *A Modest Proposal*, "The Day of Judgement," "On Poetry: A Rapsody," Swift's letters to his friends in London, and everything else he was writing in the years 1729–1733. A hundred years ago, Thackeray and others were saying that Book IV of *Gulliver's Travels* (1726) proved Swift's senility and loss of grip on reality. Some critics seem to have retreated only five years and are now fighting a rear guard action for 1731, when Swift wrote the *Verses*. Such a position is ridiculous. Swift had a great burst of creativity between 1729 and 1733, producing the Market Hill poems, "The Day of Judgement," the verses concerning Carteret and Dr. Delany, and the "scatological" poems. Numerous tracts on Irish agriculture, "The Beasts Confession" and "The Legion Club" were yet to come—a remarkable output in both quantity and quality. Twenty months after the *Verses* comes "On Poetry: A Rapsody," widely regarded as one of Swift's greatest poems, and a scorching denunciation of the sort of poetry some critics are now alleging the *Verses* to be.

This nutshell in an *Iliad* must conclude with a clear answer to a simple question—how should the poem be read? The answer, we think, does lie in an awareness of the author in his poem. Consider the basic ironies which the reader must be aware of. Swift starts off by over-abusing himself and humorously illustrating La Rochefoucauld's maxim—a humor which by no means obscures his central point, that men *do* pretty much hide behind "Indifference clad in Wisdom's Guise," willingly resigning themselves "to the Will of God" when *others* suffer. According to Murry, the poem should have ended with Wolston. Instead, Swift balances Lintot's sneers with an extravagant, sometimes untrue eulogy from his "impartial" spokesman. What does "impartial" mean? Paulson says that "this man's portrayal is as close to the truth as is possible."[44] But consider the following lines from "On Poetry: A Rapsody":

> Then hear an old experienc'd Sinner
> Instructing thus a young Beginner.
>
> Consult yourself, and if you find
> A powerful Impulse urge your Mind,
> Impartial judge within your Breast
> What Subject you can manage best.
>
> (75–80)

This gives some idea what Swift thought about the word "impartial"—certainly a loaded one in this situation anyway. To present a serious two-hundred line eulogy on himself would be pretty risky. Pope, a specialist in self-pleading, would chance no such thing. But of course the reader *knows* that the "impartial" speaker is Swift's puppet and is certainly not going to take him as anything else. How can we take the speaker's opinion seriously when we know Swift is concocting it? Having abused himself liberally in the first half of the poem, directly and indirectly, Swift now proceeds to heap magniloquent and exaggerated praise on himself. What makes the poem so delightful, and the irony so delicious, is our constant awareness of the game Swift is playing. In the exaggerated eulogy he exemplifies again, deliberately and in a new way, the maxim and announced theme of the poem, thus keeping it well tied together. He does something else as well— he insinuates a half-genuine apologia. By deliberately exaggerating and mildly satirizing his puff for himself he creates, overall, a more attractive and convincing picture of himself than Pope ever achieved by impassioned argumentation in the *Epistle to Dr. Arbuthnot*. The method should come as no surprise, for we have seen a variant of it in the "Life and Genuine Character of Doctor Swift." There he goes to elaborate lengths to suggest that he is not really the author of straight praise for himself. Here, with greater subtlety and skill, he burlesques his praise just enough that the reader should be too delighted by the multiple ironies to resist the apologia.

Notes

1. Like Sir Harold Williams, we are greatly indebted to Herbert Davis' early article, "Verses on the Death of Dr. Swift," *The Book-Collector's Quarterly*, No. 2 (March-May 1931), pp. 57–73. Due credit should be given to Mr. John Hayward, who largely anticipated Williams' text in his Nonesuch edition (1934).

2. *The Correspondence of Jonathan Swift*, ed. Harold Williams, 5 vols. (Oxford: Clarendon Press, 1963–1965), III, 506.

3. *Verses on the Death of Doctor Swift. Written by Himself: Nov. 1731* (London: C. Bathurst, 1739). Teerink-Scouten No. 771. For bibliographical details of the various editions, see *A Bibliography of the Writings of Jonathan Swift*, 2nd ed., Revised and Corrected by Dr. H. Teerink, Edited by Arthur H. Scouten (U. of Pennsylvania Press, 1963).

4. A red herring can be noted and dismissed. From an edition of *An Essay on Man* and *Verses on the Death of Dr. Swift* carrying a date of 1736 on the title page, Dr. Herman Teerink argued that this poem was in print long before 1739. ("Swift's *Verses on the Death of Doctor Swift*," *Studies in Bibliography*, 4 [1951], 183–88). However this edition has been shown to be a piracy of much later date. See A. H. Scouten, "The Earliest London Printings of 'Verses on the Death of Doctor Swift,'" *Studies in Bibliography*, 15 (1962), 243–47.

5. "The Ironic Intention of Swift's Verses on His Own Death," *RES*, n.s. 14 (1963), 249–56. [Reprinted in this volume.]

6. All references to Swift's own version (the 1739 Faulkner printing, Teerink-Scouten No. 774) are to *The Poems of Jonathan Swift*, 2nd ed., ed. Harold Williams, 3 vols. (Oxford: Clarendon Press, 1958), II, 551–72.

7. Joseph Horrell, ed. *Collected Poems of Jonathan Swift*, 2 vols. (Harvard U. Press, 1958), II, 797 nn.

8. *Essays on the Eighteenth Century Presented to David Nichol Smith* (Oxford: Clarendon Press, 1945), pp. 49–64.

9. The formula for the Bathurst printing can be summarized as follows:

Lines retained from Faulkner (i.e., MS)	Added from "Life"	Total
1–14		14
17–280		264
299–302		4
307–308		2
315–316		2

	88–89	2
	82–83	2
	95–114	20
455–458		4
	117–118	2
	121–124	4
435–442		8
319–324		6
339–344		6
	130–133	4
	136–143	8
	180–193	14
309–313		5
	197–200	4
479–482		4
	201–202	2
Totals: 319	62	381

10. *Correspondence*, IV, 151–52, 161.

11. W. E. Browning, ed., *The Poems of Jonathan Swift, D.D.*, 2 vols. (London: Bell, 1910), I, 247.

12. Browning's arrangement is as follows: Faulkner 314: add Bathurst 373–75; 318: add Bathurst 287–310; 434: add Bathurst 341–66; 474: add Bathurst 315–20; 484: add Bathurst 380–81.

13. Horrell, II, 796 nn. For a full account of its publication history, see Williams, *Poems*, II, 541–43.

14. These lines appear also in the Bathurst printing of the *Verses*. Their import is strengthened by recollecting Swift's "Character of Sir Robert Walpole" (1731), where the great patriot is described as "oppressing true merit exalting the base/and selling his Country to purchase his peace . . . the Cur dog of Brittain & spaniel of Spain." *Poems*, II, 539–40.

15. *The Fictions of Satire* (Johns Hopkins Press, 1967), pp. 190–91.

16. John Middleton Murry, *Jonathan Swift: A Critical Biography* (London: Cape, 1954), pp. 459–60.

17. Williams, *Poems*, II, 543.

18. *The Correspondence of Alexander Pope*, ed. George Sherburn, 5 vols. (Oxford: Clarendon Press, 1956), IV, 130.

19. Horrell, II, 799 nn. Murry, p. 457.

20. *Correspondence*, V, 139 (6 March). He adds, "Two editions have already been sold off, though two thousand were printed at first"— indeed a considerable success, and Bathurst issued three more editions the same year.

21. Murry, pp. 454–60. Murry says (p. 454) that the popular composite version is a conflation by Pope totaling 486 lines.

22. Remarked by George Birkbeck Hill in his edition of Johnson's

Lives of the English Poets, 3 vols. (Oxford: Clarendon Press, 1905), III, 66, n. 2. (Cited by Slepian as III, 56, n. 3.)

23. *"Verses on the Death of Dr. Swift,"* SEL, 5 (1965), 513–18. [Reprinted in this volume.]

24. "How to Die: *Verses on the Death of Dr. Swift,"* RES, n.s. 21 (1970), 422–41.

25. Fischer seems unaware that Ronald Paulson had already discussed this problem in some detail. Cf. Paulson, pp. 189 ff.

26. Fischer, p. 427 (italics added).

27. As in "The Life and Genuine Character," "A Panegyric Upon D—n S—t," "My Lady's Lamentation and Complaint against the Dean" (1728), "Lady A—S—N Weary of the Dean" (1728?), and "A Panegyrick on the D—n" (1730)—this last, like the *Verses,* employs raised style to mocking effect near the end of the poem.

28. Fischer, p. 436. The fancifulness of Fischer's methodology shows up in his constant reiteration that the points he draws from the poem are unobtrusive, oblique, not direct, not overt, submerged, and can be seen only by following allusions (see esp. pp. 427, 432, 436).

29. Fischer, p. 426.

30. Fischer (p. 435) somehow construes this as a serious statement, saying that there is "a high compliment for Pope in Swift's compassionate recognition that 'Poor Pope will mourn a month . . .'."

31. Fischer, p. 435.

32. The number of sour references to bishops' mitres seems surprising from a man who, according to Fischer (p. 439), has lost all interest in "power and fame and worldly station."

33. "Swift's Tory Anarchy," ECS, 3 (1969), 48–66; quotation from p. 64.

34. Fischer (pp. 438–39) asserts that this indifference to money and power gave Swift an ideal "liberty" as of 1731. But the reader of the *Correspondence* may doubt this indifference, and the claim is that he was *never* interested in power.

35. From Swift's note to l. 189.

36. For example, see "Thoughts on Religion," in *The Prose Works of Jonathan Swift,* ed. Herbert Davis, IX (Oxford: Blackwell, 1948), 261–63. See further Irvin Ehrenpreis, "Swift On Liberty," JHI, 13 (1952), 131–46; and Maurice Johnson, "Swift and 'The Greatest Epitaph in History'," PMLA, 68 (1953), 814–27.

37. Paulson, who rejects "Slepyan's" ironic interpretation (p. 189), says that "in the *Verses* [Swift] gives the ideal equal space with the evil, and the result is closer to the Stella poems or to the early pindaric odes of praise than to satire" (p. 204). The comparison to the odes is stylistically apt; to us, however, it suggests self-burlesque.

38. Swift, *Oeuvres* (Paris: Gallimard, 1965), p. 1843.

39. "'Verses on the Death of Dr. Swift'," N&Q, 194 (1954), 473–74.

40. Another critic who does so is Robert C. Steensma, "Swift's Apologia: 'Verses on the Death of Dr.Swift'," *Proceedings of the Utah Academy of Sciences, Arts, and Letters*, 42 (1965), 23–28. Steensma is slightly bothered because Swift "somewhat idealizes himself," but he accepts every statement in the panegyric as intended literally.

41. Paulson, pp. 207, 209.

42. Similarly Horrell complains that Swift "distorts facts," seeing the poem as evidence that "Swift's grip on reality loosens in his later years" (I, xxiv).

43. Edward Said rightly comments, à propos of the critical "house-breaking and domestication of the tiger of English literature," that "these methods are best suited to romantic and post-romantic authors" (pp. 48, 50).

44. Paulson, p. 192.